THE INNER GAME OF GOLF

REVISED EDITION

THE INNER GAME OF GOLF

W. TIMOTHY GALLWEY

REVISED EDITION

 RANDOM HOUSE NEW YORK

This is a revised edition of *The Inner Game of Golf*, published by Random House in 1981.

A portion of this work was previously published in *Golf Magazine*.

Grateful acknowledgment is made to the following for permission to reprint previously published material:
A. S. Barnes & Company, Inc.: Excerpts from *Power Golf* by Ben Hogan, published by A. S. Barnes & Company, Inc. Copyright 1948, 1976 by Ben Hogan. Reprinted by permission of the publisher. All rights reserved.

Library of Congress Cataloging-in-Publication Data

Gallwey, W. Timothy.
    The inner game of golf / W. Timothy Gallwey. —Rev. ed.
      p.   cm.
    ISBN 0-679-45760-7
    1. Golf—Psychological aspects.   I. Title.
    GV979.P75G34   1998
    796.352'01—dc21   97-41272

Random House website address: www.randomhouse.com
Manufactured in the United States of America on acid-free paper

987
Revised Edition

Book design by Jessica Shatan

To Maharaji,
with gratitude for teaching me the one thing
I most needed to learn

To be a student takes a lot of trust,
   but not in the teacher.
To be a student takes a lot of trust
   in you.

                    Maharaji

FOREWORD: LOOKING BACK

Throughout the ages there have always been two streams of advice for people who wanted to improve a skill. I call one the river of "formulas" and the other the river of "feel." One current flows toward mastery in the outer world, the other toward mastery in the inner.

The river of formulas produces a formidable flow of technical instructions arising from the detailed analysis of any skill. This approach has dominated Western thought since the broad acceptance of Sir Isaac Newton's mechanistic view of the universe. In establishing the laws that govern the movement of physical objects, the Newtonian mind attempted to subject all physical movements, large and small, to the understanding of cause and effect. The resulting picture of the universe was like a huge mechanical clock whose little gears drive larger gears, which in turn drive the movements of the hands. This understanding gave its practitioners a new ability to predict and even control a particular class of physical phenomena that in turn led to the development of countless technologies in countless fields.

The game of golf, and specifically the mechanics of the golf swing, has been a favorite subject of inquiry for the Newtonian mind. The result has been not only the most intensive analysis of the components and sequences involved in this motion but, from this, a steady generation of technical instructions swelling into the thousands. In spite of the inevitable frustration of trying to understand, assimilate, and apply so many instructions, there has been an unending appetite for and belief in this kind of knowledge. This appetite stems from the same quest that fueled the technological Newtonian revolution: the desire to know and control.

It has always been somewhat disturbing to the Newtonians that human behavior, emotions, and aspirations could not be so easily known or controlled as the physical universe. Some have claimed that human behavior is, in fact, totally subject to cause and effect but that the variables are just too complicated to understand and manipulate fully. Human behavior presents two big problems for Newtonian scientists, whose methods of verification depend on shared observation and exacting rules of description. The first problem with studying human beings is that the "gears and levers" that turn the human clock are opaque, as they are confined within the body. You can't exactly cut open the living body to observe its workings. The best you can do is observe external behavior and try to make educated inferences as to the workings of the internal gears. The second problem with understanding human behavior in terms of cause and effect is that mysterious human potential called "free choice." The ideas of freedom and cause and effect seem to be mutually exclusive when applied to the same subject. So the inner human reality has been characterized as "subjective" and the outer reality "objective." In short, the methods of objective science simply did not lend themselves easily to the exploration of subjective realities.

But well before Newton—since the days of Socrates, in fact—men of wisdom have advised the human being to "know thyself." They claimed with authority and sincerity that this was, in fact, possible and spoke of a direct way of knowing inner reality. They were not scientific in the modern sense of the word but relied on faculties of knowing called by such names as "intuition," "insight," and "self-awareness." The purpose was not so much to know the outer world as to understand the dynamics of the one living in the world—to know the subject as distinct from the surrounding objective environment.

The second river of advice has been about mastering the human dimension of existence—the domain of thinking and feeling. Some call it the "mental side" of the game. I prefer simply to call it the "inner game." In this inner domain, much of what is important to understand, such as thought and feeling, cannot be directly observed by more than one person at a time. Though the results of thought, expressed in language, can be observed and analyzed, thought itself occurs too fast to be clearly observed. Few scientists or philosophers have claimed to understand the thinking process itself. As for feeling, it can be observed subjectively by each individual but can only be vaguely expressed in the outer world through word and gesture. In short, the individual can feel and feel richly but can express, share, and compare what is felt in the inner world only partially—at best. Those who say that the human side of any activity, including golf, is important are often confined to speaking in metaphors and analogies. These are not exact and can only hint at the secrets of the game that is played from the inside out. This voice for playing the inner game has been strong and insistent for centuries, but hardly ever has it been the voice of the majority.

So these two streams, formulas and feelings, have moved through history as two great rivers, one seeming to swell as the other ebbs, sometimes crossing each other but rarely joining. It is sometimes difficult to tell if these rivers are moving toward the same ocean. It is not difficult to determine that human beings, to be effective, need something of what each stream has to offer.

Both these streams have influenced the way golf skills have been learned and performed. A few of the great teachers and players have been able to weave the wisdom of each into an integrated whole. I hope that as a result of reading, thinking about, and applying what you learn from this revised edition, you will be better equipped to forge such an integration.

When I first wrote *The Inner Game of Golf,* I knew almost nothing about the mechanics of the golf swing. I had been challenged to see how much golf I could learn just by adapting the "inner skills" that I had developed while playing and coaching tennis. The master skill was that of "relaxed concentration," which required an ability to pay close attention to the movements of ball and body and to make accurate observations of the results. It also involved the skill of trust in the body's capacity to learn and execute complex behaviors without following a complex set of instructions.

It is highly unlikely that any beginner who gets interested in the game of golf will escape being thrown into the stream of technical formulas. He or she could drown in the waters that flow from golf magazines, books, teaching professionals, and "knowledgeable" friends. The high probability of hitting some good shots, followed by some relatively poor shots, renders us vulnerable to this torrent of explanations and remedies.

But when I saw the wide disparity between my best shots and my worst, the claims from experts that there are right and wrong ways to swing the club became too compelling to ignore. So I flirted with technical instruction and admit to being seduced by a few of the leading technical formulations. I put the greatest hope in the notion that if I gripped the club correctly, assumed the correct posture, and held a single "swing thought" in mind, I would attain the "swing control" I obviously lacked.

The simple assumption behind the promise of golfing technique was that by following the correct mental formulas I could control my behavior and get the desired results.

I understood that the game of golf was about control, and I was definitely subject to the pervasive human urge to increase control, an urge that, when unmonitored, becomes compulsive and then obsessive. Yet most golfers, myself included, would love a shortcut to mastery—hitting each ball to its desired destination with the grace, ease, and precision of perfection itself. And what then? Then, all who witnessed this mastery would stand back in awe and admiration. Yes!

So much for my dream. The reality was one of high hopes followed by mini-despairs. It ended in resignation and the belief that golf could be mastered only by those of great athletic ability who had the time to practice daily. The reality was that of imposing one set of instructions after another on a noncompliant body, then judging it when it failed to perform as instructed. The reality was the tightening of shoulders, legs, hips, and both sets of cheeks. The reality was that one tip led to another to another, which in turn led to unlearning the first three. Fortunately, my experience with the Inner Game of tennis made it possible for me to step out of the technology stream before I drowned in it. Though I would continue to dangle my toes in it from time to time, I never jumped in with both feet.

Instead, I wanted to see how far I could go without the benefit of technical expertise, and my editors set me the goal of breaking 80 while playing only once a week during the writing of this book. So the original edition became a narrative of my explorations of overcoming the inner obstacles of doubt, fear, and lack of focus that prevented natural learning. It also presented the basic inner skills that facilitate learning and peak performance.

The response of the golfing world to this inner approach to the game is noteworthy. As might have been expected, there was considerable resistance among some elements of the golf instruction establishment, whose authority stemmed largely from knowledge of the "swing mechanics." Then there were many pros who knew that the essence of what I was saying was true but didn't feel comfortable talking about it. Of course, players were skeptical about anything that did not seem in line with cause-and-effect mechanics as taught by their teaching pros or as endorsed by leading playing professionals.

But the book became a best-seller in the Newton-dominated world of golf, so there were obviously enough golfers who knew that playing and enjoying golf is more than a matter of mechanics. They welcomed the book, passed it on to friends, and wrote thousands of acknowledgments to me about how it had reduced their handicaps and increased their enjoyment of the game. Sooner or later, many of the most skeptical golfers and their pros read the book and gave the Inner Game approach a try—if for no other reason than that golfers are a rare breed who will ultimately try anything that promises hope.

At the same time golfers were opening up to the mental side of golf, there was a general rise in the interest in sports psychology by athletes and their coaches. When *The Inner Game of Tennis* was published in 1974, it was considered revolutionary because it dealt directly and almost exclusively with the mental and emotional side of the game. Before then, people were nervous about expressing a need for help with the Inner Game and players who knew of its importance were reluctant to talk publicly about what they knew. The whole topic seemed to make most athletes feel just a little too vulnerable. Since then, we have witnessed the birth of a new field of study that now boasts thousands of practitioners, hundreds of facilities, and countless volumes of information about how to attain peak mental and physical states.

It was interesting for me to observe the evolution of golf instruction from the sidelines. I remember how surprised I was to see Bob Toski rise to popularity by teaching that the most important thing about the golf swing was to learn to feel it. Then there was the whole school of "imaging" led by cybervision, which taught people to learn to swing by watching slow-motion pictures of the best swing masters in the game. Without analyzing the specific movements of the swing or giving any instruction save "Watch, relax, and imagine yourself doing the same thing," it was as though the advice came straight from a single section of *The Inner Game of Tennis*.

In a recent *New York Times Book Review* article entitled "He's Tiger Woods and You're Not," author Lee Eisenberg states that there are several kinds of golf books. First, there's the instruction manual, of the cause-and-effect checklist type, usually written by leading players or their teachers. This genre of books has exploded in both volume and intricacy since the advent of the video camera, which reduces the swings of the best golfers to slow motion and provides as many freeze frames per swing as desired. This technology allows an even more minute analysis of a swing in motion and has further swelled the stream of technical instruction. At the same time, slow-motion videotapes revealed that the best golfers do a great deal that is individual or unique and that there are relatively few constants in the swings of the pros. In a book called *The Golf Swing*, David Leadbetter, one of the leading theoreticians and teachers of golf swing technique, said that the most definite conclusion he could draw from his years of study was "that there is no *definitive* method." Yet in golf, as in tennis, most teachers tend to ignore what is idiosyncratic and carve in stone whatever is not. The basic idea is to find a "model swing" that can be justified and then taught uniformly to everyone.

The *New York Times* article goes on to state that besides the books dealing with mechanical instructions there is another genre that deals with the mental side of the game, the leading examples of which are *The Inner Game of Golf* and books by Dr. Bob Rotella including *Golf Is Not a Game of Perfect*. Precursors of these books are Dr. Peter Cranford's *The Winning Touch in Golf*, Michael Murphy's *Golf in the Kingdom*, and Dr. Gary Wiren's *The New Golf Mind*. A more recent book in this genre is Fred Shoemaker's *Extraordinary Golf*. The point is that there is now a growing acceptance of the need for insight into the general domain of the Inner Game, and more information is becoming available to the average golfer. Furthermore, playing professionals as well as TV commentators are much more apt to express their thinking on the subject.

In spite of what might be called these "great advances" in golf instruction as well as advances in golf club and ball-making technology and a myriad of new training aids on the market, a very disconcerting fact has recently come to light. Generally speaking, the scores of golfers are not improving! At a recent conference of the PGA of America on Teaching and Coaching, *Golf Tips* magazine pointed out that "a question that arose repeatedly was this: Why is it that, despite the proliferation of golf schools, talented instructors, training aids, reputable instruction books and magazines as well as high-tech, game-improving equipment, the handicap of the average American golfer is at best stagnant and—more likely—on the rise, according to United States Golf Association studies." For me the undeniable conclusion is that there is a big gap between what we know about the golf swing and our ability to help people learn.

I believe the answer to this problem will not be found in the further development of either technical or feel-based instruction alone. Nor does it help to study either field as if it were an independent area of mastery. No, in life they are integrated, and so, too, must they be in golf. The integration must be one that preserves the identity of each, a true marriage, in which each kind of knowledge works together and plays its appropriate yet distinct role. There can be no true marriage when each holds dogmatically to its own perspective and vies for dominance over the other.

I have kept two main purposes in mind while revising this book. In the last four chapters, I have attempted to articulate the next stage of development of the Inner Game, a step that goes beyond the basic need to have more kinesthetic or movement awareness in learning and performing golf. It introduces in greater depth the fundamental importance of knowing *why* you play the game as inseparable from *how* you play the game. Second, in the middle chapters, I have attempted to build a better bridge between traditional mechanistic golf instructions and the newer, feel-based kind of instructions. My hope is to create a better relationship between the "inner approach" and the "outer," two approaches that have been separate for far too long.

Consistent through both editions of this book is the idea that as golfers we are often our own worst enemies. No real progress in golf can be made without an honest acknowledgment of the inner obstacles that human beings put in the way of themselves and the expression of their potentialities. Whereas there is a more widespread belief in human potential than there used to be, it seems as hard as ever for most of us to own up to our tendency to get in our own way. And when we do acknowledge it, we tend to be so hard on ourselves that we become helpless to do much about it. Only if we find the courage and honesty to admit to our own self-interference and become more alert to it as it arises will we be able to make effective use of the plentiful technical information available. Without a better understanding of the human learning process and some compassion for the vulnerabilities as well as the aspirations of learners, all the technical information and all the positive thinking in the world won't help.

Building this bridge between inner and outer can bear much fruit in every game we play. It can also bring a greater respect for the ancient and wonderful game of golf by lifting it to a level of true recreation. It will also provide newcomers greater access to the game, lessening the frustration of the initial learning process while increasing the respect of those instructors who help people learn golf.

ACKNOWLEDGMENTS

This book was completed with the help of more people than I can name. I acknowledge and thank the following, who generously contributed time and energy: Jane Blalock, Marilyn Bowden, Tom Capelety, Tony Coleman, Ed Gallwey, Sally Gallwey, Al Geiberger, Molly Groger, Arch McGill, Michael Murphy, Tom Nordland, Gary Peterson, D.P.S. Rawat, Linda Rhodes, and Prentiss Uchida.

In addition, I acknowledge the valued assistance in design and production of this revised edition from Arnie Billingsley, Sean Brawley, Leslye Deitch, Tom Fitzpatrick, Larry Joseph, William A. Kasoff, John Kirk, and Sylvia Trujillo.

Contents

THE INNER GAME
OF GOLF

REVISED EDITION

CHAPTER 1

GOLF: THE INNER AND OUTER CHALLENGE

As I laid down my tennis racket and cleaned off golf clubs scarcely used in twenty-five years, I felt two emotions. On the one hand, I had a keen sense of expectancy about exploring the application of Inner Game methods and principles developed on the tennis courts and ski slopes to the "royal and ancient" game of golf. On the other, I felt distinct uneasiness about grappling with the notorious mental obstacles evoked by the game. Somehow I sensed that, for me, golf could prove to be a dangerous game.

My uneasiness did not stem from a lack of confidence in the Inner Game. I knew that it had a real contribution to make, that its principles were grounded in basic truth, and that the methods and techniques had produced dramatic results not only in tennis and skiing but also in such varied worlds as music, business, education, health, and family life. Furthermore, I had received letters from many golfers who had read *The Inner Game of Tennis* and reported that they had not only significantly lowered their handicaps but considerably increased their enjoyment. I sincerely felt that the Inner Game would help golf and golfers in general and from time to time even indulged in wishful daydreams about instant mastery of the game.

But golf is different from tennis, a sport that I had excelled in, having played it all my life. My intention was to take up the game and in a short period of time see how much I could improve my present hacker level. I knew that helping others overcome the doubts, fears, and frustrations always seemed easy to me. But in learning golf *I* would be the student. Sometimes I felt the pressure of possible failure, but I comforted myself with the knowledge that if I really played the Inner Game I would inevitably learn more than golf. Thus I could not really lose. Results would inevitably follow learning.

"THE ONLY GAME I PLAY THAT I CAN'T LICK"

One of the first rounds of golf I played on my return to the game was at the Hillcrest Club in Los Angeles in a foursome that included Dr. F., one of the best-known surgeons in California. Somehow Dr. F, whom I had met at a celebrity tennis tournament, found time to play three times a week. On the first tee I felt nervous in this unfamiliar atmosphere and admired Dr. F's seeming self-assurance. On the second tee, however, after a par on the first hole, he pushed two successive drives out of bounds. Exasperated with himself, he slammed his driver to the ground and exclaimed disgustedly, "This is the most frustrating damned game ever concocted by the mind of man!"

Sensing that his outburst did not come out of short acquaintance with the game, I naively asked, "Then why do you play so often?"

Dr. F. paused, then finally answered, "Because I can't lick it." He seemed surprised by his remark, and thought about it for a moment before repeating firmly, "Yes, it's the only game I play that I can't beat!"

It soon became apparent that Dr. F. was frustrated not only by drives. Seeing him stand tensely over four-foot putts, I reflected that if he held his scalpel with as much apprehension and self-doubt as his putter, I'd never want to be on his operating table. Obviously, performing delicate surgery demands far more dexterity than is required to sink a four-foot putt, quite apart from the added dimension that the patient's life is at stake. Yet, clearly, golf unnerved Dr. F. more. Somehow I just couldn't imagine him angrily throwing his scalpel on the operating-room floor and calling himself a clumsy oaf, but this is exactly what happened on more than one three-putt green. As I watched all this, my respect for the challenge of the game was not diminished.

Dr. F. was not alone in frustration. Though I'd learned better in tennis, after almost every mis-hit golf shot I found myself subjecting my swing to critical analysis. I knew very little about the mechanics of the swing, but I tried to figure out what had gone wrong. Had I been off balance? Swung too hard? Maybe I'd been either too early or too late with my wrists. On the next shot I would try to correct whatever I thought had caused the mistake. But it seemed that every time I managed to fix one flaw, two more would emerge. The harder I tried to control my swing, the more mechanical and less rhythmic it became. The resulting shots were erratic, provoking my desire to try even harder for self-correction. Before long this cycle proved to be more like self-destruction than self-correction.

Away from the golf course, I took a fresh look at the game and asked myself what it was all about. The single word that came to mind was *control*. Basically, it seemed to be a matter of getting your body to do what you want it to do so that you can make the golf ball do what you want *it* to do. I saw the game as a stark challenge to a person's ability to control his or her own body. Since I had learned something from my experience in tennis about the problem of control, I decided to find a way of translating this understanding to golf.

WHAT I LEARNED ON THE TENNIS COURT

In short, what I learned on the tennis court was that the way most of us are taught to control our bodies simply doesn't work. Telling our bodies how to do something is not the most effective way to improve performance. Our muscles don't understand English, and our thinking minds don't really understand hand-eye coordination. Trying to make their bodies conform to the instructions of their last lesson, most tennis players inhibit free movement of their bodies and interfere with coordination rather than assist it. "Get your racket back early. . . . Meet the ball in front of you. . . . Don't roll the racket over on the follow-through," they say furiously to themselves during a match. Even when these drill-instructor commands are obeyed, they are usually performed with the stiffness and self-consciousness of a rebellious recruit and in a way that prohibits true excellence.

The quality of my teaching and of my students' performance took a major step forward the day I realized the extent of the disrupting effects of overinstruction. When my pupils' minds were free from both external and internal instructions, they could follow the ball better and had significantly better feel of their rackets. As a natural consequence, better results followed. In those early days of exploration of the Inner Game I was surprised at the improvement that would result after giving students the sole instruction "Forget everything you think you know about how to hit a tennis ball." Unable to forget anything they *really* knew, they could forget only what they *thought* they knew, and a natural ease would enter their game. But the Inner Game is not won with a single instruction, the inner opponent being far too crafty and well entrenched in our psyche to be dethroned so easily.

After several years the premise of the Inner Game of tennis emerged clearly. The prime causes of error in tennis are within the mind of the player—in doubt, tension, and lapses of concentration more than in ignorance of mechanics. For this reason, as coach I found it far more effective to work from the inside out, trying to resolve the mental causes of error rather than to correct all the external symptoms. Over and over I observed that the removal of a single self-doubt could result immediately in numerous technical improvements in a tennis player's swing and overall game. The changes were spontaneous and unforced; they required neither technical instruction nor the constant demand for self-analysis that had characterized my early teaching.

On the tennis courts, methods for combating most mental problems facing tennis players had been found and proven effective. Now the challenge was to find practical ways to do the same under the physical requirements and mental pressures of the game of golf.

GOLF IS AN INNER GAME

As I began to play golf more regularly I realized that it would be a unique challenge to Inner Game effectiveness. What other game invites such tension and mental anguish? Like one's own children, golf has an uncanny way of endearing itself to us while at the same time evoking every weakness of mind and character, no matter how well hidden. The common purpose served is that we either learn to overcome the weaknesses or we are overwhelmed by them. Few games provide such an ideal arena for confronting the very obstacles that impair one's ability to learn, perform, and enjoy life, whether on or off the golf course. But to take advantage of this opportunity, the golfer must accept the challenge to play the Inner Game as well as the Outer Game. He or she must recognize not only sand traps and OB markers but the existence of mental hazards as well.

Perhaps the first task for the player of the Inner Game is to become aware of the mental factors evoked by golf. I found them to be many and multifaceted, but essentially they seemed to fall into five categories: the lure of the game to the ego, the precision it requires, the competitive pressures on the golfer, the unique pace of the game, and the obsession with the mechanics of the swing.

THE LURE OF GOLF

There is, I soon discovered, a seductive quality to golf found in few other sports. In moments of frustration many players vow to quit, but few are able to. For some reason, the two or three "triumphs" during a round are remembered long after the exasperating failures and dull mediocrity are forgotten.

I could see that some of the attraction of the game lay in the results that could sometimes be achieved by sheer luck. Golf is one of the few sports in which a novice can, on occasion, perform like a champion. A nonathlete playing golf for the first time can sink a fifty-foot putt on the first green and conclude that it is an easy game. Overconfidence can run rampant. Likewise, a reasonably well coordinated twenty-year-old may hit his first drive 250 yards straight down the middle of the fairway, and by the time he's walked up to his ball his ego is telling him that it will probably be only a short time before he's ready for the PGA tour. On a given day, my seventy-five-year-old father could score better than Jack Nicklaus on his worst. And on a given hole, even I, as a beginner, could occasionally hit a good drive down the middle, make an approach to the green, and sink the putt for a birdie—an outcome even the best pros would welcome. The problem, of course, was that this doesn't happen very often for me—and in my naiveté my good holes would seduce me into thinking it was possible to be playing with the best. And the bad holes that inevitably followed would tend to plunge my vain hopes into despair. The same is not true of most sports. I am a better tennis player than golfer, but if I played Pete Sampras on my best day and he was having his worst, I would not win many points, much less games or sets. Realistic expectations about my abilities in golf were not so easy to come by in the early days.

After only a few hours on the driving range I realized that the compelling attraction of the game for me was also its major frustration. Even though I had played relatively little golf since I was thirteen, on occasion I would drive 230 yards, right on target. The sight of the ball soaring high and true was exhilarating; it filled me with a sense of mastery and power. The frustration lay in the fact that I couldn't repeat the experience at will. Fed by seemingly undying hope, I repressed my annoyance at failure and would reach for ball after ball. I wanted that feeling back to prove to myself that I could repeat what my body had shown me it was capable of doing. I was getting hooked by the game.

As I looked around the practice range I could see that others were caught in the same snare; there we were, spending hours and dollars trying for that elusive but tantalizing perfect swing that would give predictable results. Yet time and time again we were all faced with the dismal truth that we simply didn't have the self-control we wanted and somehow felt we should have. It wouldn't have hurt so much if we hadn't hit some excellent shots, giving us that cruel knowledge that the ability was there within us somewhere.

I began to understand and share Dr. F's fascination with the game. Golf seemed to raise my hopes only to dash them, to puff up my ego only to squash it. What kind of fun was this supposed to be? Could the game be beaten? What would that mean? Could I at least learn to enjoy the game and to play without frustration? I felt that to do only this would be a significant victory.

THE DEMANDS OF PRECISION

The most agonizing aspect of my own game was clearly its inconsistency. I was perfectly capable of hooking a ball forty yards left of center on one shot and then, with what seemed to be the same swing, slicing an equal distance on the next. Even more disconcerting was hitting a long drive down the middle on one hole, followed by a topped ball that barely dribbled off the tee on the next. I was used to inconsistency in tennis, but nothing on that order of magnitude! Although I might serve an ace and follow it with a serve four feet out, I wouldn't hit the bottom of the net with one shot and the fence on the fly with the next. Yet that's what golf felt like on some days.

It seemed to me that the precision required to play good golf demanded much greater mental discipline than was necessary for good tennis. The reason for the low margin of error was not hard to discover: the speed of the club head that is necessary to hit the ball a long distance. The speed of the golfer's arms on the downswing is not much greater than the speed of the tennis player's arm on the serve, but because of the greater length and flexibility of the golf club, the club-head speed is much greater. If a club head traveling over 100 mph contacts the ball with a face open a mere degree or two, the ball can be sent off target many tens of yards. With those odds, it's amazing that the ball ever does go exactly where we want it to.

In tennis, the serve is the only shot in which the player *initiates* the action, whereas in golf he does so on every shot. It is interesting to note that if you miss your first serve in tennis, you get another try. Golf is not so forgiving! Further, in tennis a much larger surface hits a much larger ball a much shorter distance. Moving from tennis to golf was definitely going to require some fine-tuning of my concentration.

The greater precision required in golf is also reflected in the manner in which the player addresses the ball. A tennis player can be pretty casual, or even a little flamboyant, as he sets up the service line, bounces the ball a few times, and serves. Most professional golfers display much more self-discipline. They seem to approach the ball in the same controlled, almost ritualistic way every time. Even their dress seems more meticulous. (I've often felt I could pick out the golfers from the tennis players at a cocktail party.)

Meticulousness has never been my strong suit. There isn't a family picture of me as a boy in which at least one shoe wasn't untied. I could usually solve all the problems given me on a math test but would seldom make a perfect score because of careless mistakes in computation. I wondered if I'd ever be able to achieve the degree of discipline that the game of golf seemed to call for. At the outset my only hope was to look at the game as a challenge to my ability to enhance this particular quality of mind. I can't say that I looked forward to the task.

The precision required in golf doesn't allow for release of the pent-up anger and frustration that one can find in more aggressive sports. Golf produces frustration, but it requires that you learn to deal with it in some way other than in your next shot. This presents a fascinating Inner Game challenge.

If I have a mediocre day on the tennis court and lose a match 6–3, 6–3, I can always lessen the humiliation to my ego by telling myself that my opponent was playing particularly well that day. But the golfer stands alone. Blame or credit for the score rests on him or her, and usually there are three other people around to pass judgment. The ego thrives and dies in such a setup.

Every shot I take in golf counts. In tennis I can lose three straight points and still win the game; many lost points will never show up in the final score. Tennis forgives a few mistakes; golf forgives none. Thus, pressure can seem constant.

Because the game of golf is inherently a game of the golfer against himself, the Inner Game is intensified. The ego is both more challenged and more threatened. The player's spirits tend to rise or sink in direct proportion to his score, the sole product of his own efforts. Although I have seen many golfers avoid this pressure by blaming various weather and course conditions, golf clubs, balls, other players, family, or business affairs, I feel that few can fool themselves for long before facing the fact that golf is a game played only against the course and oneself and that one's score is a pretty true indication of skill.

Although I have seen many "fry" under this kind of pressure, I have also noticed that often it is this very same pressure that attracts golfers to the game. As a rule, most golfers prefer the tougher courses to easy ones and like to add to the existing pressure by betting money on the result "just to make the game more interesting."

Learning to perform at one's best under pressure is a clear goal of the Inner Game. The challenge of sinking a five-foot putt on the eighteenth hole to save par and the match is clearly a lot more mental than it is phys-

PRESSURE

ical. And the player who can learn to perform with precision and power under such seeming pressure will learn an inner skill that can help him to cope with other situations in his life.

PACE   The pace of golf is unique and in obvious contrast to that of most sports. In tennis, for example, if my mind begins to entertain a flow of self-critical or negative thoughts, it is cut short abruptly by the need to respond to the oncoming ball.

But in golf we have too much time to think. Between shots a negative train of thought can become entrenched: What went wrong on that last shot? How do I correct my slice? What will happen to my score if I hit the next shot out of bounds? There is endless time to overanalyze and become confused, discouraged, or angry.

The tennis player is constantly caught up in the action—moving toward or hitting the ball. In four hours on the court I may play about sixty-four games or about four hundred points in perhaps twelve hundred to fifteen hundred separate shots. During the same length of time in golf I will hit—I hope—less than one hundred shots. If each golf shot takes me two seconds, then I am engaged in swinging the golf club for a total of only three minutes out of four hours of play.

Therefore, concentration in golf requires a unique kind of effort. In the first place, the ball just sits there and the pace of the game demands that the golfer be at an intense peak of concentration at the exact moment of the swing, supremely challenging his ability to keep from being distracted during the long intervals between shots. In tennis my concentration tends to build as the point progresses, reaching its peak as I become "lost in the action." But in the long stretches between golf shots it is easier to become lost in the thoughts on the surface of our minds.

I concluded that the walk between shots is one of the most critical parts of the game. Though this period of time is recognized by some pros as a potential mental hazard as well as a benefit, I feel its importance in most golfers' minds is generally undervalued. It is most often in the interval between shots that both the Inner and the Outer games are won or lost. It is during this time that the golfer's mental equilibrium can be destroyed by the momentum of negative thoughts or employed to shake off the tension of the last shot and to prepare for the next. The inner golfer learns to use the time between shots to relax the mind and to prepare it for the total concentration needed during the two seconds of the next swing. (This subject will be dealt with further in Chapter 8.)

I had long thought that the mechanics of the tennis swing had been exhaustively analyzed until I took a look at existing golf manuals. I wouldn't be surprised if more has been written about the mechanics of the golf swing than just about any other human movement. It has been dissected into amazingly minute segments and the information passed along to the already overloaded minds of students of the game. Hearing that I was taking up the game, a friend presented me with three volumes: *295 Golf Lessons* by Bill Casper, *395 Golf Lessons* by Gary Player, *495 Golf Lessons* by Arnold Palmer.

It is not difficult to see how superstition thrives on the modern golf course. So many players are in constant search of "the secret," and endless magic formulas are propagated by true believers. Ready to try anything to relieve frustration, the golfer finds his hopes rising as he hits a few good shots after trying a given tip. It works! he thinks to himself. "I've got the game licked," he exclaims, as my father has so many times confessed to feeling. But how long does any single magic formula help a given player? "The secret" is dropped after a few poor shots occur and hope wanes. Soon the golfer is open for the next tip. Of course, some modest tips can be truly helpful, but the all-encompassing ones only raise one's hopes for conquering a game that can *never* be mastered by a single tip. I am convinced that the happiest and best golfers are those who have realized that there is no single gimmick that works and that good golf is attained only by patience and humility and by continually practicing both Outer and Inner Game skills.

So here is the mental situation, as I see it, facing the brave soul who plunges innocently into the awesome game of golf. His ego will be attracted to the rich psychic rewards offered by success in the sport, and it will fear the imagined devastation that failure to perform up to a reasonable norm may bring. After he has played a few rounds, he will have hit enough good shots to provoke unquieting thoughts of heroism—if only he can learn to repeat consistently what he has shown that he can do on occasion. But unknown to the novice player, the mechanics of the game dictates that the probabilities of hitting those shots consistently are almost nil. Furthermore, he will be surrounded by prophets with both mental and technical golfing keys promising to deliver him from his evils and to unlock the gates leading into the heaven of good golf. Confused by the long lists of dos and don'ts, ranging from sound fundamentals to superstitious mental magic, he will tend to analyze each shot and to try to compensate for each mistake. Then he will compensate for the compensation. Between failures he will have all the time in the world to think and, while doing so, to increase his tension and doubt, while after success

OBSESSION WITH TIPS AND TECHNIQUE

he won't be able to resist the temptation to analyze how to repeat it. Put this all together in the head of one man or woman who is already suffering the tensions of modern life and what you have is an intriguing but dangerous game.

THE INNER GAME OF GOLF

It is the thesis of this book that the secret to increasing control over our bodies lies in gaining some measure of control over our minds. A basic understanding of mechanics can help, and, surely, a certain amount of physical coordination is required to play good golf. But differences in talent do not account for the fact that most of us hit much better on the practice range than we do in the thick of battle on the course or for the wide variations in our individual scores. The aim of the Inner Game is to close the unnecessarily wide gap between our potential and our actual performance and to open the way to higher and more constant levels of enjoyment of the game.

Thus, the challenge of golf lies as much in the relatively unexplained aspects of the Inner Game as it does in the Outer Game. There is a growing interest in the mental side of golf that is reflected in current books and magazine articles on the subject. Asking me to speak at a PGA meeting, a regional PGA educational director said that there was a general consensus that teaching pros were reaching a point of diminishing returns on analysis of the mechanics of golf and were turning their attention to the mental side of the sport. "We know a lot about the swing," one college golf coach said to me, "but not much about how to help golfers learn it."

This is not merely a matter of words. The issues of how to overcome self-doubt, lapses in concentration, self-anger, and low self-esteem are very real. Facing these handicaps for some is like noticing an unwelcome bedfellow; we'd rather roll over and forget that he or she is there.

But to play the Inner Game is not really a matter of choice. It is always going on, and we are playing it constantly in our various outer games. The only question is whether we are playing it consciously and whether we are winning it or losing it. Anyone who feels his performance is always equal to its actual potential, and fully enjoys and learns from his golf experience, has my hearty congratulations for winning the Inner Game. As for all others, including myself, though we may play very different outer games in different circumstances, there is still an enemy within and, thus, an Inner Game to be played.

The fundamental challenge to the golfer is to recognize the existence of interference and that winning the Inner Game may be more to the point than simply defeating the golf course.

This book describes practical ways to bring Inner Game principles and techniques to your golf game. These exercises are neither gimmicks nor tips; rather, they are ways to increase three primary inner skills: awareness, choice, and trust. Because many of the exercises were developed as I attempted to learn golf, some of this book consists of brief accounts of my own inner and outer struggles and the evolution of my game.

The next chapter begins with my efforts to gain enough consistency in my swing so I could take ten or more strokes off my 100-plus average score. I accomplished this with the help of a focusing technique I adapted from *The Inner Game of Tennis* called "back-hit-stop."

CHAPTER 2

BREAKING 90
WITH
BACK-HIT-STOP

I n *The Inner Game of Tennis*, I wrote, "Relaxed concentration is the key to excellence in all things." I realized that golf was going to offer an even more difficult challenge to maintaining this concentration than tennis. When I first began to explore the Inner Game of golf, I was not aware that this subject was not entirely new. Since almost all golf instruction at the time seemed focused on mechanics, I was surprised when I ran across an article called "The Mental Hazards of Golf" in a 1929 issue of *Vanity Fair* by none other than the legendary Bobby Jones. The article was sub-titled "Stray Thoughts on Worry, Nerves, Temperament and Lack of Concentration in the Game." Here are some excerpts:

> Golf is assuredly a mystifying game. Even the best golfers cannot step
> onto the first tee with any assurance as to what they are going to do. . . .
> It would seem that if a person has hit a golf ball correctly a thousand
> times he should be able to duplicate the performance almost at will. But
> such is certainly not the case.

> The golf swing is a most complicated combination of muscular actions,
> too complex to be controlled by objective conscious mental effort.
> Consequently, we must rely a good deal upon the instinctive reactions
> acquired by long practice. It has been my experience that the more

completely we can depend upon this instinct—the more thoroughly we can divest the subjective mind of conscious control—the more perfectly can we execute our shots. . . . That intense concentration upon results, to the absolute exclusion of all thoughts as to method, is the secret of a good shot. Few great shots are played when the mind is fixed on the position of the feet, the behavior of the left arm, etc.

In playing a golf shot it always helps if the player can shut out from his mind all worry over the result of the effort, at least while he is in the act of playing the shot. . . . After taking the stance, it is too late to worry. The only thing to do then is to hit the ball.

It is not easy, even with the assistance of a first-class teacher, for a man to develop a sound golfing style. But it is possible and practicable for a person to cultivate a mental attitude toward the game which will enable him to get everything possible out of his own capability.

These statements rang true according to my experience teaching concentration in tennis. I realized that what I may have thought I discovered had, in fact, been around for a long time and had probably been discovered by many others, perhaps by everyone who had truly achieved excellence in his or her field. Yes, the problem is ultimately a simple one of control, but most things requiring excellence are too complex to be controlled, as Bobby Jones observed, "by objective conscious mental effort."

SELF 1 AND SELF 2

A major breakthrough in my understanding of the problem of control of mind and body came when, as a tennis instructor, I became aware of a constant commentary going on inside my head as I played. I realized that my students were subjected to a similar flow of self-instructional thoughts while taking lessons: Come on, get your racket back earlier. . . . You hit that one too late again. . . . Bend your knee on those volleys. . . . Uh-oh, here comes another high backhand like the one you missed last time. . . . Make sure you don't miss it again. . . . Damn it! you missed it again. . . . When are you ever going to hit those things? . . . Watch the ball, watch the ball. . . . What am I going to say to my doubles partner if I lose this match?

As I began to take a closer look at the thoughts going through my mind during a tennis match, I found myself asking, "Whom am I talking to, and who is doing the talking?" I was surprised to discover that there seemed to be at least two identities within me. One was playing tennis; the other was telling him how. I observed that the one doing the talking, whom I named Self 1, thought he knew all about how to play and was supervising Self 2, the one who had to hit the ball. In fact, Self 1 not only gave Self 2 instructions but criticized him for past errors, warned him of probable future ones, and harangued him whenever he made a mistake. It was easy to see that the primary feeling in the relationship between these two selves was mistrust. Self 1 didn't trust Self 2 to hit the ball, and, precisely to the extent that he lacked trust, he would try to force Self 2 to conform to his verbal instructions. I noticed that when I had more confidence in my ability to hit a shot, there was a corresponding decrease in instructions from Self 1 and that Self 2 would perform amazingly well without him. When I was on a streak, there was no talk in my head at all.

Once I became aware of Self 1, it grew increasingly obvious that this judgmental little voice barking away like a drill sergeant inside my head was not the best thing for my tennis game. Self 1 was more of a hindrance than the great help he wanted me to think he was. Thereafter I began looking for ways to decrease the interference of Self 1, and to see what happened if I trusted the potential of Self 2. I found that when I could quiet Self 1 and let Self 2 learn and play without interference, my performance and learning rate improved significantly. My Self 2 was a great deal more competent than Self 1 gave him credit for. Likewise, I found that when, as a teacher, I didn't feed the instruction-hungry Self 1 of a student with a lot of technical information but, instead, trusted in the capacity of *his* Self 2 to learn, the progress of my students was three or four times faster than average, and they learned with much less frustration.

In short, I found that Self 1—the verbalizing, thought-producing self—is a lousy boss when it comes to control of the body's muscle system. When Self 2—the body itself—is allowed control, the quality of performance, the level of enjoyment, and the rate of learning are all improved.

Although after a time I realized that Self 1 was really a composite of different ego-personalities that would surface at different times, it was still helpful to group all these elements under the identifying label of Self 1 as the source of our interference with our natural selves. I found that in order to *de*crease interference and *in*crease performance, it wasn't necessary to analyze *why* doubt, fear, judgment, and lapses in concentration occurred; it was sufficient to recognize their intrusion and then concentrate the mind on something real in the immediate environment. From this realization, a number of Inner Game concentration exercises were developed for tennis players.

Some readers of *The Inner Game of Tennis* have associated Self 1 and Self 2 with the popular two-hemisphere-brain theory, equating Self 1 with the rational, analytical left hemisphere and Self 2 with the intuitive right hemisphere. I don't make the same association because both right and left hemispheres are part of the human body. I look at Self 2 as the total human organism, the natural entity. Self 1, on the other hand, does not actually have a physical existence; it is a phenomenon of mental self-interference that can and does interfere with both right- and left-hemisphere functions. Self-doubt, for example, can be as crippling in a mathematics test as in a tennis match, on a golf course or in singing a song. But when the mind is concentrated and absorbed in what it is doing, interference is minimized and the brain is able to function closer to its potential.

When Self 1 and Self 2 are clearly defined in this way, the basic premise of the Inner Game can be expressed in a simple equation: $P = p - i$. The quality of our performance (P) is equal to our potential (p) minus the interference (i) with the expression of that potential (Self 1). Or: Performance = Self 2 (potential) minus Self 1 (interference).

Thus, the aim of the Inner Game is not so much to try harder to persuade Self 2 to do what it is capable of doing but to decrease the Self 1 interferences that prevent Self 2 from expressing itself fully.

Still, I found that like most tyrants, Self 1 didn't like losing control and resisted efforts to minimize his influence. The process of decreasing his control in favor of Self 2 proved to be a challenging one, which required the development of concentration techniques designed to keep Self 1 occupied in noninterfering activity and consciously to allow Self 2 to hit the ball. Once Self 1 was focused in a concentration exercise, his interference with Self 2 decreased significantly and performance instantly improved.

THE MAGIC OF BOUNCE-HIT

What had become clear to me on the tennis court was that it was not so easy to follow Bobby Jones's admonition to "divest the subjective mind of conscious control." Neither was it so easy to focus to the extent of "absolute exclusion of all thoughts."

In tennis the most obvious focus for the attention is the moving tennis ball. But simply to encourage students to watch the ball doesn't create the level of focus I was looking for. I found that when I asked students to watch the ball's spinning seams, there was a higher degree of focus and usually smoother shots. I found even more success in a quite simple focusing technique I called "bounce-hit," which proved effective for players at all levels.

Before giving the students instructions, I would usually introduce the exercise by saying that its purpose was not to improve results but to improve *focus*, an important Inner Game skill useful in all endeavors. The exercise was to say out loud the word "bounce" the instant the ball hit the court and the word "hit" at the moment of impact with the racket. Once the player got locked in to "bounce-hit," an almost immediate improvement could be seen in the way he swung his racket and moved his feet and body, and there was usually an observable increase in relaxation and fluidity of movement. Players hit even more difficult shots with relative effortlessness while their conscious mind was absorbed in the cadence of the bounce-hit focus.

I realized there were two basic criteria for the success of any effective focusing exercise. First, it had to be interesting enough to engage the attention of the conscious mind, distracting it from its normal patterns of overcontrol and interference. Second, it had to give useful feedback about ball and body to enable more coordinated movement.

What I was looking for in golf was some simple focus of attention that in the same way would keep my conscious, thinking mind out of the way of my natural swing and natural learning process. And golfers I met who were familiar with *The Inner Game of Tennis* were asking me the very question I was asking myself: "What is the bounce-hit of golf?"

Although I experimented with a number of exercises for focusing attention on the golf ball—such as watching a dimple, the label, or a speck of dust—none of these seemed to keep my mind quiet for long. The problem was that the darn ball just sat there. I would easily grow bored looking at it, and, if I forced the exercise, my mind became strained and my swing stiff. The bounce-hit magic seemed to have something to do with the mind's fascination with the movement and rhythm of the tennis ball, and this simply didn't apply to the golf ball. Also, in order to hit the golf ball, Self 2 didn't need moment-to-moment *visual* feedback; the ball wasn't going to go anywhere until I hit it. The very lack of motion of the golf ball, which gave one so much time to think and grow tense, was exactly what was impeding concentration.

Finally, I did find one focus that helped more than the others and is worth mentioning. Instead of looking only at the ball, I began looking at the back of the ball *in relation to* one of the blades of grass just below it. By keeping both in focus, I could tell if during the swing there was undue head movement. If the relative position of the ball and the background of grass changed a great deal, it was because I had moved my head a lot. This helped, but it still was not the answer I was looking for.

Eventually I came to the conclusion that the primary focus of attention in golf should be *not* the ball but the club head, the critical moving object. The movement was *there*, the feedback needed was *there*, the rhythm that fascinates the mind was *there*—not in the ball. But I couldn't follow the club head with my eyes; if I wished to focus attention on it, I would have to use my sense of *feel*, and I didn't know how difficult this would be. How much could I actually *feel* the club head moving during my swing? I decided to go out to the driving range to experiment with club-head awareness.

At first, I had relatively little sense of where my club was. I found that if I didn't worry about whether I hit the ball or not, I could feel it better. I tried shutting my eyes and swinging and found that my awareness of feel increased even more. The movement of the club head was becoming interesting enough to hold my attention throughout the arc of the swing. Whenever I would try simply to *feel* the club head and *not* to *control* it, the club seemed to swing itself, and I got excellent results—the same kind I had in tennis when my mind became concentrated. But when I split my attention—half to the feel of the club head and the other half to trying to control the swing—the results weren't so good.

BACK-HIT-STOP

To keep my mind focused on the club and away from the process of controlling it, I came up with the following exercise. Keeping my attention on the feel of the club head, I would say the word "back" the instant I felt the club reach its furthest extension at the completion of the backswing. I would simply sense its position without worrying at all whether it was in the "correct place." Then I would say the word "hit" the instant the club face met the ball. Finally, I would say the word "stop" the moment the club came to rest at the completion of the follow-through.

This exercise kept me in touch with the club head throughout the entire arc of the swing and was exacting enough to keep my attention away from the intrusion of Self 1 commands. Staying with the club until "stop" proved to be particularly effective in keeping Self 1 from prematurely jerking my head up to see where the ball had gone. The drill actually required more concentration than the visual bounce-hit in tennis. Precisely because it was more demanding, it was even more effective.

After only a few minutes' work with this exercise, there were often dramatic improvements in swing technique and results. The only real difficulty was in the tendency to want to control the swing instead of simply doing the exercise. It is natural not to want to give up all conscious control at once. But even with 50 percent of my focus occupied in "back-hit-stop," there was significantly less interference with the swing. Then, as my confidence grew, it was easier to risk focusing more on the exercise and to leave the hitting to instinct.

It was surprising to many golfers to whom I showed this exercise how unaware they actually had been of their club head. Although most had interesting theories about where it *should* be at the back of the swing, they were often six to eighteen inches off in their estimate of where it *actually* was. One thing I had learned in tennis was that it is more important to know where your racket *is* than to know where it *should be*. The tennis ball is hardly ever where it should be but always where it is. I told my students, "*Should* and *is* usually miss each other." The same is true in golf. What the body needs to control the path of the club head is not a lot of instructions but accurate, moment-by-moment feedback about its position. Back-hit-stop was effective in increasing this input, as well as in quieting Self 1. It took practice and trust, but it paid off in results.

One problem that emerged for some players practicing this exercise was a tendency to turn "back" and "hit" from nouns into verbs. This had the effect of putting them back into the mode of obeying commands. It was as if they were telling themselves, "Now get your club back, now hit the ball." I could usually tell when this was happening, as the normal overtightness and controlling effort would appear while the accuracy of the "back-hit-stop" suffered greatly. "The word 'back' is supposed to be used as a noun," I would remind them. "It is just used to denote the moment you feel your club reach the top of its swing, and 'hit' is another noun to denote the moment of impact." The same goes for "stop"; it is not a command to stop the swing but a word to mark its completion.

DA-DA-DA-DA

To help some people avoid the temptation to command I substituted the syllable "da" for each of the words. "Da" at the back and "da" at the hit and then "da" at completion. This made the rhythm of the swing even more obvious, especially when it was turned into a four-count cadence. "Da" at the moment of takeaway; "da" at the top of the backswing, "da" at the moment of impact, and, finally, "da" at the end.

This four-count cadence had several added advantages. It gave an increased sense of rhythm and tempo as well as feedback about the position of the club head at four critical moments. It turned out to be a far more interesting focus for the mind because of the added sense rhythm. Consequently, there was less room for conscious control, better feedback for the swing, and a greater freedom in swinging the club.

This exercise can be practiced on the range to improve club-head awareness and to help discover one's natural rhythm and tempo. It can also be used during play on the course to keep the mind focused and clear.

I realized, as I had with tennis, that there is a very big difference between *observing* your swing and *trying to control* it. Most important, I found out that it's hard to do both at the same time. When I kept to the discipline of this exercise, paying full attention, I had much less tendency to overcontrol my swing, and, as a result, it seemed over time to gain control naturally.

Sometimes I felt that the Inner Game worked even better for others than for myself. Just when I was starting my search for the bounce-hit of golf, I got a phone call from a Mr. Dean Nims, from Des Moines, Iowa.

He identified himself as the president of a paper company and an avid but frustrated golfer with an eighteen or nineteen handicap. He said he had read both of my Inner Game tennis books in the hope that they would help with his golf.

DEAN NIMS'S STORY

"I tried to come up with an exercise that paralleled your bounce-hit in tennis and finally settled on 'hit-bounce,' " Mr. Nims told me. "I would say 'hit' when the club hit the ball and 'bounce' when the ball landed, wherever it landed. The results were instantaneous and dramatic for me. Playing the McCormick Ranch Golf Course near Scottsdale, Arizona, I shot a 76 for the first time using this drill. It was unbelievable! I could see the ball much better, had much less tension, and didn't turn away from my shots after hitting them as I had done before. I'd never broken 85 before. Of course, I couldn't help thinking I had the game licked after that and would only use the drill when I thought I was in trouble. Then I'd get better again."

Later Dean came out to California to take some Inner Game golf lessons and to discuss with me the translation of Inner Game principles to business practices. A few months later I called Dean and he told me he was using Inner Game principles in most areas of his life. "I can't say I've won the game," he said, "but my golf has steadily improved—not only in my scoring but in my general attitude." His handicap had gone down to eight, playing little more than once a week, and he said he was enjoying showing the methods to others.

Dean told me about an eight-year-old girl who was on the range with her father one hot, humid summer day. The father was trying to instruct her, but she was unable to hit the ball in spite of all his help. They were both hot and frustrated when Dean introduced himself to them and showed the girl the da-da-da-da exercise. The girl seemed interested, took a swing singing out "daddy-da," and hit the first solid ball of her life. She continued to do so the rest of the practice session. Her father told Dean that his daughter had been in a junior golf program and, given the task of playing one hole, had been unable to get off the tee. The next day he called Dean to say that the girl was ecstatic. She had not only gotten off the tee, she had beaten her two competitors, both two years older.

But Dean also told me that a lot of adults he'd showed the exercise to had more difficulty.

"What's the problem?" I asked.

"They seem reluctant to really try something new and different, even though they saw what it did to my game. Some say they know they're lousy golfers and didn't expect to get any better, and some don't want to entertain the hope. Others who agreed to do the exercise had a hard time accepting that they were not saying 'hit' until way after the moment of contact. But when they realized that it was their thinking that kept them from saying 'hit' on time, and then could let go of Self 1 control, they'd experience a significant breakthrough."

As an aside, Dean told me about one of his salesmen who hadn't been performing up to his potential. "Although he wasn't a tennis player or golfer, he agreed to read the Inner Game books and discuss with me their application to sales. The next year his sales doubled."

The principle behind back-hit-stop and da-da-da-da is the same. Individual preferences, however, will emerge if you choose to experiment. The only important thing is to make a commitment to doing purely the concentration exercise. Don't try to add it to another tip or to other swing thoughts.

In both tennis and golf, I found that a person's level of focus does not stay constant. Often at the beginning it would start quite purely. There would be no expectations, and the person would let go of control to do the focusing exercise as an experiment. Then if he noticed the results of his shots—either whether they improved or got worse—control would often come back. As coach, I could see the increase of tension and hear that the words spoken were no longer in sync. Then, if I asked the student if he was on time, early, or late with the words or syllables, "I don't know" was often the reply.

When either you or another person notices that your voice is out of sync with your swing, it's a sign that you are losing focus. At that point, it is often interesting to notice quickly what pulled you off focus, for example, thinking about results, mechanics, memories of past shots, and so forth. Then determine to renew your focus on back-hit-stop or da-da-da-da. When these exercises are done with discipline, the result is almost always a freer swing made possible by less Self 1 control. Obviously, no exercise can promise a flawless swing every time, nor should it be a replacement for learning the important technical aspects of the golf swing, a subject that will be addressed in more detail starting with Chapter 5.

PRACTICING FOCUS

My recommendation is that you practice the exercises for at least a short time on the driving range and putting green before attempting them on the course. It is difficult enough to let go of conscious control over your swing in practice; it is almost too much to ask under playing conditions. Once you have found the exercise that works best for quieting your mind, you should stick with it and give it a chance to work. Eventually it will be difficult not to want to use it in the pressure situations. One can expect, however, that the greater the pressure, the harder it will be to quiet Self 1 and attain the same level of concentration as in practice. But then, that's just when you need it, so persevere.

When first learning how to use these exercises, it is a good idea to say the words out loud, and even to have an observer check your accuracy. When your voice is markedly out of sync with your club position, it will be because your mind has wandered—probably to the task of trying to hit the ball. Most players need some practice with this exercise before developing a concrete feel of the club head.

After a brief period of practicing back-hit-stop or da-da-da-da, your concentration will probably improve, and so your swing will be freer and you will get better results. At the first sign of success, be careful! Don't start thinking that these are magic words and that whenever you say them the ball will go where you wish. Remember that if it works, it's not the words that make it work but improved concentration.

Don't try to reduce the exercise to a magic formula, another superstition. If you do, the exercise will soon stop being effective, just like all other gimmicks. Then Self 1 will tell you, "Well, that sure doesn't work—throw it out. This whole thing is nonsense." Don't listen. Just remember that the words were just an aid to concentration and that it was the concentration that helped. Every time you succeed in blocking out Self 1 and allow Self 2 to hit the ball, you will get better results. But you have to make the effort *every* time; momentary relaxed concentration is easy, but it has to become constant and continuous. Techniques to help gain that concentration are only as effective as your steady use of them.

BREAKING 90

The positive effects of back-hit-stop and da-da-da-da were soon very apparent on my own golf game. As a result, primarily from doing this exercise, my average score dropped from about 95 to about 88.

When Joe Fox, my original editor at Random House, asked me to write about applying Inner Game methods to my own game of golf, I was hesitant at first. At that time I played golf fewer than four or five times a year and usually shot between 95 and 105. "Let's see if you can break 80 by the time you turn in the book and by playing no more than one round of golf per week," Fox challenged. He argued that many readers could not play more than that. At the time, I had slightly over a year to complete the book and break 80. Needless to say, I felt sufficiently challenged.

My game at the time was not hard to characterize. I hit a fairly long drive, but without consistency. Out of ten drives, no more than three would be likely to land in the fairway, four would have a moderate to severe slice, and three would be dubbed or hooked. Such a variety was not encouraging to me, even though distance itself seemed somehow to be a compensation. My mid and short irons were a little more reliable—but only a little. Even though I hit some greens and sunk some long putts, they were too few and far between. My game was not a cautious one. If I had a chance to cut off distance on a dogleg or hit through a flock of trees for the green, I would almost always go for it. I hated to play it safe and all too often was willing to give up prudence.

Still, hope was kept alive by the two or three spectacular shots I would hit every eighteen holes. Deep down there was a dream that I could repeat my best swings and that perhaps what I had learned in tennis about the Inner Game would bring me instant success in golf.

The day I accepted my editor's challenge, I set myself a regimen of no more than eighteen holes of golf per week and only one hour of practice on the range and putting green. In spite of a certain feeling of pressure about having to break 80, I started this golfing experience with high expectations. Somewhere in the more naive part of my mind I entertained the thought that perhaps I could discover such an effective concentration exercise for golf that I would be shooting par in a couple of weeks.

Such was not to be. Finishing my first round at Rancho Park in Los Angeles with a 98, I realized that despite my confidence as an Inner Game tennis professional, my abilities did not automatically transfer to golf. It wasn't until after a few weeks, once my dreams of glory had died down and my tension had subsided, that I began to apply focusing techniques in a disciplined way. By that time I had played three rounds and given myself three hours of practice. My scores averaged about 95.

When I made the decision to make the practice of focus a priority over my results, my first real breakthrough occurred. I decided that the discipline of whispering to myself the syllables "da-da-da-da" in cadence with my swing was worth committing to for at least my next ten rounds of golf. Near the end of the second month I had broken 90 once, and by the end of the third my score was averaging 88.

During this time, I focused almost exclusively on the rhythm and cadence of my swing, and I had the sense that my club head was doing the swinging rather than my trying to control it. I could feel my consistency increasing and with it my self-confidence. Soon I began to feel a little more like a golfer than like a tennis player trying to play golf. I also knew that I hadn't yet attained the limit of my capacity. I still had a lot to explore about both the Outer and Inner games of golf.

Not too much later I began to wonder what would happen if I were to play one of the great golf courses. Was I ready for it?

90 AT ST. ANDREWS GOLF CLUB, SCOTLAND

I flew to London on business but with the firm intention of heading up to Scotland to play the historic St. Andrews course. When my editor heard about my plans, he bet me ten dollars that I couldn't break 100 on the Old Course, whose generally adverse conditions of heather and weather make it one of the world's toughest.

The day I finally got a chance to play I flew to Edinburgh from the Inner Game Center in London and rented a car at the airport to drive to St. Andrews. I barely made my 1:00 tee time. I played in a threesome with Peter and Daphne, an English couple who live on the first tee at the Canterbury Golf Course in Kent. I felt nervous as I stepped up to the first tee, where crowds of onlookers line up to watch. The souvenir scorecard described the hazards on each hole, complete with pictures. They were formidable. The first hole presents only one hazard, called Swilican Burn, a wide ditch full of water right along the edge of the green. I made an effort to concentrate, targeted, and landed left of center on the fairway. From there I hit a seven iron twenty feet from the pin, but only ten feet from Swilican Burn. I wished I'd brought my own golf clubs; the putter of the set I'd rented at the caddie house was much lighter than my own. I kicked the thought out of my mind, focused on the heel of the putter head, and barely missed the putt. Par.

I'd come to St. Andrews on a day of rare good weather: 80 degrees, with a warm wind at our backs. Though I'd heard a lot about the beauty and majesty of this oldest course, I was nonetheless spellbound by its incredible meandering greens, like broad expanses of meadowland, and its treacherous and unusual traps. Some were eight to twelve feet deep; others had vertical sides that dropped six feet to fine white sand—more like small cliffs than lips. All bore provocative names: The Coffins, The Cat's Trap, The Principal's Nose. The sense of ancient tradition permeates the atmosphere; the town itself is built around the course, physically and culturally. I gave in to the magic of the place and the ambience of the day. I had anticipated pressure from my desire to make my one chance to play this course a good performance, not so much because of my bet with my editor as because I wanted to write about it in the book. (Self 1 was eager for renown.)

On the second hole I hit a hesitant chip shot for a bogey; I parred the third and bogeyed the fourth. Then I noticed that I wasn't nervous anymore and, mistakenly, I took this as a propitious sign. On the fifth hole I was a little discouraged to take three putts and a double bogey; I was getting casual, at St. Andrews of all places! I went to the sixth tee without really shaking off my three-putt green.

Thus far I hadn't been reading the descriptions of the hazards on the scorecards, and my caddie, a Scot with wild reddish-brown hair tucked up under a plaid ski cap despite the heat, hadn't told me about them either. He would simply point his crooked finger to tell me where to aim. Trusting his experience and my own Self 2 to hit where he pointed, I had managed to stay out of real trouble for five holes. On the sixth, aptly named Heathery, Peter read me the description of the hidden bunkers. For the first time my caddie, Fred, offered some advice, telling me to keep right because I'd been hooking. I aimed right for a draw, forgetting to do the da-da-da-da with my swing, and the ball landed deep in the heather, nestling neither on the surface of the thick heather nor on the ground, but suspended midway between the two. I knew I would need a heavy club to budge it, so I asked Fred if he thought I'd be crazy to use a driver. He shrugged and said it might work. I swung hard, but succeeded only in driving the ball down to the ground no further ahead of where it had been. I switched to a sand wedge and this time managed to scoot it along ten feet, still in the heather. "Making progress," Peter commented dryly. Using the sand wedge again for the next shot, this time I moved it twenty-five yards, but at least I was out of the heather. My three iron drove it 170 yards to the left edge of the green—but this green was no ordinary one. I was still thirty-three yards from the hole and would need to sink the putt for a double bogey. I hit fifteen feet past it, then missed the return putt, ending the fiasco with a quadruple bogey! Heathery had gotten to me!

It's this sort of experience that makes the hazards of St. Andrews so notorious. Daphne ran into similar trouble on the next hole, "High." The green is guarded by a bunker about eight feet deep, and Daphne hit into it. Peter told her to keep her head down and swing through. She strained, but stayed in. After three swings she said, "Hopeless!" and picked up. She then had to ask Peter to haul *her* out of the bunker!

I ended the first nine with a 46, ten over par. I was feeling generally settled, not nervous, and strangely unbothered by the pressures I'd anticipated. Peter was playing better than I and was ribbing me a little; I found his chiding helped me increase my concentration. On the next six holes, I got two pars and four bogeys. On the sixteenth hole I pushed a drive OB and ended with a triple bogey.

Approaching the eighteenth hole after a bogey on seventeen, I was thinking that this would be my last opportunity to enjoy St. Andrews. I wanted to let out all the stops. Crowds were watching the golfers, mostly American tourists in plaid pants. I let go with my longest drive of the day and then hit a six iron twelve feet from the pin. I wanted to birdie the finishing hole but left it short.

Par on the first hole, par on the last. Almost poetic. I felt pretty good about both my Inner and Outer games. I'd scored a 90 and was able to find the often elusive balance between tensing too much and overrelaxing to the point of sloppiness.

Some barrier broke for me as I played those eighteen holes. I knew St. Andrews was one of the toughest courses I could play, for both Inner and Outer games, and I had survived it. It was as if I no longer felt that I had to prove anything. Being in Europe had jarred me out of my usual routine and given me new perspectives, and although my desire to do well at St. Andrews could have been an opportunity for a lot of interference from Self 1, it hadn't turned out that way. The obstacles of the course created a natural pressure that I welcomed. I felt a healthy desire to pit myself against them and take golf beyond the limits of mere score. In the place where the game began I got a better sense of what golf could be. Some underlying self-doubt I hadn't been aware of disappeared, and I felt the effects of this even in my business dealings before returning to the States.

Coming home, I felt again a humility and appreciation for what the Inner Game could teach me, with golf as a medium for discovering both my own potential and my existing limitations.

CHAPTER 3

OVERTIGHTNESS: THE MOST COMMON CAUSE OF ERROR

The single most common physical cause of error in golf, and perhaps in all sports, is overtightness. It is generally understood by golfers with even a little experience that the overtightening of muscles in an effort to produce power is responsible for many poor drives. "Don't try to hit the ball so hard, dummy," is a familiar criticism from Self 1 on the course.

But it is equally true, though less recognized, that tightened muscles cause most slices, hooks, topped balls, and fat shots. Overtightening of the shoulders prevents a full backswing and follow-through, and overtightening of the hands turns the putter blade closed or keeps it open at contact, sending the ball off course. Involuntary tightening lies behind the dread yips in both chipping and putting.

Commonly, the observation of a beginning golfer watching the pros is, "Wow, they make it look so easy. They don't seem to be swinging hard at all." On almost any driving range the muscled jerkiness of the average golfer's swing is in obvious contrast to the pro's powerful fluidity.

Yet overtightness need not plague even the most inexperienced golfer. The purpose of this chapter is to explore the dynamics of this phenomenon and to give the reader some tools with which he can significantly reduce overtightness in his swing, whether he is a beginner or an intermediate or advanced player.

Actually, "overtightness" is an inaccurate word when applied to mus-

THE PRIMARY PHYSICAL CAUSE OF ERROR

cles, since no individual muscle unit can be over- or undercontracted. It is either relaxed or flexed. When the muscle fiber is relaxed, it is soft and pliable. When it is contracted, it folds in upon itself and becomes rigid enough to support many times its own weight. Strength is measured in the amount of weight that can be supported by contracted muscles. This is not the same as power. Power is the ability to *use* strength, and it requires a very sophisticated cooperative effort between contracting and relaxing muscles. Some muscles pull, while opposing muscles remain relaxed and pliant so as to allow the movement to take place.

What we experience as overtightness in golf is often the contracting of too many muscles—more than are necessary to accomplish the task at hand. For example, if all the muscles in the wrist are tightened before impact with the ball, there may be a lot of strength in the wrists, but little or no power will be generated because the tightness of some muscles will restrict the free movement of others.

Another kind of overtightness occurs when rigid muscles fail to release. For instance, the shoulder muscles involved in moving the club back on the backswing have to release fully to allow for other muscles to produce the forward swing. If they remain contracted because of tension, the muscles that initiate the forward swing have to fight against them in accomplishing their task. This creates a classic case of interference with the expression of power and control.

A third kind of overtightening stems from the mistimed contractions of muscles. If your arms are moving toward the ball and the wrist movement occurs at the optimum timing before contact, the momentum generated by this is added to the momentum of the arm movement and produces power. But if the wrist muscles contract at the top of your swing instead of just before contact, the momentum is lost and the club will not be moving much faster than your arms when you hit the ball.

Different kinds of errors in the swing are caused by overtightening in different parts of the body at different times. A restricted backswing is caused by overtightening in the left shoulder, restricted hip rotation by tightness in the hips, casting and scooping by tightness in the wrist and arms. Most of the subtler errors in the swing can likewise be traced to overtightness in certain parts of the body.

But to attempt to remedy the problem by analyzing each instance of overtightness would be exasperating and self-defeating. Literally thousands of muscle units are involved in the golf swing; their timing and coordination are exquisitely precise and are simply not accessible to intellectual understanding. The body coordinates these muscles in response to our general command to produce accuracy and power, but only when the execution of those goals is entrusted to it. The best conscious effort we can make is to be clear about our goal and to keep from interfering with its execution.

Though some experience of overtightness may be unavoidable in the process of learning the golf swing, by far the greatest amount of it comes from the ways in which we interfere with the workings of our bodies when we attempt to control the swing. This interference can be greatly reduced if we are willing to admit that it is present and notice it when it happens.

Just as instructing your muscles to contract is obviously futile, telling yourself to relax is not a solution. The command from someone else or from yourself to relax, often spoken as if to an idiot, only causes more tension and tightness. On the other hand, overrelaxing is liable to give you the swing of a wet noodle.

The first step in decreasing overtightness in one's swing is to determine if it is present. This may sound obvious, but trying to cure a flaw without really accepting and experiencing it almost always leads to greater problems. So the first step is to swing while focusing attention on your body as it does so. Don't try to do anything; just swing and see if you notice any overtightness, any lack of fluidity, or any forcing. In many cases, simply by paying attention to any restrictions in the flow of movement, you will begin to experience a reduction of overtightness without any conscious effort to loosen up. Ten or fifteen swings may be enough to produce a significant change if you are attentive and don't try to relax.

However, if you have played a good deal of golf, patterns of overtightness may have become so ingrained in your swing that it is hard to notice them. One can grow so accustomed to an overtight swing that it's difficult to feel it and therefore difficult to change it. The following exercises will help you detect tightness in your swing as it occurs; once it is brought to your awareness, it can be controlled.

HUMMING YOUR SWING

One day, quite by accident, I discovered an exercise that is remarkably effective in reducing overtightness. I was out late one afternoon hitting seven irons on the driving range while waiting for Tom Nordland, with whom I was going to do an Inner Game practice session. I was not concentrating on anything in particular, simply hitting balls and humming to myself. Suddenly, something struck me. I could hear differences in my humming, depending on how I was swinging the club. The experience was such a surprise that I wish everybody could become aware of it as spontaneously as I did. The next time you're on the practice tee, take a few swings and try humming to yourself while swinging. *Listen to the humming.*

I hadn't considered my swing particularly tight, but my humming told me differently. I could actually hear the tightness of my swing in the sound. While I was going back the sound would be nice and smooth, but during the change of direction my voice would become strained, and at contact my throat would constrict and the humming would increase in volume, in pitch, and, most noticeably, in tightness. Sometimes, when I really went after the ball, the hum would stop after contact and I would notice that I had also cut off my follow-through. Using a tape recorder, I later recorded the sound of my practice swing and compared it with a recording of a swing at a ball. The increase in tension was painfully obvious.

This phenomenon turned out to be very practical. I realized that I was amplifying feedback from my body by the use of sound. Overtightness that I previously was not very aware of now became glaringly apparent. The audible alterations in sound while swinging told me a lot about what was happening to my body. What to do? The answer was easy: Simply keep swinging and humming. Use this humming as a biofeedback machine to increase control.

For those who are not familiar with biofeedback methodology, it is a way of hooking up subtle physiological functions—such as blood pressure or even brain waves—to an electronic device that gives you feedback, either in sound frequencies or in visual patterns on a screen, enabling you to perceive slight changes. By simply attending to this feedback it is possible to gain control over bodily functions previously thought to be beyond volitional control. For example, we can learn to control our own blood pressure or temperature, though we won't know *how* we are doing it.

The sound method works in the same way. The sound amplifies the feedback you are receiving from the overtightening of muscles. By listening to changes in the sound, you can soon gain more control over subtle muscular tightness than you might have thought possible by simply trying to relax or to hit smoothly—efforts that often impel you to swing too loosely and with low club-head speed. The best way to use this exercise is to make no effort to swing more smoothly and simply keep listening while you hit balls on the range. Automatically, and in specific ways you won't understand—and don't need to understand—your swing will start changing. You will begin to hear less tightness in your humming, notice that you are making better contact with the ball, and get more distance while making no conscious effort to get those results. Just accept them and don't ask too many questions about how they happen. Otherwise, you will start thinking you know how to relax and giving yourself instructions about how to do it—which is one of the ways the overtightness was created in the first place. A name for this exercise might be "singing your swing"—or, if you don't mind bad puns, "hum, hum on the range."

It should be noted that although it is useful to hum loudly enough to make variations in sound easily audible for the sake of giving maximum feedback when first experimenting with the use of "singing your swing," later on I found it sufficient to hum in a voice audible only to myself. Even if the hum is very quiet, overtightness in the swing will usually change the sound. Muscles in the throat constrict with bodily overtightness, and the sound is choked off, giving you the necessary feedback. The principle behind this exercise has nothing to do with sound per se. It is *awareness* that is the curative and controlling factor, a subject discussed more thoroughly in Chapter 5. The sound simply serves as a device to increase awareness of what is happening, just as a biofeedback machine does.

I went to the practice range with two friends, Tom and Linda, both excellent golfers who were interested in learning to teach as well as to play the Inner Game of golf.

We started doing the humming exercise to try to locate any blockage to the fluidity of our swings. Watching my swing and listening to my hums, Linda observed, "The sound is mellow during your backswing, but then it has a sudden surge of tension on the way down toward the ball." She asked me if I could locate the tightness in my body that was responsible for the strain in my voice. I told her that I thought it was coming from my stomach, and she asked me to try to discover when the tightness occurred. I was able to notice the exact moment my stomach began to tighten and could give her numbers for the amount of tightness I felt on each swing. But when she asked me to lower the tightness, I couldn't.

Then she suggested that I deliberately *tighten* my stomach as much as I could. I found that after I released the contracted muscles, they seemed to relax more completely and I could start swinging without any contraction in my stomach at all. I realized that I had first learned this technique in a beginners' class in hatha yoga and that it had been used for thousands of years as a means of bringing about deep body relaxation.

To gain maximum relaxation in the body, first tighten it to the maximum extent, and then let go. For total body relaxation this exercise can be done on each part of the body from foot to head, holding the muscles in each part as tight as possible for five or ten seconds before releasing them. In a golfing situation you may not have the time to do all this, but it might help to tighten the stomach muscles and then let go and perhaps do the same with the arms and shoulders. The tightening will make it easier to relax many muscle units that might otherwise not let go, thereby giving

MAXIMUM
TIGHTNESS

the swing more flexibility and fluidity. An added benefit of this exercise is that it increases circulation of the blood and makes it easier to feel movement. There is one final benefit. When you tighten *before* the swing, you reduce some of your tendency to do so *during* it. A lot of our tightening comes from anger and frustration that build up at an unconscious level. By providing an escape hatch for these emotions, you reduce the chances of letting tension destroy your swing.

As effective as physical techniques may be, they can't be expected to solve the entire problem of overtightness. If they could, golf would be a very easy game and not nearly so interesting. But because golf is a game of such precision, it takes the overtightening of only a few muscles at the wrong time to produce a slice or hook. Therefore, the more basic causes of tightness must be addressed and reduced.

"WHEN IN DOUBT, WE TIGHTEN"

In most cases, dealing with causes is more effective than dealing with symptoms. Most players admit readily that golf is largely mental, but when it comes to confronting the mental *cause* of physical error, we become shy. We'd rather stick to the physical symptoms, analyzing one error after another, satisfied if after each bad shot we can point to the technical mistake we made. But since it is so difficult to correct the myriad technical mistakes that can result from a single mental lapse, in the long run this is fatiguing and frustrating.

One becomes a player of the Inner Game only when one is willing to see the existence of mental self-interference. If there were no self-interference with the expression of our potential, there would be no Inner Game. It is only because doubt, fear, poor self-image, lapses in concentration, and anger are present in all of us that the Inner Game exists and is played by those who want to excel and to enjoy themselves doing so. Dealing effectively with these mental obstacles need not involve deep introspection or self-analysis. Golfers don't need to lie on the couch or repent their sins; they need only to be open enough to admit to the presence of internal interference and be willing to employ pragmatic methods to reduce that interference. Once the understanding is there, relatively simple techniques can reduce tension and cure many physical faults simultaneously without your even being aware that this is happening. Such an approach is powerful because it deals with causes rather than symptoms.

Over the years I have done a lot of thinking and exploring on the subject of the mental causes of errors in sports. In tennis it seemed that the primary mental problem was fear of failure; in skiing it was clearly fear of falling. In golf the anxiety and tension seemed related most obviously to fear of failure and to its brother, fear of success. But the simplicity of golf—just one action at a time—encouraged me to delve further, and I now believe there is a more basic mental cause of error.

One of the steps that led to the recognition of what I now believe to be the prime mental cause of error in all sports occurred during an informal exchange on the golf range with Archie McGill, a business executive and student of the Inner Game of tennis, who, in his golfing days, played to a scratch handicap. The brief lesson was a fortuitous one.

I had just hit a few drives when Archie stopped me and asked me to put down my club and hold his finger as if it were my golf club. I did so. He then asked me to hold his wrist as if it were my tennis racket, and I did so. "Why do you grip the golf club so much tighter than you do the tennis racket?" he asked. Not realizing that I was, I replied, "I don't know. I guess it's because I'm more sure of myself in tennis."

"Right," Archie said. "When confronted with the unknown, we tighten." This turned out to be an important moment for me. The words registered and began ringing all the proverbial bells. I looked at Archie, who himself had never made that connection before and was realizing that he had said something of more than superficial wisdom. "That's close to being a universal principle," I said.

This phrase captures a tendency that applies to many different aspects of human experience. When faced with the unknown or the uncertain—a common condition—human beings tend to enter a state of doubt and to tighten instinctively to protect themselves. Metaphorically, when we doubt our mental capabilities, we tend to constrict our minds or become closed-minded; when we doubt ourselves on the emotional level, we constrict our feelings. And on the physical level, when we doubt that we will achieve the results we want or think we may "do it wrong," we tend to overtighten our muscles.

I immediately recalled tennis players who tighten their shoulders, forearms, and wrists when confronted by a ball that they're not sure they can return. As I thought more about this response, it did seem a common tendency. When we have faith, we stay open. A child is constantly confronted with the unknown but is a sponge for all kinds of experiences until at some age he begins to learn to doubt himself. It is the questioning of whether we can meet a given challenge that seems to trigger the tightening action.

Doubt is the fundamental cause of error in sports. It is self-doubt that causes the skier to tighten to the point of rigidity at the top of the run and the tennis player to tighten on deep backhands. And it is doubt that causes the stiffness in the putter's arms and body as he tenses over a three-foot putt. It was the problem, I realized, that had caused a lot of my own suffering and worry for a great deal of my life whenever I was in a challenging situation. In many ways I could see that much of the work I had been doing with the Inner Game up to now had been an attempt to solve the single problem of self-doubt. If self-doubt was the underlying cause of overtightness and overcontrol, I wanted to understand it better and learn what could be done to overcome it. I felt that if I could make some meaningful headway with this affliction, I would have made a meaningful contribution to golfers, to say nothing of the contribution to myself.

I tried out this idea on Archie. "Would you think it fair to say that self-doubt is the prime cause of error in golf?" Archie paused and reflected. "Absolutely," he answered. "And I do not know of a single golfer who can say that he has overcome it." Just about every playing or teaching professional I asked about this agreed that self-doubt is his biggest enemy and that it inflicts itself without warning not only on the weekend player but even on the seasoned tour player.

The next chapter explores the anatomy of self-doubt and the techniques for reducing its negative influence on one's golf swing.

CHAPTER 4

OVERCOMING

SELF-DOUBT

I once asked a leading professor of psychology at the University of California at Berkeley where I could read something substantial about the phenomenon of self-doubt. He hesitated, then said that he remembered reading only two articles on the subject. "Why do you think so much has been written about fear, anxiety, and stress and so little about doubt?" I asked. His answer was, "The only thing I can think of is because it is such an uncomfortable feeling."

In my experience it is a very uncomfortable feeling and one I wish I were not familiar with. It is not within my interest or capability to take a scholarly approach to this subject, but I just want to shine the light of some common sense on the subject, to understand it in a practical sort of way that might help those who have tangled with this culprit on or off the golf course.

One of the reasons why doubt has not been more closely studied is that it is easy to confuse with fear. Doubt and fear are definitely friends, perhaps even relatives, but they are not identical twins. We often experience fear in the presence of a real or imagined threat—that is, when we are vulnerable to harm or imagine that we are.

But self-doubt relates neither to our vulnerability nor to danger, though it does question our competence to avoid the danger or, even worse, our very sense of worth. No matter how much pressure we may feel is riding on a given putt, we do not feel anxiety if we do not first doubt our ability to sink it. Fear increases as our sense of our competence decreases. Therefore, if we can lessen our self-doubt, our fear automatically wanes.

In my dictionary, doubt is defined as "uncertainty of mind" or mistrust in the reliability of something. These are not complicated definitions. They are everyday occurrences. Whether doubt is useful to a person or not is determined by where it is directed. I can benefit myself by doubting the validity of many advertisements. Certainly this book has been saying: Don't buy into all that is said about the golf swing. But isn't it a different matter when that doubt is directed toward yourself?

I asked a teenager recently if he had experienced self-doubt, and he said, "Sure. Everyone does, don't they?"

"How would you describe it?" I asked.

"Well, it's a voice in my head that says I'm stupid and that I can't do something."

"And what helps when you hear that voice?"

"If I recognize it, then it's okay."

"What do you do when you recognize it?"

"I call it stupid!"

I thought this was a wonderful answer. Recognizing the voice meant to him that it wasn't exactly his voice but one he had a little separation from. And because of that separation, he could call it stupid. He did what many of us could benefit by doing. He doubted his doubt.

I first became aware of this voice that undermined self-confidence when I played tennis. Even as a child I would walk out onto the court for the first time that day and there would be uncertainty. "How am I going to play today?" would be the big question in my mind. I didn't realize at the time how important it was for me to play well, or why. That came later. Then, after I hit two or three balls, the voice would make some kind of assessment: "Oh, my backhand is off today," or "I'm having a bad day today." What is now interesting is how short a time it took me to make this assessment about how I was going to play all that day. Many golfers experience the same kind of uncertainty on the first tee. It's the first shot of the game, and they are uncertain what is going to happen. Then, based on the first few shots, either some confidence or some doubt appears.

Of course, the voice of doubt does not stop there. After a few more missed backhands or golf shots, it makes another assessment, like "I'm a lousy tennis player (or terrible golfer)." Things get worse, and the voice concludes, "I'm not very good at sports," a not so judicial statement about one's abilities in all sports before the first set—or first nine holes—is finished. Finally, there's an awful feeling in your chest and you find yourself believing "There's something wrong with *me*." "I'm not a good enough person" is heard and sometimes believed.

It's not hard to see that when you believe in the power of these kinds of statements, they have a tendency to become self-fulfilling prophecies. When doubt is directed toward one's potential to learn and perform or toward one's very self, it can be quite detrimental. A needless questioning of one's value and potential as a human being, for whatever reason, may be the primary cause of the gap that exists between what a person is *capable* of doing and experiencing and what he or she actually *does* do and experience. Self-doubt is like a shadow that creates an uncomfortable feeling of separation within ourselves and, if believed in, can affect every action that comes from that feeling. This feeling can be covered over by a false sense of self-confidence or lost in a frantic pursuit of proving to the world the opposite of self-doubt. People don't try to prove certainties, only uncertainties.

So let's see if we can shed some light on this shadowy subject. Can we understand something about what will undermine self-doubt instead of letting it undermine us? The first step is to acknowledge that we are not born in self-doubt. It's hard to find a very young child who doesn't believe in himself. Children may trip and fall when learning to walk, or the castle that they are building may topple with a misplaced block, but such occurrences are not yet occasions for questioning oneself. In fact, observations of children before school age show they have an unquestioning faith in their abilities. It is wonderful to behold and, I might add, terrible to undermine. So doubt is not our original state of mind but something learned or accepted somewhere along the way.

A second step is to acknowledge that doubt hasn't totally destroyed this original faith. All human action is based on an innate faith in the body's ability. A person cannot take a step without the conviction that he can take the next. To walk down a flight of stairs, the body flings itself out into space, taking fully for granted that one leg and then the other will move forward and support it. This faith does not function at a conscious level in the sense that we choose to have it or not have it; rather, it is an essential part of continuous movement.

If you begin to doubt that your legs will move correctly to carry you downstairs, hesitancy may ruin the natural continuity of the action. Then you might start *thinking* about how you *should* walk downstairs. To correct this, you might start giving yourself a set of instructions to correct your way of moving. If you allow doubt to build, it will eat away at your inherent faith, and the natural fluidity of your movements will deteriorate. Soon your movement downstairs will look as mechanical and self-conscious as many of the golf swings you see on the practice range.

A third step is to make an important distinction: the distinction between the voice of doubt and you. When doubt knocks at your door, no one says you have to open it, much less invite it in for tea. However, if, like me, you were raised in an environment of doubt and always having to prove yourself, it's possible to become so emmeshed in it that you can't tell the difference between yourself and the doubt. If you do invite it in, you may listen, but you don't have to believe everything it says.

Most golfers are aware that there is a conversation going on in their heads on and off the golf course. When speaking to audiences of businesspeople, I ask how many are golfers. "What would you do," I ask them, "if players in your foursome started talking to you the way you talk to yourself on the golf course?" There is instant recognition, some nervous laughter, and an array of proposals from "Hit them over the head with my driver" to "I'd never play with them again."

The value I find in recognizing this internal dialogue is that it allows me to separate myself from the undermining voice of self-doubt. What I call Self 1 is the one criticizing my swing on the court or the course; he is also the one making me try shots beyond my capability and then calling me stupid when I fail; more than anything he is the one trying to make sure I hit the ball "right" according to his most recent set of concepts about what is right. Self 2 is the one who has to hit the golf ball, the one being addressed by this criticizing, doubting, overcontrolling voice of Self 1.

There are many ways to characterize Self 1, but we all have to do that for ourselves. For me, Self 1 expects the worst of Self 2 and then, in compensation for the doubt, tries to overcontrol.

Most of us would not put up with someone else sowing seeds of doubt in our minds. If that person persisted, we would know he was trying gamesmanship on us and we would ignore him. But, for some reason, when the voice of doubt is coming from inside our own heads, we find it harder to ignore. Yet ignore it we must.

In my father's golfing days, there used to be a tournament called the "Boo Tournament" held at Pasatiempo Golf Club, near Santa Cruz, California. The rules of this tournament were the same as for other tournaments except for the suspension of one of golf's long-standing rules of courtesy: silence while your opponent is striking the golf ball. In this tournament you could say or shout anything to rattle your opponents,

THE INNER GAME OF GOLF

48

and they could do the same to you. What is notable about this tournament is that the average scores were no higher than in any other tournament at the club. Knowing they could expect any trick in the book and some that weren't, and being in no doubt about the intention behind the cajoling, many golfers quickly learned to tune out everything that came their way and focused more completely on each shot.

The effects of self-doubt can be minimized if we attempt to see what it is. One of its characteristics is that it tends to strengthen as the challenge increases or as it represents increasing risk. For the golfer, progressing from low to higher challenges in the following imaginary sequence increases doubt:

THE DYNAMICS OF SELF-DOUBT

1. Chipping in your backyard.
2. Driving at the driving range.
3. Hitting a drive to a wide fairway on the first tee of your club in a five-dollar Nassau with your archrivals.
4. Narrow fairway, trees on left, OB on right; eighteenth hole; par needed to win club championship; your competitor's drive has landed in the middle of the fairway 250 yards out.
5. You have a five-foot breaking putt to be the dark-horse winner of the U.S. Open; national television cameras are focused; thousands are watching in hushed silence; you've never won a tour championship; you've been putting well all day, but choked on the seventeenth green, leaving a ten-foot putt short by three feet.

The first physical symptom of doubt is weakness. When a golfer stands over a crucial putt, he experiences weakness in his knees and wrists, light-headedness, and a general loss of feel and of muscle memory. In short, he loses command of his own resources. There are two common ways of reacting to this sensation: One is to give in to it; the other is to resist it. Giving in to the challenge, or avoiding it, decreases effort, motivation, and concentration and produces what I call "the unconscious mode," a state of mind characterized by inattentiveness, lack of motivation, lassitude, and sloppy performance. When this response to doubt becomes habitual both on and off the course, one's life becomes one of underachievement.

In our culture the more common reaction to self-doubt is to "try harder." Since our culture values achievement and censures laziness, most of us are encouraged by parents, teachers, or employers to overcome our shortcomings. "When in doubt, try harder," we are exhorted. In other words, we learn to compensate for doubt by exerting increased Self 1 control over ourselves. Although the "trying mode" could be considered a better solution than the "unconscious mode" (since trying tends to produce greater alertness of mind and stronger will to overcome obstacles), it nonetheless produces significant interference with the expression of our potential. Since you never try to prove what is certain, trying to prove oneself is, in effect, a mode based on doubt. It always creates mental tension and conflict, which are reflected on the physical level as overtightness; in turn, this restricts fluid coordination of muscles and thus limits the quality of our performance.

In many ways golf is a perfect vehicle for the trying mode. The challenge is so clear and the demarcation between success and failure so distinct that it is hard not to overcontrol. In tennis a double fault by a professional is not as big a failure as a topped ball or shank by a professional golfer. At every level of the game the difference between one's worst and one's best is embarrassingly large. When I am standing over a chip shot and entertain doubt about hitting a decent shot, I try harder for control, tighten in doing so, and to that extent make it harder for Self 2 to execute the shot. But when I don't doubt myself on a putt, I don't *try*; I simply putt in a spontaneous and natural way. The natural Self 2 effort expresses itself without overtightness, as when you walk down a flight of stairs or put food in your mouth—actions that don't generally call forth doubt but still require considerable coordination.

In short, "trying" is essentially compensation for mistrust in ourselves and generally leads to poor performance. Fritz Perls, the father of Gestalt therapy, observed that human beings are the only living species with the capacity to interfere significantly with their own growth. How? Mostly, Perls said, by *trying* to be something we're not. Perls was fond of remarking succinctly, "Trying fails."

Five Common Types of Trying Too Hard in Golf

Basically there are five kinds of trying too hard in golf. All of them are compensations for a present or long-standing doubt and involve an overtightening of muscles that interferes with your swing. Once doubt is identified, practical steps can be taken to eliminate its influence.

Trying to Hit the Ball

As a beginning golfer I experienced the same doubt as almost every novice: doubt that I would hit the ball at all. Most golfers remember their initial experience of failure. We stood far above a small white ball that we were supposed to strike with a long, unfamiliar club in such a way that the ball would travel a long distance. Both the ball and the club face seemed very small, and the chances of the two making contact seemed remote. Taking the club back farther and farther from the ball, we aimed, swung hard, and missed the ball entirely—an embarrassing and frustrating experience. This first association of failure remains with many throughout their golfing careers. Somewhere deep inside is that memory of missing the ball and thinking that it's really hard to hit. From this doubt comes some of our overtightening on the downswing and our tendency to *try* to hit the ball, instead of letting Self 2 swing the club.

I still find it remarkable to observe the difference in the swing of most golfers when the ball is not actually in front of them. An amateur who was having a tough time playing in a foursome including Sam Snead during a pro-am tournament at Rancho Canada Golf Course finally asked him for help. Snead replied, "The only thing wrong with your swing is what's wrong with most amateurs'; you don't hit the ball with your practice swing." Something about the presence of the ball invites doubt.

Trying to Hit the Ball Up into the Air

After the beginner has managed to make contact with enough balls, his focus often shifts to trying to hit them up into the air. It appears doubtful to him that swinging *down* on the ball will make it go *up*. Trying to lift the ball up by scooping under it is one of the most common causes of error cited by professionals.

On a round with a teaching pro, I bladed an approach shot over the green. What's happening? I asked myself. As if I'd spoken aloud, the pro said, "You're trying to lift the ball up into the air. You actually elevate your body as you hit the ball. *Don't try to lift the ball; let the club do it.*"

Trying to Hit the Ball Far

There has never been a golfer who has not once succumbed to the temptation of trying too hard to hit the ball far. During my first month on the driving range my favorite club was the driver! I had an almost compulsive urge to see if I could knock each ball past the last marker. Of course I couldn't, so I tried harder and fell into a familiar pattern: trying to muscle the ball to get maximum distance.

Equating power with physical strength and physical strength with the tightening of muscles, I would whale away, using, in particular, the muscles of my right arm, which had been developed through thirty years of playing tennis. Every once in a while I would connect and send the ball what seemed to be a mile. This would whet my appetite, and my over-efforts would continue. But you can't be around the game for very long before you hear the platitude "Swing easy." I had to admit that the pros on TV didn't seem to be using as much effort as I did. The interferences caused by trying to hit with more power actually inhibit power. If you try to be strong, you only get in your own way.

The way to achieve power *without trying* is discussed further in Chapter 8.

Trying to Hit the Ball Straight

The closer we get to the pin, the greater our doubts about hitting the ball straight. This results in the kind of trying often called "steering." This is the kind of overcontrol that doesn't work any better in golf than it does in tennis, football, basketball, or baseball. When I try to steer a putt into the hole, I seem to flub it in the very act of trying to make sure it gets there. Sometimes after the putt I can feel the tightness that comes from the steering, and I realize that it corresponds exactly to the degree of doubt I had in my mind before putting. In the same "Mental Hazards" article quoted in Chapter 2, Bobby Jones described how he once hit one of his worst golf shots at a golf course called Brae Burn:

> The seventeenth hole is 255 yards and requires a very accurate brassie shot. The more serious difficulty there lies to the right, and this was the side I determined to avoid. But, as I addressed the ball, I was thinking more about keeping away from the danger on the right than about driving to the green, and, as I hit the ball, I did something—Heaven knows what—that sent the ball an inconceivable distance into the very woods I was trying to avoid. I was very lucky to get out of that scrape with a four. This desire to *guide* the shot is the most difficult fault in golf to overcome.

Trying to Hit the Ball "Right"

Although the first four kinds of trying cause overtightness and introduce error into the swing, they are self-induced and relatively simple compared with the fifth kind of doubt. When trying hard to hit the ball far and straight fails, as it inevitably will, the golfer turns to trying to hit the ball "right" and in so doing involves himself in a web of such complexity that it is almost impossible to extricate himself from it. Once a player starts "taking apart" his swing and analyzing its mechanical elements, he not only lets himself in for endless self-criticism, doubt, and trying too hard, but handicaps himself in putting it together again. Every "shouldn't" invites mistakes, and every "should" challenges both our memory and our ability to make our bodies conform. Chapter 5 explains in greater detail this major pitfall of traditional golf instruction.

Most golf pros are aware of the difficulties imposed on students by too many "shoulds" and "shouldn'ts" of the golf swing. One professional I know wrote the following satirical piece about how easy it is to play golf:

IT'S AN EASY GAME: Everyone can learn to play golf. Once a player has mastered the grip and stance, all he has to bear in mind, in the brief two-second interval it takes to swing, is to keep his left elbow pointed in toward the left hip and his right arm loose and closer to the body than the left . . . and take the club head past his right knee . . . and then break the wrists at just the right instant while the left arm is still traveling straight back from the ball and the right arm stays glued to the body . . . and the hips come around in a perfect circle; and meanwhile, the weight must be 40 percent on the left foot and 60 percent on the right foot at the start . . . and at just the right point in the turn the left heel bends in towards the right in a dragging motion until the left heel comes off the ground . . . but not too far . . . and be sure the hands are over the right foot, but not on the toe more than the heel . . . and be sure the hands at the top of the swing are high and the shaft points along a line parallel with the ground . . . and pause at the top of the swing and count one, then pull the left arm straight down, and don't uncock the wrist too soon. Pull the left hip around in a circle . . . but don't let the shoulders turn with the hips. Now transfer the weight 60 percent to the left foot and 40 percent to the right . . . and tilt the left foot so the right side of it is straight . . . watch out for the left hand, it's supposed to be extended . . . but not too still or the shot won't go anywhere . . . and don't let it get loose or you'll smother the shot . . . and don't break too soon but keep your head down . . . then hit the ball. That's all there is to it!

Technical instructions are easy to give, but not so easy to execute. Because Self 1 is not designed to translate complex instructions into actions, doubt is incurred when it receives them and is expected to be able to make Self 2 perform them.

"WHATEVER YOU'RE TRYING TO DO, DON'T."

Once during an Inner Golf clinic I walked down the golfing range asking the participants what they were trying to do on their swing. There were varied answers: "I'm trying to keep from slicing"; "I'm trying to make sure I follow through"; "I'm trying to swing from inside out"; "I'm trying to keep my left arm straight"; "I'm trying to swing easy." And, of course, there was a beginner who said, "I just want to lift the ball off the tee!"

To each person I gave the same simple instruction: "Whatever you're trying to do, *don't*. Don't try to do it and don't try *not* to do it. Simply don't try at all and see what happens."

What happened was that each person improved—without trying to. The slicer sliced less, the left arm stayed straight all by itself, and the beginner was so exuberant over hitting every ball up in the air that she kept jumping up and down, saying, "This is easy, this is easy."

The less the golfer *tries*, the more fluid his swing will be and the easier it is for Self 2 to achieve the optimum coordination and timing that produce the true golf swing.

The very nature of Self 1 is to doubt Self 2. Self 2's attributes of spontaneity, sincerity, natural intelligence, and desire to learn are beyond Self 1's ability to conceptualize. Instead, he says that they don't really exist and programs his computer with beliefs and concepts about the way you are in order to take Self 2's place. The self-image Self 1 creates is a cheap imitation of the living, limitless real you, the you whose capabilities and attributes surpass anything that Self 1 can conceive with his thinking mind.

THE LIMITATIONS OF THE TRYING MODE

Many people are perplexed at the suggestion that trying hard is a questionable virtue. Over and over in our culture we've been told, "If at first you don't succeed, try, try again." Hence, for many of us the word "try" means to succeed, and not to try has come to mean accepting failure. But the point of this chapter is that success comes easier when we make an *effort* but don't try.

Part of the difficulty of this concept is semantic. I use the word "try" to refer to the kind of Self 1 effort that is a response to self-doubt. "Effort" is the necessary energy expended by Self 2 in order to complete an act successfully and is based on faith, or self-trust. Faith is the natural underpinning of all successful acts, and it doesn't have to be learned. Babies don't *try* to learn to walk or talk, but they do make an effort. They don't overtighten when grasping your finger firmly; they use only the necessary muscles. (By the way, this would be a good image to keep in mind when gripping your golf club: hold it with the kind of firmness with which a baby grips your finger.)

When we realize that Self 1, having introduced doubt, attempts to take control over our acts himself, we are near the heart of the matter. Having weakened faith in Self 2, he makes his bid to take over as much as we will allow him to. His first ploy is to set himself up as your internal judge, to judge your actions as good or bad, and then to judge *you*. After bad shots, he tells you what you did wrong and what you should do next time to avoid the error again. After a good shot (which probably happened when you weren't thinking about any instructions) he wants to tell you how you did it so that you can do it again—but next time it almost never works.

Self 1's control is essentially coercive. He praises you and punishes you. He is a sergeant who wants to run the show and thinks that the private (Self 2) is stupid. He uses concern over results to entice you to depend on him. The natural outcome is that Self 2, who knew how to succeed all the time (or could easily learn), is so overridden that failure follows. No matter how familiar we may be with it, and no matter how far we've progressed in spite of Self 1, the fact is that control through self-judgment—that is, *trying*, with ego reward and punishment—is neither effective nor very satisfying.

Golf is traditionally a game played in silence. Few players will tolerate another person saying a word to them once they have addressed the ball. Then why are we so tolerant of Self 1's distracting voice chattering within our own head? If another person in the foursome were to remark, "You'd better watch out for that sand trap in front of the green," we'd probably accuse him of trying to psych us and try to ignore him. But if Self 1 whispers the same sentence in our heads, we listen as if he were a trusted friend and may even reply, "Thanks for reminding me: I'll try hard to avoid it." Of course disaster in one form or another usually follows. My own best golf is played when everything is quiet inside as well as out.

There is a state of mind more conducive to excellence than either the *trying mode* or the *unconscious mode*. The true professional in every field performs from a base of solid faith in his potential to act successfully and to learn to do what he hasn't yet achieved. He keeps his goals high, without letting himself become so emotionally attached to them that he fears failure. His sense of his own value is independent of external results. He doesn't listen to self-doubt, nor does he perform by rote. He dances to the tune of his Self 2 intuitions. In this state of mind his attentiveness to detail is sharp and selective. He sees each situation as it is, not as he would have liked it to be, and nonjudgmentally he perceives in each situation opportunities to propel himself toward his goal. Though he gets more done than most, his acts seem relatively effortless. What appears difficult to accomplish in the trying mode seems easy to him. This state of mind— what I call the *awareness mode*—is conducive to optimum performance and is a subject that will be discussed at greater length in the next two chapters.

THE DOCTRINE OF THE EASY

Obviously, golfers experience self-doubt and start trying hard when they look at the game as difficult. Part of this sense of difficulty is, of course, inherent in the exacting requirements for precision and power in the game. On the other hand, it is within almost everyone's experience that when we hit our best shots they seem easy, in comparison with the difficulty so often experienced during our worst shots. Some experts say that the golf swing is a natural movement. Others assert the opposite—that golf is difficult because the swing is so unnatural and contrary to instinct. This issue is worth some examination because it is the sense of difficulty of the game that is responsible for much of our mental tension and our despair about significantly improving.

In his introduction to *Power Golf*, Ben Hogan took the position that golf was a tough game to learn:

> In order to develop a golf swing your thoughts must run in the right direction. Otherwise it will be impossible. Perhaps you will understand me better when I say that when you grip a golf club to take your first swing at a golf ball every natural instinct you have to accomplish that objective is wrong, absolutely wrong.
>
> Reverse every natural instinct you have and do just the opposite of what you are inclined to do and you will probably come very close to having a perfect golf swing. However, every golfer, even the so-called "natural player," learns the hard way. Some are just a little more fortunate than others in being able to learn a little quicker, that's all. . . .
>
> My approach to golf in this book will be positive rather than negative. In other words, you will not read anything in this book which will make you self-conscious and frighten you by emphasizing all of the faults you can acquire in trying to develop a golf swing.

At the other extreme is Ernest Jones, called on the book's jacket "America's foremost golf teacher," in a book called *Swing the Clubhead*. In the first chapter, entitled "Good Golf Is Easy," there appears a sequence of pictures of Diane Wilson swinging a wood with near perfect form at the age of five. The caption reads: "At her age Diane can swing so beautifully because she does not let her imagination interfere with the feel of the clubhead. She has shot a 71 for nine holes, and her father, a well-known professional, is now entering her in junior tournaments. Diane makes golf look easy because it is easy." Mr. Jones writes:

If a five-year-old child can learn to swing, there is no reason on earth why you cannot. All you need to do is to repeat the action of that child. She was not distracted in her swing. Her mind was not cluttered by the countless don'ts which fill the air whenever people talk golf. She merely took the club as it should be taken, in her two hands, and did with it what comes naturally. She swung.

So who's right? Is golf easy or hard, natural or unnatural? Tennis professional Vic Braden, my friend and occasional critic, has stated that one flaw in the Inner Game approach to teaching tennis is that it assumes that tennis is as natural as walking or talking and that in fact it isn't. Since tennis calls for movements that are not instinctual or "natural," he contends that tennis strokes must be learned through close analysis of patterns based on the law of physics.

My own belief is that Hogan, Jones, and Braden are all correct. Golf and tennis are both difficult *and* easy. On the one hand, it is probably true that our genes do not carry instinctual information about the most effective way to hit a golf ball. It is also true that the most effective way to hit the ball is the opposite of what you might at first think. As we've discussed, students learn that hitting down on the ball makes it go up and that tightening muscles doesn't necessarily produce power. But whether the golf swing is natural or not, it is exacting enough to call for our full attentiveness in learning it. The true issue is not whether golf is natural; the point is that *learning is natural*. Even what might be called unnatural can be learned naturally. Natural learning is easy, but being taught something *un*naturally can make it very hard. Speaking, for example, would be virtually impossible if you tried to learn how to pronounce words by studying the necessary tongue positions. So however difficult golf actually is, we can make it harder or easier by the way we learn or are taught the game.

There is one other way in which we make the game harder for ourselves. What does "harder" mean? In this context it means close to the limit of our capabilities to learn. Hence, the lower the image we hold of our innate capabilities to learn or perform, the more difficult a particular task seems. When we assume too readily that poor performance is based on a lack of innate capability—that is, when we blame Self 2 for our failures—we automatically make the game seem harder. The main point of this chapter has been to establish that the more probable cause of error is Self 1 interference rather than Self 2 deficiency. Self 1 usually prefers to blame the difficulty of the game, Self 2, or various external causes, and it is this very perception of Self 1 that something is harder than it is that sets the self-doubt cycle in motion. The doubt produces "trying," which produces tightness, which produces error, which produces more self-doubt.

The "doctrine of the easy" states that acts done well are done easily and that that which seems hard is usually not being done well. Since it is always hard to perform with the interference of doubt, the difficulty of golf lies not so much in the precision required by the Outer Game, but in the task of circumventing the tension that results from thinking how tough it is.

Of course we think golf is hard because most of us make frequent errors. Since we have failed more often than we've succeeded in our attempts to hit almost every kind of shot, we are likely to entertain doubt about how we will do on the shot confronting us. Some degree of mental tension is apt to be present even if we do not remember our past failures consciously.

Below is a description of a technique that, with practice, can reduce or entirely circumvent this kind of tension. I call the technique "easy link." It works to relax the mind in the same way as associating with past failures works to produce tension. The technique is simply to remember or associate with a seemingly difficult task (in this case the golf shot) some action that is simple, preferably one that has never failed. For example, when addressing a ten-foot putt, you might remember the action of simply picking up a ball out of the hole. By vividly associating with this easy act, there is no room left in the mind to associate the upcoming putt with failure. Therefore there will be less tension and less trying.

The first time this technique occurred to me I hit ten golf balls out of ten into a target across the carpet in my office ten feet away. What amazed me was that after doing so it didn't seem remarkable. It was easy to pick up ten balls.

Before trying the technique again I asked Molly, an Inner Game assistant, to experiment with it. First I asked her to make ten putts toward another golf ball about fifteen feet away. Measuring, I determined that her average putt landed about nine inches from the target. Then I said, "This time, Molly, I want you to think to yourself that all you are doing is reaching out and picking up that golf ball. Mentally I want you to associate these next putts with that simple action, not with the harder task of putting."

Molly got the idea and hit ten putts very close to the target ball—an average of only four inches away. Afterward she said, "The target ball somehow seemed more in my immediate world, not something out there. I had no doubt that I could reach out and touch it." Her stroke looked different, too; it was not consciously controlled, yet it was authoritative and followed through in a much less tentative manner. This technique uses a trick of Self 1 against itself. If doubt is engendered by association of a present action with past failure, why can't confidence be engendered by associating with an act you never fail at? I reasoned that it wasn't necessary, as it is sometimes suggested, to remember past successful golf shots; it would be more productive to associate with actions that you have *never* doubted you can do. Each time I succeeded in totally immersing myself in this concept, there was not a trace of doubt in my mind about sinking the putt, and Self 1 seemed to be entirely fooled. He didn't even become excited over shots better than my expectations; anyone can reach out and touch an object, and there's no need to congratulate oneself for that. And because the putt seemed easier, my stroke was easier, with no tendency to overcontrol.

This technique is easily adaptable to any part of your game. When I next had a chance to go out to the driving range, I asked Molly to come along.

I looked out at the yardage marker 150 yards away, a six iron in my hand. It just didn't feel right to associate hitting a shot that far with reaching out and touching it. Realizing that I was searching for something, Molly asked, "Well, what could you do in relation to that sign?" I thought for a moment. "Well, I know I could throw a tennis ball pretty close to it."

"Okay, you're just throwing a tennis ball to your student, who is right at the one-hundred-fifty-yard marker."

This association had the same magical effect for me. I held in my mind the memory of tossing a tennis ball and felt so comfortable inside that I didn't steer. Ball after ball went straight toward the marker. Only when I got sloppy with my technique or started thinking about my swing would accuracy desert me.

Then I asked Molly to try the same association. At first there was no noticeable improvement. I realized that she hadn't thrown a tennis ball much, so we tossed balls back and forth for a few minutes so that she could experience how easy it was. Her next shots were not only significantly straighter, but were more cleanly hit and had better distance. "It may be hard to play golf, but it's easy to toss balls," she said, grinning.

When I started experimenting with drives, fairway woods, and the longer irons, I found it natural to associate with throwing a baseball. Projecting a fairway to exist between two trees about thirty yards apart on the range, I would have thought that my chances of driving a ball into that opening were about fifty-fifty. There definitely would have been some doubt that I could do it consistently. But I had no doubt that I could throw a ball into a thirty-yard-wide opening, and neither would anyone else who has ever spent much time throwing. This association seemed to make it easy for me to let power out in the swing without fearing that I was losing control; I knew I could throw the ball hard and still keep it within the opening. The effect this had on the consistency of my drives was even more surprising than in the irons. There were no severe slices or hooks, simply straight balls, gentle fades, and a few slight draws—all in the fairway.

What excited me about all this was that I wasn't getting excited. This may not seem to make sense, but it was important to me. I had played enough to know that whenever I became aware that I was playing particularly well, the wave I was riding on would soon crash.

When I experimented with this technique on the putting green, I found I had the best results by associating mentally with reaching in the hole and picking up the ball. Another association I liked was that of threading a needle. Remembering that action not only relaxed my mind but concentrated it and automatically put in me a state of mind conducive to precise action. For chipping, I liked thinking about the simple action of taking the stick out of the hole.

Although there are other ways of circumventing self-doubt, this one is simplest to learn, for both the beginner and the advanced golfer. There are just three guidelines I found useful for successful association. First, the associated action should in some way include the target; that is, putting your hand in the hole is a better association than picking a daisy in a field. Second, the associated action should be not only a simple one but also one that you have actually done frequently. Details such as distance are not important; it didn't matter to me that my tennis students had never been 150 yards away, or that I had never thrown a baseball 240 yards. Third, it seems to help if the action is generically similar to the one you are doing, but not so close that you might try to physically substitute one for the other. The technique is *not* to swing a golf club the way you toss a ball. The association signals the mind to relax, but does not tell the body how to swing. It is effective in inducing a state of mind that is optimal for performing a physical action.

This technique is effective and simple, but it is not a panacea; don't expect it to make your ball go where you want it to every time. But when done with concentration and not as a gimmick, it can reduce the elements of self-doubt and tension that interfere with performance. Especially when you are prone to associate a particular golf shot with past failure, I recommend using this technique as a kind of shield to block out doubt. After a while you won't have the negative association any longer, and you can put away the shield.

It is likely that if you succeed in convincing Self 1 that golf isn't difficult, it may start thinking that the game is easier than it really is. You'll know this is happening when, instead of getting overly tense, you grow too casual and sloppy. This is not a bad sign. Be thankful for being rid of your tension and make one adjustment: *Do the easy with full attentiveness*. For example, it is easy to pick up a golf ball out of a hole, but it requires effort and concentration to do it with maximum attentiveness. In this case, you might think of picking up the ball as if it were a valuable diamond you wanted to examine, or performing the act with maximum grace, care, and coordination. Since it is easy, you have no fear of failure, but since you want to do it well, it requires concentration. A commitment to attentiveness will result in the best from both worlds: you step closer to that state of mind in which performance is optimized, while avoiding the tension associated with past failure.

CHAPTER 5

THE AWARENESS
INSTRUCTION

The previous chapter made the case that self-doubt, fear of failure, and self-judgment can significantly interfere with your ability to learn and perform. And one of the practices that invites all three of these inner obstacles is imposing on oneself a complicated series of technical instructions. When I first wrote this book, this was a rarely acknowledged fact. Golf instructors taught technique, and golfers tried to apply that technique to their swings. That's the way it was. Though it felt mostly awkward at first and frustrating much of the time, it was still generally accepted as the only way to learn. Now there is a greater understanding among players and professionals that the mind should be relatively free from instruction while you are swinging the golf club—at least during the round itself. Most golfers agree that carrying more than one instruction in your head at a time is counterproductive to good golf. Yet there is still a great deal to learn about how to learn golf.

Psychologists confirm that most of us learn more in our first five years than in all the rest of our lives. Yet small children don't go through this torturous process of self-evaluation, analysis, and trying to do it *right*. They don't have to *try* to learn; they simply do so. Until adults teach them otherwise, learning is so natural for children that they don't even know it's happening, and, in contrast with the experience of most adults, they have fun doing it. The talent to learn is one that we adults still possess, and if we can let go just a little of our attachment to conceptualization, it can be used and developed to great advantage.

This chapter explores a different and more natural approach to learning. It introduces the awareness instruction, which focuses attention on what you *are* doing instead of telling you what you should be doing. It shows that if you use awareness instructions, you can learn most golf technique directly from experience without being taught. This is a more empowering way for the student to learn and much more user-friendly.

HAS SOMETHING GONE WRONG WITH THE WAY WE LEARN?

Most of my life, I have been involved directly in the process of education. For seventeen years I was a student in the culture's educational system, which culminated in four years at Harvard University and a year on a government fellowship studying "Change in the Four-Year College" at Claremont Graduate School in California. After graduating from college, I taught high school English at Exeter Academy in New Hampshire and then became a training and education officer in the U.S. Navy. Still interested in the learning process, I went on to become one of the founders of a new liberal arts college in northern Michigan whose mission was to create an educational environment for students who wanted to accept leadership responsibilities in their lives. Five years later I took a leave of absence from formal education to reconsider my direction.

It was during this leave that I discovered a new and very different way to learn and to teach. I offer this brief history because I would like to address the problem of learning and teaching golf within the broader context of education in our culture at large. With a little understanding about the imbalance that permeates the way we learn and the way we are taught in formal settings, it becomes easier to apply whatever you learn about learning golf to learning in general.

If asked to state the imbalance concisely, I would say that institutional education has overemphasized conceptual learning to such a degree that the value of, and trust in, the natural process of learning directly from experience has been seriously undermined.

Based on the assumption that the mind is an empty receptacle that develops as it is filled with facts, conceptual learning is concerned primarily with the accumulation and ordering of concepts and theoretical information. Experimental learning has more to do with the development of innate potentialities and skills. The word "education" comes from the Latin *educare*, meaning "to lead out," and indicates that the potential intelligence sought already exists within us and needs to be drawn out. This drawing out by a teacher, a system, or an environment is the primary function of true education. Thus, talking, for example, is not a skill imposed on the child from without; rather, it develops from an innate capacity encouraged and supported by parents and the youngster's experience of his environment.

Balanced education requires a proper relationship between cognitive and experiential knowledge, but in the teaching of physical skills, learning through direct experience should take priority over learning through formal instruction in concepts.

As a result of formalized education, we tend to think that learning virtually ends when we graduate from school. We enter the workplace thinking that learning will happen only when we get sent to a training course. But our lives—at work, in relationships, and in any other activity that needs competence and understanding—require that we become better learners from our ongoing day-to-day experience.

LEARNING FROM EXPERIENCE

I sometimes wonder what man's fate would have been if in the development process he taught himself to understand language before he learned how to walk. No doubt parents would have coached us when to shift our weight from left foot to right, and we would have spent a lot of time on the floor analyzing the causes for falling down again. Undoubtedly, many of us would have developed negative self-images about our motor skills and would still be tripping over our own feet.

Instead we learned from experience as a natural process, just as kids teach themselves how to balance on bicycles and skateboards. It is a demanding process that engages one's complete attention and is enjoyable, although the desired results are not always reached overnight. The foundation of the Inner Game approach to learning is that experience itself is the primary teacher and each individual must learn to learn directly from his or her own personal experience. Another person's experience, through teaching and instruction, can be helpful only if it does not compromise a student's all-important relationship with his or her own direct experience.

Learning is about change, making an inner change. The change can take place in a person's understanding, perceptions, and/or capabilities. It is provoked by new meaning given to experience. It is what enables us to grow and to cope more successfully with external changes.

Awareness is the primary faculty we have for *knowing* and learning from our experience. To some the word "awareness" sounds vague and impractical, but it is, in fact, one of those words that refer to something so basic that it is difficult to find a satisfactory definition. My *Webster's New Twentieth Century Unabridged Dictionary* does not even contain the word as a noun. It briefly defines "aware" as an adjective meaning "knowing, cognizant, informed." As a synonym it suggests the word "conscious." It is by this primary faculty of being aware or of being conscious that human beings can know or learn anything. The entire evolution of life, from the single cell to the complex arrangement of cells called the human body, is based on the power of the living organism to be aware of external stimuli and to respond selectively to them. Yet throughout my education, I heard almost nothing about the power and fundamental role of awareness.

THE LAW OF AWARENESS

The Inner Game approach to learning is based on a fundamental and powerful principle of change. I call it the "law of awareness." In simplest form, this law states that *if you want to change something, first increase your awareness of the way it is*. In a more concise form: *Awareness itself is curative*. Whatever helps to increase awareness of *what is* will promote learning; whatever hides or distorts awareness of *what is* will block or distort learning.

Attention is the faculty of focusing awareness and the principal means of increasing awareness. Stated in simplest possible terms, where you focus your attention determines what you learn. An "awareness instruction," then, is an instruction to the attention to focus on a particular area for the purpose of becoming more aware of what is there. Unnecessary judgment, fear, or doubt about what is there will distort awareness and thus distort the opportunity for learning. It is the use of the awareness instruction in learning golf that I want to bring to your attention in this chapter. Before doing so, I want to take a critical look at what we are more accustomed to in learning golf, "the do-instruction."

THE DO-INSTRUCTION

The do-instruction is basically a command to *do* something or *not do* something. It is most commonly given in the form of "you *should* do this" or "you *should not* do that." As such, it carries with it an aura of rightness and authority that sets up the actions by the student to be judged by the giver of the command. When such instructions are not easily understood or easy to accomplish, they tend to evoke a fear of being judged that threatens the natural learning environment. It is only when the instructions are needed yet easy to understand and to follow that interference is not apt to be evoked. For example, to be told by a trusted instructor to stand with your feet about as wide apart as your shoulders is not apt to evoke fear or resistance. But can you say the same if you were given Ben Hogan's instructions about your downswing?

All tension should be released from the right leg and hip. The right knee should break in toward the left knee. The wrists uncock, the right arm straightens and then turns over going forward over the left shoulder. This all takes place in that sequence and you will find that it will bring you to the complete finish.

Such instructions cannot help but create a sense of doubt in the student about his ability to put all this together. And with the doubt comes the fear of being judged for doing it wrong and often an understandable resistance, conscious or unconscious, to the instructor. When these instructions become internalized, as when Self 1 gives them to Self 2, the doubts and fears come with them and become part of our internal learning environment.

How do do-instructions incur doubt? How do you write your name? How do you tie your shoe? How do you walk down a flight of stairs? Think about one of these actions and see if you can come up with a set of instructions about how to perform it. Then try to do the action by following your own instructions. It's not easy if you described the action in any detail, but why?

The primary difficulty lies in our inability to translate any but the simplest verbal command into a bodily action. When asked to do more, we invite self-doubt because the brain cannot consciously control the body with words; the part of the brain that analyzes, conceptualizes, and instructs us verbally is incapable of moving a muscle and has only a limited capacity to communicate to the part of the brain that does control our physical behavior.

Besides the general tendency of the ego to resist being told what to do, there are five basic ways in which do-instructions engender doubt.

The first is the communication gap between teacher and student. The student doubts that he even intellectually understands what the instructor means. Teachers are notorious for developing their own jargon and assuming that everyone speaks the same language. For example, I'm still not sure exactly what the famous golf instruction "Pronate the wrists" means. Not knowing the meaning of the instruction obviously invites doubt that I can follow it.

The second is the internal communication problem with the student. Intellectually the student may understand, but his body doesn't. This is the most prevalent gap and a universal invitation to doubt. Because the mind understands, the student assumes that he should be able to make his body conform. He also knows that his teacher expects conformity. But unless the body can associate that instruction with an already familiar action, it can't conform. Without *muscle knowledge* of the instruction, the student finds himself unable to meet his own or his teacher's expectations and doubt increases.

Third, the student may understand intellectually and his body may understand, but the action called for is outside his present capability. For example, it was some time before my body was ready to deal with the subtleties of leg motion at the outset of the downswing. It's easier for instructors to see what's wrong in a person's movement than to know which particular correction should be focused on in a given development process. Doubt increases as the student is asked to do something out of line with his natural learning progression; this reinforces his "I can't do it" self-image.

Fourth, in many cases do-instructions given by teachers to students and by students to themselves are just plain incorrect. Trying to follow commands that do not conform to the mechanics of golf or to the physiology of the body obviously causes doubt.

Fifth, there *are* do-instructions that are understood intellectually and in body language, are correct, are within the natural progression of learning, and are easy to accomplish. Such do-instructions need not cause doubt and can aid learning in some cases. But doubt arises when one tries to conform to too many of these at a time. Almost every time we receive a "should" instruction, there is a spoken or implied "shouldn't," which leads to another and then another, until the mind is clogged with more instructions than it can handle.

Much of modern physical-skill teaching relies heavily on do-instructions in spite of their inherent limitations and general misuse. In fact, most golf students feel cheated if the instructor doesn't tell them what they're doing wrong and what they should be doing. But it is this process that we have become so accustomed to that actually cheats us of recognizing our potential as learners. It persuades us subliminally to mistrust ourselves, and the resulting gap between our performance and our potential is large. Unfortunately, we learn from our teachers how to teach ourselves, and soon we all develop a Self 1 who continues to sow seeds of self-mistrust whenever we listen to it, whether or not we are taking lessons from a pro. To redress this problem is, in my opinion, one of the most important challenges before education in general, and it would be interesting if sports teaching could lead the way.

Before addressing the alternative to the do-instruction in the teaching of golf, I should point out that there are excellent instructors of every sport who understand the limitations of do-instructions and who have developed the art of speaking a language the body can understand. The best teachers have always used image-rich language that invokes not an abstract description of a movement but a concrete picture or "feelmage" associated with acts already familiar to the body. Bob Toski's book *The*

Touch System for Better Golf attempts to establish the primacy of feel and muscle memory in the swing. For example, he suggests that your swing should feel like a canoe building up momentum and then going over the falls and that "the left wrist should feel as firm through impact as it would if you were backhanding a rug-beater." Gary Wiren in *The New Golf Mind* points out that Sam Snead used to think of the word "oily" as he swung, thus engaging his right-brain hemisphere and avoiding the pitfalls of conceptual left-brain thinking. Unfortunately, as Ben Hogan pointed out, the golf swing is not easily associated with other common movements, so most of us do not have many useful analogies in our muscle memories.

Fundamental to the Inner Game approach to teaching is a workable alternative to the do-instruction, one that engages the student in learning from experience and increases his self-trust. I call it the "awareness instruction." Simply defined, it is a command to the *attention* of the student rather than to his body. Instead of saying, "See if you can do this or that," it says, "See if you can *see*, *feel*, or *hear* what is happening right now and right here." The back-hit-stop exercise introduced in Chapter 2 involves an awareness instruction that requests that the student focus on the club, with special emphasis on its position at the back of the swing and at its completion. None of these three instructions calls for a change in *behavior*—they all simply call for heightened awareness of what is happening.

"See if you can *feel* whether the blade of your club is open, closed, or square at impact" is also an awareness instruction, circumventing the doubt about *doing it right* by involving the pupil's mind in the process of just noticing what is happening. The instructor might ask the student to shut his eyes, then arrange the club in different positions—open, square, and closed—until he can feel the difference in his hands while the club is motionless. The next step is the challenge to the student to see if he can feel the angle of the face at the moment of impact when the club is moving at normal speed. If the student thinks that this is a gimmick to help him to hit the ball square, he is apt to *try* to do it right and to be caught in the same trying mode as if he were simply told to make sure that his club was square at impact. But if he takes the awareness instruction for what it is—simply a request that he attempt to feel what is happening with the face, no matter what it is—then there is no question of right and wrong, the mind focuses on the experience, and soon experiential learning will take place as he learns to differentiate the sensations of the different angles of the club face.

Awareness instructions are radically different from do-instructions and tend to put the student in another frame of mind entirely. They engen-

THE AWARENESS INSTRUCTION

der a mode of learning that is free of doubt, frustration, and discouragement. They induce a natural state of learning, which, once rediscovered, progresses organically and rapidly. Most important, they strengthen the student's faith in his own capacity to learn from experience; the instructor's role is only to help him in focusing on the most relevant parts of his experience.

Let me add that when a student has been helped by an Inner Game teacher to regain trust in his ability to learn from experience, certain do-instructions *can* be given at appropriate moments in such a way that they neither cause doubt about their achievement nor undermine the student's basic trust in his own learning capacity. But so conducive are awareness instructions to learning that I use them 95 percent of the time and employ do-instructions only for simple tasks or when a high degree of trust in Self 2 and the teacher has been established.

Most do-instructions can be better framed as awareness instructions, and their translation becomes easy after a little practice. When I first heard the tip "On the downswing swing from the inside out," I was confused. Even after I understood the instruction intellectually, I had little confidence that I could do it, so of course I *tried*. I didn't get it right, so I tried again and, of course, only became tighter. A couple of times my friend Tom Nordland said, "That time you got it," but I couldn't feel the difference between those "right" swings and all the others.

The translation of this doubt-producing do-instruction into an awareness instruction might sound like this: "Just swing the club without trying to do anything, but feel whether, on the downswing, it's moving from outside the ball—that is, further away from your body—to inside—closer to your body—or the other way around." Before beginning, the instructor might move the student's arms from outside to inside and then from inside to outside to give him a *feel* of the difference. As soon as he can distinguish between these two broad categories of movement while actually swinging, the student can be asked to distinguish more subtle changes. He might be asked, for example, to see if he can tell after each swing whether it was more or less inside out than the last. In this case, in order to pinpoint his focus more subtly on the swing, awareness can be heightened by the use of a rating scale. If a downswing that is square to the target line is 0, a swing that is slightly inside out could be called a +1; more inside out, +2 or +3. Likewise, outside in downswings would be rated −1, −2, and −3. (With advanced golfers, the scale can be refined indefinitely to focus on smaller and smaller fractions of differentiation.) This fine-tuning of the student's attention creates more refined differentiation in feel and allows learning to take place. By experimenting, Self

2 discovers which stroke feels and works best for his body at his level of development.

Sometimes a golfer's swing becomes stuck in a groove, and, despite focusing on the downswing it remains stuck. If the student feels that his normal swing is a −2, the instructor might say, "Why don't you see what a minus 3 feels like? . . . Now try a plus 3, a plus 2, a plus 1." After he has broken out of his rut by experiencing different swings, he can go back to swinging without trying, and if he sincerely doesn't *try* to swing "right" but sticks to awareness exercises, his body will automatically select the swing that feels and works best. Through such a natural learning process the student can groove his new swing without *thinking* about it but by concretely *feeling* it.

Here are some examples of translating do-instructions into awareness instructions. As you read them, try to imagine the difference in the way you might react to each instruction.

1. Keep your head still throughout the swing. It's imperative to keep it still. Keep working at it until you get it.

1. See if you sense any movement in your head during the swing. Notice whether there is more or less movement on each succeeding swing.

2. Early in the downswing, the right elbow should return to the right side. (Sam Snead)

2. During the next few swings, pay attention to your right elbow. Don't try to change it in any way; just see if you can tell what it does, especially after you begin the downswing. Notice any changes in its position.

3. Keep your left arm straight.

3. Notice whether your left arm is straight or whether it bends on each swing, and scale the amount on a scale from 1 to 5.

4. The most common fault of the inexperienced player during the downswing is hurrying into the downswing before the backswing is completed, rushing the right shoulder around before the club head reaches the hitting area, and turning the upper body into the shot too quickly. (Ben Hogan)

4. On the next twenty shots, pay attention to your body and see if you can detect any rushing during the swing. If so, tell me how you rushed—that is, which muscles you used to rush and when. Don't try to avoid rushing; just notice what you are doing, and any changes in degree.

5. Try to be certain the back of your left hand faces down the target line as you strike the ball. (Arnold Palmer)

5. Take a few swings paying attention to the back of your left hand. Notice if it is square, open, or closed in relation to the target line.

6. It is the consensus of *Golf Digest*'s professional teaching panel and advisory staff that the ideal position of the club shaft at the top is parallel to the intended line of flight. (*Golf Digest*)

6. Without looking, sense whether the shaft of your club is parallel to the target line, inside the line, or outside it. It might help if you shut your eyes during the swing to increase your sense of feel.

In each of these examples one difference between the two kinds of instructions is consistent. The do-instruction asks the golfer to achieve a certain result that he may or may not feel he can produce. Because there is a potential for success or failure, he is likely to be overconcerned with getting results and thus be open to doubt and to straining. Even if he succeeds, he will think that he has to remember that tip every time he wants the same results—along with all the other instructions already in his head. The awareness instruction, on the other hand, asks only one thing of the conscious mind: Pay attention to what is happening. There is no doubt because there is no right way or wrong way, and there is no fear of failure because there is no externally implied standard for success. Yet the body learns because it is now free to focus on what feels good and to see for itself what works.

One of the primary characteristics of the awareness instruction is that it is nonjudgmental. Awareness simply sees and accepts what is; it doesn't place a positive or negative value on the result. Some instructors who have tried to make awareness instructions work for them fall into the use of quasi-awareness instructions, such as "Are you aware that you're taking your swing back incorrectly?" or "Be aware that you're not turning." But it's impossible to be aware of *not* doing something because awareness can focus only on what *is* happening. What's not happening is a concept based on a judgment about what you think *should* be happening.

The most difficult thing about awareness instructions is to realize that they work, when all your life you've believed only in do-instructions. It's not hard to see that they circumvent self-doubt and frustration, but perhaps it's not so easy to believe that they get results. If it's any comfort, I have the same problem; even though they improve learning and performance whenever used, each time I am surprised. It blows my mind that a change for the better can take place so effortlessly. It is not always the change I anticipated, but that only makes it more interesting. Nothing but my repeated experience that awareness instructions do work has given me the confidence to rely so heavily on them. It is results, not theory, that warrants their use. Therefore, I don't suggest that you make a heroic effort to forget about results or to convince yourself that your score is really not important. What I do suggest is that you experiment with awareness instructions long enough and sincerely enough to discover their effects for yourself.

Ever since I heard of Al Geiberger's score of 59 at the Colonial Country Club in Memphis, I had wanted to meet him and talk with him about what he had done in the Inner Game to achieve such Outer Game success. When I called him, we made a date to meet at a private club in Santa Barbara.

I arrived at the club first and went to the pro shop to meet the club pro, with whom Geiberger had arranged to use the putting green and range. When I introduced myself, he expressed some curiosity about what I intended to do with Mr. Geiberger on the range. "You're not going to do anything that looks like teaching, are you?" he asked somewhat threateningly. I asked him what he felt would look like teaching.

"Well, I just don't want you showing him how to swing a golf club or him standing over you showing you how to address the ball or anything like that." I couldn't help being amused at the prospect of teaching Geiberger *anything* about how to swing a golf club, and, though I knew that he was certainly competent to teach me, I didn't want to learn that way. "No, I can assure you that what we do won't resemble that kind of teaching," I answered.

When Al arrived his bearing and manner reminded me immediately of Jimmy Stewart. He told me that he'd been interested in the mental side of golf for some time and that he was particularly open at this point; he had just had a disastrous time trying to learn the hows and how-not-tos of the parallel turn from a skiing instructor who'd made him dizzy with instructions. "Finally, I said, 'To hell with all this,' just skied down the hill and began to get the hang of it."

I asked Al about his Inner Game experiences in golf. He recalled that several times when he was practicing putting before a tournament and someone came up to talk to him, he would continue putting and be surprised that it would improve while he was engaged in casual conversation. When the interruption ended, he would say to himself, Now I'll get back to some serious putting—only to find that his performance would drop off significantly. "From this and other experiences," Al said, "I've come to realize that I perform best when I'm letting my subconscious

INTRODUCING AL GEIBERGER TO THE INNER GAME

mind hit the ball and my conscious mind is otherwise occupied. Is that what you're talking about in the Inner Game?"

"That's a part of it," I replied, "but it's possible to use the conscious mind in a productive way while still allowing what you call the subconscious mind, part of what I call Self 2, control the hitting of the ball. You don't have to distract the conscious mind away from golf; you can involve it in a task that helps Self 2 in his task."

I offered to give Al an example of one way this might work in putting and began by telling him that I had found that one of the greatest single obstacles to performance among tennis players was trying too hard for results. "The same seems to be true in putting, where the goal desired is within immediate reach. The overconcern with results produces tension, tightening, and consequent loss of touch, which makes achieving the goal more difficult. So the key to increasing one's putting feel is to switch games—to change from the game called 'trying to get the ball in the hole' to an awareness game called 'see if you can *feel* where your ball goes in relation to the hole.' " The hole would still be the target, but the primary object of the game wasn't to drop the putt, but to be able to tell, without looking, where the ball stopped in relation to the hole. Only by focusing on the feel of the swing can you make an accurate guess.

At first Al had a hard time really letting go of trying to sink the ball. He would putt and guess, then look up to see where the ball had actually gone. If he had missed by what seemed to him too wide a margin, he would shake his head in mild disappointment. Finally, I insisted, "Al, don't try to get the ball into the hole. That isn't the game right now. Pretend that we're betting a hundred dollars a putt that you can come within six inches of telling me exactly where your ball comes to a stop."

"You don't *want* me to try to sink it? Should I try to miss it?"

"No, don't try to sink it and don't try to miss it. Just putt toward the hole and see if you can tell by feel alone where it goes."

This time Al prepared to putt with much less tension in his face. Instead of looking at the hole two or three times, he looked once, shut his eyes, and stroked the ball right into the cup. I caught it before it could make a sound and asked him where it had landed. "It was pretty good," Al said. His eyes were still closed, but there was more certainty in his voice. "Maybe it went three inches past the hole on the right edge."

"Nope, you're off a little. It went directly into the hole, though it probably would have rolled a few inches past if you'd missed. See if you can do better next time," I challenged. Al was beginning to see what this drill was about, but the surprise to him was that he was putting considerably better when he was sincerely playing the awareness game than when he was trying for results.

Thereafter Al became absorbed in the awareness game, and I could tell from the diminished tension on his face, both during his setup and after the putt, that he had let go of some of his concern about results. Most of his focus was now concentrated on increasing his feel in order to be more accurate in his guesses, and within a few minutes he significantly improved his ability to tell where the ball stopped. Simultaneously, his putting stroke became smoother and slightly less deliberate. Instead of looking at the ball, then back at the hole three or four times, he would sight once, close his eyes, putt, and then, even before the ball stopped, guess.

"How can you tell whether the ball went right or left of the hole?" I asked.

"I don't know for sure, but I can feel it."

"Putt a few more and see if you can discover what gives you the most accurate feedback about the direction of the ball," I suggested.

After three more putts Al decided that he could feel the direction by paying attention to the points on the thumb and forefinger of his right hand where they touched the leather of the putter handle. When I asked him to focus his attention on those points, he was able to tell me with amazing precision just how far to the right or left his putts went. As the accuracy of this feedback process increased, so did the accuracy of his putts, and soon they were considerably more consistent in their direction. Then I asked the same kind of question about how he could best determine the length of his putts. Although there were several factors here, by focusing on what seemed the most reliable feel he was able to increase the accuracy of his guesses, and automatically the accuracy of the length of the putts themselves increased.

As happens with almost everyone I have taught, after Al noticed the improved results he was getting during this awareness exercise, he would sometimes lapse into trying to repeat the "good results" by a conscious effort to control the putter. Inevitably, the results would be worse. "Can you feel the difference when you try?" I would ask. "Yes, I tried to sink that last one," he'd say. Then he would return to awareness-putting for a while until he couldn't seem to help trying again to sink the putt. There wasn't much for me to do, since his own experience was teaching him that trying for results instead of simply focusing on the feel of the stroke was giving him worse results. The fact that he could physically detect the difference, depending on which "game" he was playing, fascinated him. He seemed about to discover something important, but was a little afraid to accept the full implications of what he was learning.

"This might be really hard to do during a tournament," Al finally remarked after sinking three twenty-foot putts in a row.

"It's always hard to let go of long-standing patterns," I replied, "but the fact that it works makes it easier. I suggest you don't try it in a tournament until you have spent more time with the exercise on the practice green. Even if you don't radically change your approach to putting in tournaments, doing this exercise ten or fifteen minutes every time you practice putting can't help improving your feel for length and direction."

"That's the crux of putting—just feel of length and direction," Al agreed. I could see that he was wrestling with himself about his experience. Somehow he couldn't quite bring himself to trust not trying to control the putter and sink the ball, in spite of his clear experience that he putted best when his Self 2 was engaged. On the other hand, he had experienced such surprising results that he couldn't dismiss the difference.

"Let's go to the driving range," Al suggested. There we started with an exercise similar to awareness-putting. I asked him to swing without looking where the ball went and then see if he could describe its trajectory. At first Al was surprised that this exercise was so difficult. He said that he was in the habit of looking at the ball in flight to determine what, if anything, he had done wrong on his swing. I knew that this was a traditional method but suggested to Al that perhaps there was a better one. "What if you could actually *feel* the first tendency of the swing to leave its groove? Then wouldn't it be possible for correction to take place even before the ball was hit? I don't know much about the mechanics of the golf swing, but I feel confident that if I could feel the difference between a hook and a slice or even between a draw and a fade, I could then control which kind of shot I produce. On the other hand, I'm not sure that even if I correctly analyze a given error, I will succeed in trying to correct it on the next swing."

Al agreed that during a tournament round most pros don't attempt to make mechanical corrections, though perhaps they might modify their address to the ball if something seemed wrong there. "We save mechanical corrections for the practice range," he said.

So with renewed motivation we began the awareness game, beginning with an eight iron and then moving on toward the longer clubs. As with putting, after he had developed by feel a general awareness of where the ball went, I asked Al to try to be more specific. "What part of your body is most reliable in telling you whether you're getting a fade or a draw? And how can you tell the height of the trajectory?" These questions piqued Al's curiosity. He had never really tried to locate what cues from his body gave him this feedback, since he had relied primarily on his eyes and his analytical mind to figure out what his swing was doing. As time passed, he became more accurate and confident in his descriptions of his trajectories, and it was easy to tell that he was more aware of his swing.

Increased control was inevitable. "I think you're on to something here, Tim," he said, "but what about the fundamentals? Surely you have to teach the fundamentals."

I answered that of course I felt the fundamentals were important for advanced players as well as for beginners, but that before we discussed how to deal with them, I wanted him to give *me* an Inner Game lesson. Al agreed, and I told him of a simple awareness process that I had used in both tennis and skiing. It seemed to me that in golf, too, it would be useful in correcting errors and reinforcing strength.

"First you ask the student to forget about results and simply focus on the kinesthetic sensations of his body while swinging the club. When you see that the student is not trying to hit the ball but is simply focusing on the feel of his body, ask him if he is more aware of any particular part of it. My experience is that if there is an important flaw in the swing, the part of the body that is critically related to that error will draw itself to the student's attention. On the other hand, if there isn't an error, generally the part of the body that is critical in controlling the optimum swing will receive the student's focus and be reinforced. When the student locates the part of his body that is in the foreground of his attention, he can then be asked exactly *what* he is feeling there. For example, if he is most aware of his right shoulder, he may answer that he feels a little tightness or jerkiness there during the swing. At that point the coach may ask him to take a few more swings while focusing his attention on his shoulder to see if he can locate the exact moment in the swing in which the tightness occurs. It's important that the coach not give the student the impression that the tightness is "bad" and should be eliminated, only that it is there and that we want to find out more about it. Perhaps after a few swings the student determines that the tightening occurs just at the beginning of his downswing. At this point his feel has progressed from general body awareness to a specific "where," then to a specific "what," and finally to an exact "*when*." The final step in the process is to discriminate the *degree* to which the action is occurring. To help the student do this, the coach might say, 'I want you to take a few more swings paying attention to whatever is happening in your right shoulder at the moment your downswing begins, and specify the degree of tightness you feel. If you feel the same tightness as on the last few swings, call it a five; if there's more, give it a number from six to ten, depending on how much; if there is less, number the degree of tightness from four to zero.' By helping the student differentiate between degrees of tightness, his body unthinkingly starts to select the kinesthetic sensation that feels and works the best."

"So you never try to help him actually make the correction even if you can see what's wrong?" Al asked.

"No, because the whole point of the exercise is to help the student recognize that his body has the inherent capability of correcting itself. It's not that a novice golfer can't benefit from outside instruction; of course he can. But most of us have become so reliant on external authority to correct ourselves that we've lost confidence in the extremely sophisticated mechanism we have within us for self-correction. This process is designed to strengthen that confidence, and it also allows the student to gain more from external instruction at those times when it is useful."

After this explanation, Al watched me take a few swings with a seven iron and then began to give me an Inner Game lesson.

After five swings Al asked me if I was particularly aware of one part of my body, and I answered that I seemed to focus on my right hand. I also remarked that my shots seemed to lack consistency and that I really couldn't tell if they were going to go straight, draw, or fade. "Don't worry about that," Al said. "Just tell me what you are noticing about your right hand." I said that its grip seemed a little loose, and he asked me exactly which part of the hand. After a few more swings I said that I could actually feel my fourth and fifth fingers leave the club handle. "When does that happen?" Al asked. "At the back of the swing, before coming down," I answered. Of course I realized that this was probably a flaw in my swing, but, sticking to the process I'd outlined, Al said, "Don't try to hold the club any tighter; just keep swinging and give me a number that indicates how loose your hand is on the club at the back of the swing. Zero will mean that your fingers didn't leave the club at all, and a plus figure means the degree of firmness of your grip."

I took about ten shots, calling out numbers after each one: "Three, two, three, zero, one, zero, minus one, minus one, minus one, minus one." "The last four shots were the best I've seen you hit," Al said. "They felt more secure somehow," I replied, "but it also felt as if I was getting less power." "It may have felt that way," said Al, "but in fact they were a good five to eight yards past the others."

Al was not surprised that keeping my hand on the club produced better results; in fact, he said, the standard instruction to combat this common error is "Keep the last two fingers of your right hand firm on the grip." But he admitted that while watching my swing he hadn't picked up the fact that my fingers were coming free and that the Inner Game method had been an effective way of detecting the error.

"What if you had seen the error and given me the traditional instruction and I had asked you *how* firm I should hold my fingers?"

"Yes, I see what you mean; the numbers do make it more precise."

"Not only that, but the big difference is that now I don't have to try to remember to do something right and therefore won't tighten up or become frustrated about my fingers. All I have to do is to feel what's happening and get feedback from the results. This state of mind is very different, even though the technical correction may be the same, and it will help me maintain poise and self-control."

Al remembered a lesson he had recently given his son and how frustrating it had been when the boy couldn't seem to master a particular mechanical detail. "I threw his whole swing off by trying to get him to do one simple thing right. Finally, I told him to forget about it and just swing the club, and his rhythm began to return. Maybe the Inner Game approach wouldn't tie him up in knots the way I did."

After a round at Los Robles Greens in Los Angeles, I went out to the range to hit some balls and was joined by Pete, one of the golfers in the foursome I'd just played in. Pete was a long-iron hitter with a ten handicap who seemed to rear back and attack the ball. On the sixth hole he'd hit a nine iron 150 yards downwind and sunk it for an eagle. He said he'd been having trouble with his drives; he was slicing all of them. I asked him if he wanted to try an Inner Game exercise that wouldn't tamper with his swing but would help his concentration. He agreed, and I explained the back-hit-stop exercise to him. At first he couldn't do it at all, but when he started paying attention to the club head instead of trying to correct the slice, there was an immediate, dramatic change in the trajectory of the ball. "Wow," he said, "it works! That's the first draw I've hit all day."

"Okay, but don't try to do it again. Just let the club head go where it wants."

Again Pete hit a draw. "This is incredible. I thought the stiff shafts of my new clubs were making me slice and that I had to learn to really come through with them."

"The problem seems to be more that you *thought* there was a problem. Most of our problems come from trying to correct problems, and when we stop trying to correct them and just pay attention to the club head, the body makes its own corrections."

I could see that this was an entirely new idea to Pete and that he wasn't buying it easily. Still, he went on practicing the back-hit-stop, and I returned to practicing with my five irons. Jack, another of our foursome, came over to offer Pete some help, and they began a very technical discussion. Pete started slicing again. Soon I heard him say to Jack, "Hey, watch this. I don't know why it works, but you ought to try this back-hit-stop stuff."

A Lesson in Lesson Taking

After a while Pete came over and offered to give *me* a lesson. He wanted to teach me how to hit down into the ball on my irons, to take a divot from inside out and make the ball jump off the club.

He gave me about four do-instructions and I felt pretty awkward, but I was eager to learn. I knew that my irons weren't going as far as I could hit them. Actually, the lesson turned out well. He'd give a command like "Hit a goddamn divot this time!" and I'd translate this mentally into "Let's see how much earth my club takes." Then there'd be a divot and Pete would say, "Good, do you see what that does? The ball jumped off the club, and look how far it went." Then he said, "Okay, this time stand farther away from the ball, and make the divot go in this direction." He placed a cigarette 30 degrees outside my target line. It didn't look possible to me; I'd never come close to swinging in that direction. All right, Self 2, I said to myself, somehow swing so that the divot goes toward the cigarette. I haven't the slightest idea how to do it.

After a few swings Self 2 got it. Pete was jumping up and down saying, "That's it! You're hitting it inside out!"

I knew that Pete's technical information was helpful, but I also realized that if I'd tried to follow his instructions literally, I'd probably have ruined my swing. I had to smuggle his tips safely past Self 1 somehow and hope that Self 2 got the picture. This wasn't easy, particularly because I didn't want Pete to think I wasn't trying to do what he was asking, and I had no idea whether Self 2 would do it. But Pete must have thought I was trying hard to do exactly what he said, because the results got better and the swing easier, and in the process I picked up a good ten yards per club on my irons. Pete left feeling that back-hit-stop had cured his slice and that his technical advice had helped put distance on my irons.

I finished the practice realizing that what another person has learned from experience can help Self 2 to learn and that it is possible to circumvent the doubt and overcontrol that usually attend do-instructions.

CHAPTER 6

DISCOVERING
TECHNIQUE

Chapter 5 attempted to show that there is a fundamental difference between the awareness instructions and the traditional technical instruction, or what I called the "do-instruction." I hope it's now clear that increasing proficiency at any skill is a function of awareness, choice, and trust. Whatever interferes with any of these functions will inhibit the process of learning. If one's self-confidence is undermined in the process of receiving instructions, the possibility for learning will be impaired. If on top of this there is pressure from the instructor to do it "by the book" at the risk of displeasing him, Self 1 has the opening to inject fear, doubt, and distraction into the learning environment. It is ironic how often instructions designed to help the student will do precisely the opposite.

By using awareness instructions alone, you can make a great deal of progress in evolving a golf swing that is truly yours. But a large question may remain in your mind: Am I supposed to throw out all the technical knowledge I have accumulated over the years? Am I supposed to ignore all that I am being taught or might read? In short, what is the role of technical knowledge in learning golf according to the Inner Game philosophy of learning?

This chapter attempts to answer that question by suggesting that there is a way to integrate the best of the Outer and the Inner, technical knowledge and learning from experience. What I hope to provide here is a way to use both awareness techniques and technical information to help you *discover technique for yourself*. The purpose of all good instruction is to help the individual learn better and better ways of doing something. I first introduced this concept of the "marriage" of awareness and technique in the revised edition of *The Inner Game of Tennis*, and it is equally applicable to any sport. In the next two chapters, I will try to illustrate the integration between awareness and technique in my discussion of the specific skills of putting, chipping, and swinging. First, I have some general comments on technical instructions as they relate to learning from experience.

To me it makes sense to build any system of instruction on the best possible understanding of the natural learning process you were born with. The less the instruction process interferes with the process of learning built into your very DNA, the more effective your progress is going to be. Said another way, the less fear and doubt are imbedded in the instructional process, the easier it will be to take all the steps in the natural learning process.

WHICH CAME FIRST, THE EXPERIENCE OR THE TECHNIQUE?

In the effort to understand how to use technical knowledge or theory I believe that it is most important to recognize that, fundamentally, *experience* precedes technical knowledge. We may read books or articles that present technical instructions before we have ever swung a club, but where did these instructions come from? At some point did they not originate in *someone's* experience? Either by accident or by intention someone hit a ball in a certain way and it felt good and it worked. Through experimentation, refinements were made and the golf swing finally became a repeatable one.

Then, perhaps, in an attempt to repeat that way of hitting the ball or to pass it on to someone else, the golfer attempts to describe that swing in language. But words can only represent actions, ideas, and experiences. Language is not action, and, at best, it can only hint at the subtleties contained in any complex behavior. Although the instruction can now be stored in the part of the mind that remembers language, it must be acknowledged that remembering the instruction is not the same as remembering the swing itself.

It is, of course, very convenient to think that by giving ourselves a correct instruction like "Swing from the inside out," we will hit wonderful draws over and over. We have been taught to trust Self 1's conceptual process of learning technique more than Self 2's natural process. Self 1 wants the credit for the good shot and wants to ignore the role of Self 2. This sets us up for disappointment when we give the same instruction again and the same good shot does not occur. Since we think the instruction was correct, the conclusion we come to is that we failed to obey it properly and that led to the error. Then we may get angry at ourselves for this "failure," make disparaging remarks about our abilities and call ourselves stupid, or blame ourselves in a variety of other ways.

But maybe the error was in not trusting Self 2 more. It is as if we think of ourselves as an obedient computer rather than as a human being. Consequently, we are apt to lose the direct access to the muscle memory that carries the most complete knowledge of the desired action. In a society that has become so oriented toward language as a way of representing truth, it is very possible for us to lose touch with our ability to feel and with it our ability to "remember" the way the shots felt. This remembering is a fundamental act of trust in Self 2 without which excellence in any skill cannot be sustained.

When the verbal instruction is passed on to another person who does not have in his bank of experience the action being described, it lives in the mind totally disconnected from experience. Then, as the student continues to learn in this way, there will be an ever-widening split between the memory of theory and the memory of action. And if we use an instruction to pass judgment on our shots instead of attending to the lessons of experience, the gap between experience and the instruction is further widened. The instruction, used as a conceptual "should" or "should not," puts a shadow of fear between Self 2's intuitive knowledge and the action. Many times I have observed golfers hitting perfectly decent shots but complaining about them because they thought they did something "wrong." By the time they have brought their swing into conformity with their concept of the "right" way to do it, the shot has lost both power and consistency as well as naturalness.

In short, if we rely too heavily on instructions, we lose touch with the ability to feel our actions and undermine our natural learning processes and our potential to perform. Instead, if we swing the golf club while relying on the instincts of Self 2, we reinforce the simplest neural pathway to the optimal shot.

By using awareness instructions, you can learn a great deal of technique naturally by paying close attention to your body, the club, and the ball. The more awareness you can bring to bear on any action, the more feedback you get from experience and the more naturally you learn the technique that feels best and works best for you or any given player at any given state of development. We may need to learn how to feel again and learn how to learn again. The saying of an old master is pertinent here: "No teacher is greater than one's own experience."

How to Make the Best Use of Technical Instructions

So the question remains: How can one person's greater level of experience help another person? The short answer is that a valid instruction derived from experience can help me if it guides me to my own experiential discovery.

For the student, the question is how to listen to technical instructions and use them without falling into the Self 1 traps of judgment, doubt, and fear. For the teacher or coach, the question is how to give instructions in such a way as to help the natural learning process of the student and not interfere with it. If the teacher succeeds in this effort, then he will have taught more than golf, and the student will walk away with skills that can be used for the learning of any skill.

How Do You Learn to Grip the Club Correctly?

Let's say you've read a set of instructions about how best to grip the golf club. There is not much doubt involved in learning the grip. It may feel a little awkward, and you may not have much understanding of why the club should be held in the prescribed manner, but those problems diminish with time. You look for the grip that suits your hands. The instructions are there to "get you into the ballpark" so you can go on to discover what will work best for you.

But how firmly should you grip the club? You will probably not find a technical description that is more specific than "Grip the club firmly but not in a death grip." Or perhaps "Grip the club with the same firmness of a handshake." You can tell that there is no way you are going to learn the best amount of pressure to apply to your wrist by reading about it in a book. The book can give you a hint, but after that you are going to have to learn directly from your experience. And that is probably how the person writing the book had to learn, too.

Just as the originator of the instruction discovered from experience what was too firm and what was too wobbly, so the individual golfer has to find out the same way—by experimentation. This can be done only by paying close attention to the feel of your hands, wrists, and arms during your swing. You don't need to put your findings into words; *it is the feel itself, not the description of the feel, that you will remember.*

A "discovery" frame of mind is very different from a "dogmatic" frame of mind. If I try to define "firm grip" and obey it as an instruction, in the effort to grip the club "correctly" and "firmly," I will usually overtighten the wrists. This prevents them from moving as freely as they need to through the ball and thereby robs me of both power and accuracy. Then, in an effort to get more control and more power, the dogmatic Self 1 is apt to let the tightness move up the arms to my shoulders and neck until the swing is generally constricted.

Soon someone will tell me that I should relax and not try to hit so hard. But how much should I relax? Do I know how to relax? If I can't "feel" the overtightness, I am not going to be able to find the proper amount of relaxation. It just can't be spelled out in words.

So I believe the best use of most technical knowledge is to communicate a *hint* of a desired destination. The hint can be delivered verbally, demonstrated in action, or observed in a picture or video, but it is best seen as an *approximation* of a desirable goal waiting to be discovered first-hand by the individual golfer through paying close attention to his own experience.

If you asked a group of golf instructors to write down all the important elements of a golf swing, most would find it easy to distinguish at least fifty instructions. Imagine the difficulty for the golfer who must deal with this complexity. No wonder self-doubt is so easy to come by! On the other hand, understanding the swing and remembering its feel is like remembering a single picture. The mind is capable of that, and it can recognize when one element in one picture is slightly different from another. The other advantage of using awareness to "discover the technique" is that it doesn't tend to evoke the overcontrolling and judgmental tendencies of Self 1.

HOW TO WATCH THE PROS

When I was a child, I used to play touch football, and I noticed that I played a lot better when I'd just come home after my dad had taken me to see the San Francisco 49ers play. I hadn't studied Frankie Albert's passing technique, but I had picked up something, and it made a difference when I played. I think most people have had experiences very similar to this.

Although it is obvious that we can learn a great deal by watching better players play golf, we have to learn how to watch. The best method is simply to watch without assuming that the way the pro swings is the way you should swing. In many cases, asking a beginner to try to swing like a pro is like asking a baby to walk before it has crawled. Formulating technique while watching the pro or by trying to imitate him or her too closely can be detrimental to your natural learning process.

Instead, allow yourself to focus on whatever most interests you about the pro's movements. Self 2 will automatically pick up elements of the swing that are useful to it and discard whatever is not useful at the time. Observe how each new swing feels and how it works. Allow the natural learning process to lead you toward your best swing. Do not force yourself to make the change. Just allow Self 2 to "play around" while it searches for new swing possibilities. In doing so, it will use what it is ready for from the "hints" picked up in its observation of the pro.

Self 2 has very good instincts about when it is time to work on any particular element of your swing. In learning how to learn by watching pros play, you may want to alternate between external observation and experimentation on the range until you have the confidence that you can access the particular swing technique you are working on.

Throughout this approach to learning, the ultimate choice stays with you as you alternately shift attention between observation of the pro's swing and focus on your own. There is no judgment necessary in the process. You see differences between what you are doing and the external model, but simply notice them, and continue to observe, feel your own movements, and check the results. This "learning mind-set" lends a freedom to search for the feel that works for you.

In summary, I do believe that someone who has discovered his or her best swing can help you discover *your* best swing. Knowledge of technique learned by one person can give another an advantage in discovering what technique works best. But it is dangerous to make that person's swing or any swing description into your standard for right and wrong. Self 1 easily gets enamored of formulas that tell the body what position it should be in and when. It likes the sense of control it gets from doing it by the book.

But Self 2 likes the feeling of flow—sensing the whole swing as one thing. The Inner Game encourages you to keep in touch with the Self 2 learning process you were born with while avoiding getting too caught up in trying too hard to make your movements conform to an outside model. Use outside models in your learning, but don't let them use you. Natural learning is and always will be from the inside out, not vice versa.

With this approach I do not have the feeling that I am fitting myself or my students into an external model. After an Inner Game tennis lesson, a golf professional told me what he liked about this approach: "What I consider to be the right technique for my swing is ever-changing day by day. My model is always being destroyed and rebuilt as I learn more and more. My technique is always evolving."

Self 2's nature is to evolve every chance it gets. As your technique evolves, you will become better at learning technique and you will be able to make big changes in a short period of time. As you discover Self 2's learning capabilities, not only will your golf swings improve but you will have increased your capacity to learn anything.

Strategy Number 1: Trying to Figure It Out on Your Own

You think you're a good athlete and things come naturally to you, so you'll just rely on your knowledge of other sports and figure things out as you go along. What happens to such a player? He starts with the enthusiasm that's natural for a person who is going to be independent and learn on his own. But he doesn't know how to learn. He makes good shots, and he makes bad shots. Every time he makes a good shot, he thinks, What did I do right? Every time he hits a bad shot, he tries to figure out what went wrong. He is caught in this culture's good-bad mode of learning, but he is basing his own rules of "good" and "bad" on relatively little experience. What he doesn't know he fills in with unfounded assumptions. His thinking is both judgmental and groundless. His criteria for right and wrong are founded on an all-too-narrow base of experience. He becomes superstitious: "Before that last good shot, I wiggled this way or waggled that way, or thought this particular thought before starting my swing . . . and it worked. Now I've got the secret to the game!"

Confident in his new discovery, he addresses the next ball with high hopes and expectations. In this state of mind, it is not unusual for him to hit another good shot—not because of the wiggle, waggle, or special thought but because of his momentary self-confidence. Maybe two or three good shots, then the inevitable flub. "What went wrong with that one?" he wonders. "Maybe I didn't wiggle or waggle enough. Maybe I didn't think my thought strongly enough." So he redoubles his efforts, but now doubt has crept in. Another shot misses the mark. "Maybe it's something else I'm doing wrong." The latest "secret to successful golfing" is discarded after three holes, and the same thinking that dreamed it up in the first place is now looking for the next secret. Uncertainty sets in. Just enough good shots are being hit to make him think that his latest explanation of cause and effect is grounded in reality. At the same time, inexplicably poor shots are fueling the uncertainty. Frustration deepens. Amazingly enough, some players hold on to this approach throughout a lifetime of golf. To compensate for the continuous disappointment of broken beliefs, they brag to their friends that they are self-taught and don't really need the help of a teacher.

THE LADDER OF EFFECTIVE WAYS TO LEARN GOLF (FROM LEAST EFFECTIVE TO MOST EFFECTIVE)

Strategy Number 2: Taking Lessons from a Golf Professional Who Understands Only the Mechanics of the Game

This strategy starts with the commonsense assumption that if you don't know how to do something, someone who does know can teach you. If you don't know the law, you go to a lawyer. If you don't know mathematics, you go to a math teacher. This is a sensible approach, and, if you have enough humility, it can work much better than Strategy Number 1. The instructor, like any trained expert, understands the game and will be willing to pass his knowledge on to you for a reasonable fee. This is the same kind of knowledge you can find in a golf magazine or book. It is cause-and-effect knowledge, based on a mechanical understanding of the golf swing (even though the theories of mechanics vary greatly among experts and they disagree vehemently on certain elements of the proper swing).

The underlying fallacy of this approach is the assumption that someone who knows the mechanics of a golf swing therefore knows how to help someone else learn how to play golf. Although, typically, both professionals and students share this assumption, it is not necessarily true that if a person can describe, demonstrate, and correctly analyze the golf swing, he can teach it to another person. The conceptual knowledge of a golf swing can indeed be passed via book, article, or qualified golf professional, but, as explained earlier on, there is quite a gap between knowing something conceptually and being able to do it. Fortunately for golfers, the PGA and many golf instructors have been making strides to understand the learning process better and to improve ways of helping students learn.

The biggest downfall of learning from the professional in the traditional way is that the student becomes overly dependent on both the professional's knowledge and the learning process. When things go wrong, he will return to the pro or refer to one of his many instructions. The student undoubtedly will be caught up in the process of analyzing each bad shot just as he did in Strategy Number 1. The natural learning process is still missing. Most of golf simply cannot be learned by imposing external instructions on the swing elements. Fortunately, the body is such an amazing learning mechanism that, over time, it will begin to learn in spite of the interferences that are an inevitable part of learning by instruction and analysis.

Strategy Number 3: Natural Learning Without the Help of a Professional

Almost anyone who does not interfere with natural learning is capable of developing a good game of golf without taking lessons. The fundamental skill is nonjudgmental awareness—a way of looking that does not judge good or bad, a way of focusing attention without consciously trying to correct. Learning by this method requires trust, not in a formula but in your body's ability to learn directly from experience, without judgmental analysis. Though golf may be more complicated than riding a bike, for example, it can be learned in much the same way. When you can relax in face of the challenge of golf and are not overwhelmed by the shoulds and shouldn'ts of external models, you are much better able to feel what is happening in your swing. Your attention naturally gravitates toward what needs to be noticed. By trusting that attention, and giving freely of it, learning takes place. The process is continuous as your attention shifts spontaneously to the next focal point. You are learning to stay out of the way of the natural learning process, secure in the knowledge that you'll be hitting shots that work and shots that don't. Improvement will be gradual, but natural, and you will skip the frustration that drives so many away from the game. Moreover, you will be able to employ these skills of focus and trust in the development of other skills. Strategy Number 3 is the primary method described in this edition of the book and the one I used to learn the game while writing the original version.

Strategy Number 4: Natural Learning Plus the Help of an Inner Game Coach

Even though I am capable of focusing my own attention, I have been consistently surprised at the relative effectiveness of using a focus suggested by another person. As individuals operating within our own mindset, we inevitably develop blind spots, areas of our behavior that we simply overlook or ignore. We become accustomed to what we repeat, and this familiarity breeds unconsciousness. So, as effective as natural learning is, there is no substitute for the help of another pair of eyes, especially if they belong to someone who understands the natural learning process.

The value of Inner Game coaching, even when done by individuals without any special knowledge of the mechanics of a particular sport, has been driven home to me by how much I have learned from my students. Though few of them know much about the mechanics of golf, most have begun to absorb the principles of natural learning. First, I would coach them, then I would ask them to coach me. I would ask them to watch my swing, not for the purpose of correcting anything but just to observe. I knew that their attention would spontaneously focus on some aspect of the swing. It might be my posture at setup, an aspect of the backswing, or the follow-through. It might be balance, tempo, or some little detail that didn't seem significant enough to mention. Whatever it was, I would ask them to tell me. Recently, a student said she saw that the first thing I did on my takeaway was to make a slight movement with my right hand that opened the club face. I had no idea what I was doing and no idea if it was working or not. My response was twofold. First, I had to be careful not to jump to any conclusion about whether this movement was helpful. Second, I had to focus my attention on that movement and notice if it increased, decreased, or stayed the same, trusting that any necessary learning would take place.

The big difference between this kind of coaching and that of the traditional professional is that the first holds up a mirror. The Inner Game coach says focus here or focus there, without any hint of trying to induce a preconceived change. It is this noncorrective attitude that helps the student make nonjudgmental observations of his own swing, increase the sense of feel, and trigger the natural learning process.

Strategy Number 5: Natural Learning with the Help of a Golf Professional Who Understands How to Coach Natural Learning

The coach who understands the natural learning process, but not the mechanics of the golf swing, can still help the student get the most out of his or her own learning abilities. But the professional who grasps both the mechanics and the Inner Game can be even more helpful, since the student will be able to keep faith with his own learning capabilities while benefiting from the teacher's experience.

Whereas the Inner Game coach might just give the focusing instruction "Notice the extent of turn made by your left shoulder," the knowledgeable professional can give a hint about the direction of change he expects to take place. He might believe, for example, that to gain maximum power it is important to take a complete backswing and that, in most cases, the shoulders should turn until the back of the left shoulder is just behind the ball. But how would he "coach" the learning of this movement? Not with an emphasis on "doing it right." The emphasis should be on exploration. He might say, "Notice the degree of turn of your shoulders during your backswing. Let me know if the back of your left shoulder [pointing to the exact spot] stops turning before or after the ball." He might ask the student to scale −3, −2, −1 for positions in front of the ball and +1, +2, +3 for after the ball. After the coach is confident that the student is able to feel accurately what her shoulders are doing, he might add the suggestion "As you keep exploring this turn, you will probably find the position you are looking for in the vicinity just behind the ball." If this instruction is given in such a way that it does not cause the student to stop exploring and to start "obeying," the learning can take place naturally and with firsthand knowledge of what works. It will be more confident, quicker, and more lasting. Under such instruction, a student gets the best of both worlds. He retains his trust in his own natural learning abilities yet benefits from the pro's knowledge. The dignity and joy of Self 2 learning are kept intact at the same time that experience and knowledge of golf are brought to bear unobtrusively.

CHAPTER 7

THE SHORT GAME: INNER PUTTING AND INNER CHIPPING

Much has been written about the importance of the short game in golf. It accounts for nearly half the strokes taken in any given round, yet it often gets only a small fraction of the attention and practice. Even more important, the simple back-and-forth movements of putting and chipping are the easiest places to build the foundations of both your Inner and Outer game technique and to understand the relationship between the two.

The short game is clearly the place where mental focus comes most into play. Awareness and feel are critical. It is also where a little yip in your chip can cost you a quick stroke while sending a piercing dart into the heart of your self-confidence. A putt that misses by a hair's width is still a missed putt, and sending it that last millimeter will count as a full stroke the same as your 200+ yard drive. The ultimate goal of every shot is to hit the golf ball in the hole, but the only time you actually succeed is on your last shot on each hole.

Finally, the short game is the great equalizer in golf. Every golfer has the *physical* ability to sink a chip or a putt and on occasion will hit shots that the pro would gladly accept. Age and lack of skill can put a three-hundred-yard drive out of reach, but not the hope of holing a thirty-foot putt. If you don't happen to live near a practice range, or perhaps don't feel like spending another five to seven dollars for a big bucket of balls, there's always the backyard lawn, a grassy park, or a living-room carpet. Each will provide you with a learning environment for practicing this crucial part of the game of golf.

This chapter is about developing your awareness and trust skills in putting and chipping. It also explores how to integrate technical knowledge in a way that does not undermine what is most important—your feel and your self-confidence.

INCREASING AWARENESS OF THE PUTTING SURFACE

Almost all golfers could make a significant improvement in their putting by *seeing* the putting surface more clearly. The most common mistake is to *look too hard* and *think too long* about the line of the putt. Near the hole, the final target, tension tends to increase; we know that a small error can add a stroke to our score, so we tend to strain as we look back and forth between the hole and the ball trying to fix the line in our minds.

But this isn't how to see something well. The eyes work best when they are relaxed. As with other tryings, *"trying* to see" fails. Even a slight tension in the mind can cause a tightening of the muscles that regulate the shape of the lens. In effect, this means that staring or tensing the eyes will actually make the hole appear either farther away or closer than it actually is. Tension can also make the hole look smaller and distort the slope of the green. The eyes don't need help to see; you don't have to squint or stare. What we see *comes* to our eyes, not the other way around. When looking at the hole, don't take a "hard" look, as in straining to see detail. It is better to use "soft" eyes that are receptive and allow the important details to come to you. This will also allow a more tension-free stroke. In this state it is natural for our eyes to move around; trying to hold them still prevents them from absorbing information. Only when you are relaxed and receptive does the light reflected from external objects fall on the most sensitive part of the eye, and only then are details seen in full clarity.

Thinking too much can also hinder the seeing process. Most golfers feel they should mentally calculate the break when they line up a putt: "Let's see, it's a downhill lie, so I should hit it soft, maybe with a longer, smoother swing. . . . There's a break to the right, so I guess I should aim about six inches above the hole. . . . But I left the last putt like this short, so I don't want to hit it too soft. . . . I wonder what the effect of the grain will be . . ." This kind of thinking can interfere with seeing.

It's not your intellect that needs to analyze the putt because, as I hope you now believe, it is not your intellect that can direct your putter to hit the ball effectively. You can see the slope of the green and the distance to the hole without saying to yourself, "It's eight feet downhill, with a break to the right." To translate the situation into words invites intellectual analysis and Self 1 interference with your stroke.

The other possibility is to observe the putting surface, including any changes in its contour, and let Self 2 pick the line. Often I stand in front of a breaking putt and think I know how much break to allow for. But then I let Self 2 make the decision and often watch the ball take a completely different line to the hole.

Self 2 doesn't learn how to read greens by looking at the green alone. It learns most by observing the balls roll over the surface of greens with different contours and different kinds of grass. A good way to educate Self 2 is to roll golf balls across a given contour and study the shape of the trajectory of the ball's path relative to what you imagined it would do. When the ball does something you didn't expect, take a closer look at the green to determine the cause.

GOING TO SCHOOL ON OTHER GOLFERS' PUTTS

It is commonly felt that you can learn a lot about the contour of a particular putt if one of your opponents has a line similar to yours and is putting first. But it is to your advantage to go to school on *every* putt both before and after your own. If you do this exercise, it will not only sharpen your awareness of the speed of this particular green but give Self 2 further information that will help you in the future. Estimate the length and slope of each player's putt; then, before the putt is halfway to the hole, decide whether the ball is going to stop short or beyond the hole and by how much. This gives Self 2 valuable practice in reading greens, as well as precise information about the relationship between the speed of the ball and how far it travels. I find it's also more fun than just standing around pretending to be interested when I'm not and keeps me from analyzing my last putt or worrying about what will happen when it's my turn.

INCREASING AWARENESS OF DISTANCE

I have found that it's not necessary to try to calculate the number of feet to the hole of any given putt. But it is important to allow yourself to increase your awareness of distance. Standing behind the ball, I sometimes divide the line between the ball and the hole in half and then divide those segments in half one or two more times. If the green is contoured, my eye doesn't follow a straight line to the hole but whatever line Self 2 is picking out to allow for the break. Having visually focused my attention on the distance in this way, I will take a practice swing or two, without any effort to control the force of the swing. I don't rehearse the swing in the normal way of trying to repeat the "right" amount of force. I really don't know how hard I should hit the ball, so I ask Self 2 to show me. This active admittance of not knowing is important. "Show me how hard to hit this one," I say as Self 2 takes a few swings. I can tell when it is comfortable that it has found what it was looking for. Even then I don't try to reproduce that swing but let Self 2 make any adjustments it wants to in the final swing. It takes some trust, but when I don't interfere, I usually find out that my trust was well placed. I don't believe there is anything magical about this, and Self 2 definitely improves with experience on different kinds of greens.

Another way to sense distance is to walk to the hole with your eyes shut and attempt to put your putter handle in the hole. This brings "distance" to the body in a way that is more than just visual and adds to the information Self 2 can use in doing its calculations. As you get good at this exercise from short distances, you can test your distance awareness from longer and longer distances from the hole.

A SIMPLE SOLUTION TO A COMPLEX PROBLEM

Self 2 has to calculate both the direction and the force with which to hit the ball, and these variables are related to each other in a way that is almost impossible for the conscious mind to grasp. When a problem is clearly too hard for me, I sometimes find it easier to trust Self 2, and then the putt comes out much better than I expected. The best putter on the 1996 Tour was Brad Faxon. When asked for advice about what to think about while putting, he was quoted in *Golf Magazine* as saying, "Believe it or not, I'm not really thinking about anything when I putt. . . . It's hard to teach. I let my instincts take over. I like to see which way the break is going and use it. When I'm putting well, I feel as if I can make everything." A better statement of trusting Self 2 in putting will be hard to find. Yet other pros still like to rely on the technical aspects of putting.

JUST HOW TECHNICAL IS PUTTING?

At one L.A. Open, I ran into a touring pro who had the negative experience of falling from a consistent top five place on the tour to a position well down in the pack. We were introduced in the locker room, where he made the following comment about *The Inner Game of Golf*.

"I read your book," he said, "and I think what you have to say applies pretty well to the golf swing, but not to putting. Putting is just much too technical for the Inner Game to work." If anything, I expected quite the opposite, so I asked him, "Tell me, how old were you when you putted the best?" The pro thought for some time and then, with an almost nostalgic look, said, "I guess I've never really putted better than on certain days when I was fifteen or sixteen years old. I used to go out with three adults and one-putt sixteen out of eighteen greens. When they saw that I was in that kind of a zone, they would let me putt their balls as well. And I would generally sink them from wherever they were on the green."

I then asked what I thought was a question with an obvious answer: "Well, just how much technical knowledge could you have had at fifteen years old?" His answer truly shocked me. "Oh, of course I had very little technical knowledge. It's true that I putted best at the time, but that really doesn't count because at that age I didn't know how technical putting really was."

This conversation has stuck with me over the years as an example of just how deep belief in technique can go. It was particularly poignant because with all his accumulated technical wisdom about putting, it was his deteriorated putting game that was largely responsible for his declining standing on the Tour. When belief in technique becomes stronger than belief in our fundamental abilities, there will inevitably be loss in both confidence and performance.

Of course, not all touring pros who have technical know-how put their primary belief in it. Jack Nicklaus, in *Golf My Way*, writes, "Such is putting! 2% technique, 98% inspiration or confidence or touch . . . the only thing great putters have in common is touch, and that's the critical ingredient . . . none of them found it through mechanizing a stroke, nor do I believe they could maintain it in that way." That says it very clearly, and I believe the principle behind what Nicklaus is saying applies to more than putting.

But the question remains: How do you develop this "critical ingredient" called "touch"?

BODY AND CLUB AWARENESS

After you have begun to learn about reading the green, the greatest challenge is to increase awareness of body and club while putting. Developing feel in putting can be broken down into two simple components: feel of distance and feel of direction. Feel in putting, as with any golf swing, is transmitted primarily through the hands, wrists, arms, and shoulders. What is different about putting is that these are the only necessary transmitters of feel. Because most putts do not require great force, the legs and the hips are not required to be in motion. They simply provide a solid and stationary base for the delicate movement of hands, arms, and shoulders. It is because putting requires such precision that simplicity is the most important characteristic of the putting stroke. The less unnecessary movement there is in the rest of your body, the easier it is for Self 2 to focus attention on the critical arm and hand movements. You want to eliminate all unnecessary variables in the stroke so that the remaining essentials can be felt and translated into precision in both distance and direction.

The grip of the club is your feeling contact with the putter. Therefore, you want a grip that (1) allows your two hands to act as one and (2) allows for maximum feel of the putter's movement. I like to get as much skin as possible in contact with the handle to allow for maximum feel. I also like to have the back of my left hand and the palm of my right hand parallel to give me a better feel for direction. Within those guidelines each individual can explore and discover the grip that gives the best touch.

The way you stand over the putt is also important to maximizing feel. If you were to stand in a different way on each putt, you would make it harder for Self 2 to learn consistency. You want to stand in such a way that is comfortable, again so that you are not robbing yourself of an ounce of awareness of the movement of the stroke itself. For the same reason, you will probably want to have the ball in the same position in your stance. Most professionals advise that it be placed just far enough toward your front foot so that the putter is at the bottom of its arc or just barely on its way up at the moment of contact with the ball.

Don't be afraid to experiment with different grips and postures. Often a change will increase your sensitivity to the feel of your body. Similarly, changing putters can often increase your awareness of different putting sensations. This is one reason why golfers often putt better for a short time after switching putters.

If you continue to follow the principle of simplicity in putting, the stroke itself will begin to resemble a pendulumlike motion. The shoulders, arms, and wrists can form a relatively firm and consistent triangle as they rock back and forth in a rhythmic and steady motion. Again, the fewer unnecessary movements there are in the motion, the more feel you will gain of the stroke.

THE TOUCH GAME

I devised the "touch game" to increase my own sense of feel in putting. It is a simple awareness game, yet it is the most effective practice I have found for this purpose. The minds of most golfers, even when just practicing putting, have one dominant thought: Try to get the ball in the hole. The difference between success and failure in putting is so definite and the goal so precise that putting tends to make us very goal-oriented. But too much goal-orientedness will rob you of feel—the feel you need to reach your goal. So the touch game changes the goal of putting. Here's how it works:

You putt the ball without looking where it goes, and then you form a mental image of where you *guess* the putt has come to rest. Success is not defined as getting the ball in the hole but as *knowing* where the ball went. In other words, if the putt goes right of the hole six inches and stops eight inches beyond the hole and you guessed it right, by feel alone and without looking, then you win! If the ball went in the hole and you thought it went two inches left, then you lose!

There is only one way to win this game, and that is to feel as accurately as you can what effect a particular putting stroke has had on the ball. You do not try to sink the putt, nor do you try not to. You trust Self 2 to make the putt, and you're totally absorbed in trying to feel what happens. Where the ball ends up compared to where you thought it did is the measure of just how aware you were of the feel of your body and putter.

This is a very challenging and beneficial learning game. It takes the tension out of the putt by changing the game's external goal. At the same time it gives you an ever-increasing awareness of the two all-important variables in golf—distance and direction. After a little practice, most golfers find that they are quite accurate in knowing where their putts end up without looking. At the outset of this practice, I suggest you divide the touch game into its two components. First, just play for accurate sensing of distance. Then, switch to direction. Go back and forth between the two games until you feel you want to combine them.

To get the most benefit out of the touch game, I recommend putting with your eyes shut. Even though it is more difficult to make precise contact with the ball at first, this disadvantage can soon be overcome and you will find that closing your eyes gives you a much greater sense of feel and surprisingly good results. It proves how much putting is a matter of touch and shows that after the putt is lined up, how little need there is for the eyes.

PUTTING WITH YOUR EYES SHUT

The Next Step: Knowing How You Know

After you have gained an ability to feel where your putts go, you can take another step to heighten both feel and control. After making your initial guess about where your ball ended up, ask yourself, "How did I know?" With this question you are searching for the "feel clues" that contributed to your guess. For example, you may have guessed that your putt went six inches left of the hole. When you ask yourself what made you guess that, you might realize that you sensed the putter blade was slightly closed at impact. Then, on the succeeding putts, you put extra attention on the club face at impact, trying to "read" even more accurately its effect on the ball. Because the goal is not trying to get the ball in the hole, you do not try to control the putter face, you simply observe it. You attempt to feel if it is more closed, less closed, or the same as it was during the preceding putt. This requires a lot of attention, which almost always increases feel and control. Without conscious effort, the law of awareness will tend to bring the putter into proper alignment.

But let's say the putter face doesn't change its angle of impact and you continue with the awareness process. You then ask yourself, "If the putter is square at address to the ball, at what moment in the putting stroke does it change?" In this way you search for the source of this critical variable. When awareness is at the source, it will tend to change naturally in a way consistent with the desired results.

It is also possible that the club face is not the only variable contributing to your leftward putts. As you continue the touch game, you discover another indication—a sensing of a right-to-left direction (a push or pull) in your putter stroke. Then you apply the same awareness process to the direction of your swing as you did to your club face. You simply notice the direction of your next putts and again guess at the results. Learning to sense this direction is a very different process from "trying to keep it straight," which ends up in a tendency toward Self 1 control and over-tightening of muscles that decrease feel. The awareness *without effort to correct* increases feel and as a result increases true control.

The process of attempting to increase your awareness of particular sensations—no matter what they are—is the same. In all cases, you are trying to trace the *feeling* that contributed to the result back to its source. Then you focus attention there and allow the change to take place where it is most needed.

The Touch Game for Beginners

The beginner can go a long way toward achieving the foundation of feel by playing a simplified form of the touch game. I recommend the following exercise for the more advanced golfer who is getting ready to play a round: Line up three or four balls a few inches apart. Putt the first, and look where it stops rolling. Then putt the second without looking. Guess if it went farther, the same, or not as far as the first putt. Then check. Do the same with the remaining balls, comparing the feel of "distance" to that of the first putt. The same exercise can be done with regard to direction by guessing whether the second and following putts are right or left of the first ball. Again, the idea is not to hit the "target" ball but to use it as a reference for feeling distance and/or direction. The advantage of using the first ball as a reference as opposed to the hole is that it takes away all implied pressure of "succeeding" and "not succeeding."

This process of discovering and then attending to the variables that are affecting your stroke apply equally to putting and to chipping. By using the touch game, any golfer will find subtle changes taking place in the short game, making it more consistent and reliable. Listed below are a number of critical variables that can be attended to that apply to both putting and chipping. Focusing attention on one of these variables at a time without trying to make any changes can provoke spontaneous swing improvement.

- Awareness of the alignment of feet, hips, and hands
- Awareness of the club-head speed
- Awareness of the direction of the path of the club head
- Awareness of the length of the backswing and the length of the follow-through
- Awareness of the angle of the club face before, at, and after contact
- Awareness of the spin imparted to the ball
- Awareness of the position of the ball between your feet

The natural way to learn putting and chipping technique involves using awareness and trust together to move toward one desired learning goal—control over distance and direction in the short game. Awareness is used to focus on the critical variable, and trust allows you to let go of technical controls and trust Self 2's sense of feel and the natural learning process. After you gain firsthand familiarity with this process, it is possible to incorporate knowledge of technique into the equation. As stated in the last chapter, technical knowledge will not be used as a direct instruction (except in the case of easy-to-follow instructions regarding grip and ball positioning). Instead, technical knowledge will be used as a "hint" to the student about the learning that is likely to take place as the student increases awareness of his or her current putting or chipping stroke.

The chart on the following pages is divided into three columns. The one on the left describes a commonly desired outcome of a putting or chipping stroke. This column represents what might be your end goals in achieving control over distance and direction. The second column lists a few of the critical variables that contribute to achieving the goals in the column on the left. These variables are to be taken not as instructions but as places to focus your attention in order to discover the technique for achieving your desired outcomes. For example, it is very important that you not read the phrase "any unnecessary movements" as an instruction to limit your movement. Instead, read it as an instruction to *look for* or *sense actively* any unnecessary movements. Follow the law of awareness—if something needs to change it will as you increase your awareness of it.

SOME CRITICAL VARIABLES IN PUTTING AND CHIPPING

DISCOVERING YOUR PUTTING/ CHIPPING TECHNIQUE

Also, this is not meant to be a complete list of critical variables, but it should be enough to give you some practical examples. You can compile your own list based on your understanding of your own short game as it continues to evolve.

Finally, the column on the right represents some hints based on the technical knowledge about the short game commonly held to be valid by golf professionals. This list is also not complete and of course can vary depending on the professional who is asked. This column is meant to give you a hint about the direction of desired change. I believe this is the most effective use of technical knowledge in a verbal format for the person who wants to discover putting and chipping technique. It is there to prompt and/or validate the spontaneous change that occurs while you are paying attention to the corresponding critical variable. To the extent that you treat it as a hint and not an instruction to obey, Self 2 will be able to guide you to the technique that works best for you and will produce your desired outcomes.

Inner Putting and Chipping Chart for Self-Discovering Technique

DESIRED OUTCOME	CRITICAL VARIABLES FOR FOCUS	LEARNING GOAL (TECHNICAL HINT)
Consistent, simple motion	• Unnecessary movements, especially in wrists, legs, and head • Unnecessary variations in movement of arms or hands • Consistency of grip • Consistency of stance • Consistency of preputting routine • Position of ball in stance • Change in distance between elbows	• Approximately like the motion of a pendulum made by rocking your shoulders—left shoulder down, right shoulder up on the backswing, and vice versa on the forward stroke • Backs of hands square to putter face • Weight favors front foot • Have the same routine • Left eye over the ball at address

DESIRED OUTCOME	CRITICAL VARIABLES FOR FOCUS	LEARNING GOAL (TECHNICAL HINT)
Consistent, simple motion (*cont'd*)	• Speed of backswing compared to forward swing	• Keep distance consistent • Keep them even
Stability	• Movement of head during swing	• No head movement until ball is well on its way
	• Stability of lower body	• Knees and hips slightly bent, no movement from waist down
	• Distance between feet	• Approximate shoulder width
	• Stability of triangle made by shoulders, arms, and wrists	• Keep the triangle intact throughout putt
	• Center of gravity	• Keep it low and even— belt-buckle level
Control of distance	• Length of backswing • Length of follow-through	• Backswing and follow-through approximately same length
	• Applied force (acceleration)	• Smooth as possible acceleration
	• Sound of ball on putter face	• Solid
	• Quality of contact with ball	• Strike ball on putter's sweet spot
Control of direction	• Contour of path to hole	• Putt toward apex in a breaking putt
	• Position of ball in stance	• Under your left eye; beneath your sternum. Contact at bottom of arc

DESIRED OUTCOME	CRITICAL VARIABLES FOR FOCUS	LEARNING GOAL (TECHNICAL HINT)
Control of direction (*cont'd*)	• Direction of shoulders, hips, knees, and feet	• Parallel to target line
	• Angle of putter face through impact	• Keep putter face square to target line through impact by working back shoulder under forward shoulder
	• Position of hands relative to ball at setup and at impact	• Slightly forward of ball
	• Angle of lead wrist	• Constant angle
	• Direction of putter movement in relation to path to hole	• Straight line, except on long putts when it works from inside the target line at the back of swing to inside at completion

MORE AWARENESS EXERCISES FOR INNER PUTTING

Looking at the Hole

After you have practiced the touch game with your eyes shut and have gained confidence that Self 2 can make solid contact with the ball without looking at it, a new possibility opens up for your putting. The technique is simple. Look at the *hole* while putting instead of the ball. The effectiveness of this technique depends on how developed your sense of feel is in your putting movement. It is best to control movement through feel rather than through vision. And since you know where the ball is, the best place for your eyes is on the target and/or on the intended line of the putt. After all, where does an archer look?

I tried this technique first on the putting green and then on the course with very good results. Once I learned to "see" the ball with my hands, I could keep my eyes on the hole and see both at once. With the target in my immediate vision, I felt more confident that Self 2 could find the *feel* that would put the ball where my eyes were focused.

A second advantage of this technique is that it avoids the tendency to lift your head up to see where the ball is going. And because the putting stroke is so short, looking at the hole does not restrict necessary body movement.

A third and not unimportant advantage is that I found the technique helped my confidence. When I am looking at the hole, I can imagine that it is an easy matter to place the ball into it. I imagine that I am just reaching out to touch the hole or to take something out of it. This reduces the tension that arises from assuming that I am attempting something "hard." With reduced fear of failure, there is also less chance of steering the ball or having a breakdown in my wrist or a dreaded yip. I also find that the more I use "soft eyes" to focus on some interesting aspect of the hole, the more I keep myself in the present and allow for a tension-free swing. You can always find something about the hole to engage your specific interest. Perhaps it is the richness of the dirt at the back of the cup, the light reflecting off several blades of grass at the point of desired entry, or the hole's oval shape. The particular focus doesn't matter. What is helpful is finding something that engages your visual attention and allows Self 2 to make the putt without any interference from Self 1.

One-Handed Putting

One way to notice the effect of doubt on performance is to putt one-handed. First take a few strokes and ask a friend to notice if your hand wobbles. Then putt a ball toward the hole. If there is no wobble, it's not a bad way to putt. Try it in competition on the course. Any wobble? Doubt has a greater effect on our small muscles, and with no left hand to steady them, their movements become more obvious.

Now that you have a clear feedback system, you can work to decrease the effect of doubt. Keep putting and simply observe the wobble with detached interest, noticing everything about it without trying to suppress the doubt or curb its effects. If you can do this, the wobble will diminish by itself. The doubt will have no fuel; you will realize that doubt doesn't have to be fought and that it will go away if you don't resist it but stay focused on what *is*.

Listening

Hearing can be more of an asset than it is generally given credit for in golf. It can give you input that you don't get from other senses, especially about the contact you are making with the club. By listening to the sound of the ball as it is struck, you can learn to discriminate whether it is being hit inside, outside, or directly on the sweet spot. As this awareness increases, so does the percentage of solid putts.

This exercise reminds me of the blind golfer who was playing in a foursome and was being ribbed by the other players. After one of his opponents left a sixteen-foot putt five feet short, he remarked, "That has to be the worst putt I've ever heard!"

Threading the Needle

Precision in putting is as much a state of mind as it is a technical accomplishment. One of the ways I find the state of mind that produces precision is to imagine that I am threading a needle. I think of the delicacy required, the accuracy of hand and of eye required to put a thread through the narrow teardrop at the end of the needle. Immediately, my mind is focused and geared for precise movement. I notice if my left and right hand move the club at exactly the same moment, if the club is resting just above the grass so it touches it but without the slightest friction. These are simple things to notice, but they require a fine-tuning of the attention that prepares for the surgical accuracy required in putting. In this way, I feel less that I am accomplishing precision by "doing things right" and more that I am simply uncovering the precision that is already there and expressing it. The first attitude makes me tense as I think of what I have to do to be precise. The second attitude is knowing that Self 2 is capable of great precision and that I can relax and appreciate the expression of this quality.

INNER CHIPPING

Chipping is like putting in that it requires only a short swing, with at least part of the shot rolling along the putting surface. But it also shares many components with the full swing, and I've been able to learn a great deal about golf just by chipping on the lawn. I like to take a bunch of balls out to the front yard and chip them toward a target, trying to find a rhythm and feel that works for me. Most of the important elements of the game are there, and I can hit several hundred balls in less time than it would take me to play nine holes. In a relatively short time I can explore my awareness of alignment and posture, rhythm, tempo, and most of the aspects of body and club awareness. The touch game works as well with chipping as it does with putting. And there is an almost endless list of critical variables I can focus on. Here are just a few:

- Awareness of weight distribution on my feet
- Awareness of the position of the ball in my stance
- Awareness of the position of my wrists and hands in relation to the ball
- Awareness of the distance of backswing relative to follow-through
- Awareness of where the club makes contact with the ball
- Awareness of the smoothness of transition from back to forward motion
- Awareness of the acceleration of the club's forward movement
- Awareness of the direction of motion relative to the target line
- Awareness of the angle of the club face
- Awareness of the angle of both front and back wrists
- Awareness of back-hit-stop
- Awareness of the tightness of the grip
- Awareness of the sound at impact
- Awareness of any jerkiness in the swing
- Awareness of the angle of takeaway and the angle of descent

CHIPS AND TIPS

Tips are Self 1's favorite weapon against the awareness progression, and there is no harder task than ridding ourselves of the hunger for tips. Self 1 constantly offers hope that there is some one thing it can do that will work.

Perhaps I hit a putt while thinking about something specific, and the ball goes into the hole. "That's it!" says Self 1. "You thought that thought and the ball went in! It works!" If you think the same thought on the next hole and sink the putt again, you're really in for trouble. You'll be sure you have The Answer and will probably start telling other people about it, too.

Of course there isn't any such tip; there is no thought, no technique, no theory, in either the Inner or the Outer Game, that is going to make the ball go in the hole. Taken as such, a tip is really nothing more than a superstition, and it carries the implication of a superstition that if you *don't* do it, something terrible will happen.

On the other hand, it is perfectly consistent with the principles of natural learning to find a focus of attention that works for you one day and move to another on the next. Focus on a critical variable is very different from following a tip. Focus does work, and the particular variable you focus on can and will change.

Chipping on the lawn today, my attention goes naturally to the back of my left hand. As long as I let it rest there, the feedback I receive seems to give me maximum feel about where my leading edge is and lets me feel confident. This doesn't mean it's my secret for chipping; it's merely what my body finds useful today. I have to be willing to let go of it and may have to find another focus tomorrow.

A lot of golfers try to figure out how long the chip shot will be in the air and how far it will roll along the ground: "Where should my shot land on the green?" I suggest that it is good practice to try to guess at the shot's trajectory but to avoid thinking, "This is what I am going to try to do." Many combinations are possible between the variables of height and force applied. I suggest that you line up your shot, then guess what its height will be and where a shot of that height should land to make it to the hole. But don't try to get that result. Just let Self 2 do it, then watch the loft, where the ball lands and how it rolls. With each effort, Self 2 will get more experience and thus more skill.

The human body and the energy that moves it make the ball go in the hole, and we have no choice but to rely on them. All we have to learn is to concentrate the mind and keep ourselves out of the way of the body so it can either do its job or *learn* to do it better than it now can.

WHAT TO DO WHEN YOU LOSE THE FEEL

Nowhere is feel more crucial than in putting and chipping. Everyone experiences days when the club feels like an extension of the body and control seems simple, and everyone has times when the feel just isn't there—especially when playing under pressure.

The greatest cause of loss of feel is self-doubt, usually brought on by missed putts. Using the doctrine of the easy can help by taking your mind off negative associations with past putts and bringing positive associations into your swing.

But the basic strategy for increasing feel is consciously to switch games from a game of results to one of awareness. Usually, it is overconcern with results that leads to overcontrol and decreased feel, so change your goal to increasing awareness. Pick any awareness technique and increase your focus on whatever feel is there. Don't judge it as good or bad; merely observe it. Feel will pick up immediately, and improved results will follow as a matter of course.

Another reason for losing feel is boredom. When a player becomes bored, awareness declines, and although his swing may be so grooved that it achieves satisfactory results for a while, he will soon stop learning, and shortly thereafter performance will drop off. Boredom is best combated by taking conscious risks and concentrating on enjoyment. Experiment with a radically different putting stroke, or even change putters. It doesn't have to be a *better* stroke or putter, just a different one; it is the change that will increase awareness and decrease the boredom.

Equally effective is putting for pure fun. Playing the results game without ever giving yourself a break is dull and, ironically, leads to a decline in results. Take a break. Do whatever is necessary to introduce pleasure and excitement into your putting. Use your imagination; risk a few failures. An increase in feel is the inevitable result of an increase in the quality of your experience. Results will inevitably follow.

For some reason the chip shot seems to invite a tendency to mis-strike the ball. The ball is hit thin and sculled along the ground, or it is hit fat with an embarrassing thud that reveals that the "big ball" (planet Earth) was hit before the little one. And when doubt raises its ugly head, the dreaded yip can enter, seemingly grab the club, and make such an awkward stab at the ball that both score and pride have a hard time recovering.

The best preventative first aid against the yips is back-hit-stop or da-da-da-da. These focusing exercises are simple yet usually engaging enough to distract the mind from doubts. But I am among those golfers who did not find the occasional yip so easy an obstacle to overcome. It was not unusual for me to stand over a chip shot and feel quite uncertain. I would take five or six practice strokes mainly for the reassurance, only to stand over the real ball—and yip. I really hated the sensation and hated the result. I hated it much more than hitting a drive out of bounds or failing to get out of a bunker. I even hated it more than missing a short putt. It was especially embarrassing when I was playing with people who knew I had written a book on "the mental side of golf." I think the yip gods took a special pleasure in inflicting their tortures on "the Inner Game guy."

Chips and Yips

Welcoming the Yips

I tried many remedies for the yips, both technical and nontechnical. Some of them worked for short periods, but none cured the disease. Finally, the only way out that I could find was not to fight them. Like all manifestations of Self 1, the yips don't do well in the light of awareness. I would say to myself, "Okay, if you are going to yip, I am going to feel exactly how you do it. If you show yourself on this shot, I will study you with full awareness and without judgment." With this statement I declared that I would not be pushed around by a yip—even if it happened, which it usually did, at the most inopportune moments. When I caught the yip in action, I could feel a kind of weakness occur in my right wrist a split second before impact. That weakness wasn't real, but it seemed real, and the result would be that my club face would not move squarely through the ball but either stub the ground behind it or open at the last instant, sending the ball way off to the right.

I believe it was my intense dislike for yipping that made this error so enduring. And it wasn't until I could accept a yip or two without feeling terrible about it that the yips seem to decide to leave me more or less alone. Again, as with other habits, awareness itself is curative. But the awareness has to be accompanied by a true acceptance, without judgment, for the magic to work. I remember Mike Murphy's comments on yips when we played Pebble Beach together. "The most excruciating moments in all golf," he called them. "The short putts or easy chip shots that are impossible to miss unless you do something grossly wrong will make something inside you say, 'You'll do the impossible. You *will* miss.' And blink! You hit the ball sideways. It's the simplest movement fouled up, the most insidious opening to your demons. Those are the real character testers."

So the short game is a great place to learn the fundamentals of Inner and Outer golf. Here you can develop feel and consistency that will stand you in good stead whenever you are close to the green. And here you can also learn to overcome whatever demons of doubt might have crept into your game. It's not only a place to test character but a place to build a little.

CHAPTER 8

INNER
SWINGING

The physical requirements of a consistent golf swing are both precise and complex. The demands of power and accuracy accentuate the central problem facing the golfer on each swing, exacting control of the body. The development of a swing to meet this demand can be either daunting and frustrating or a relatively easy and natural process. We have a choice. As earlier chapters pointed out, if you give the control to Self 1 by trying to impose all the shoulds and shouldn'ts, dos and don'ts, you will travel the path of complexity. If, on the other hand, you can find your way to the natural learning process that you in fact already have, then the continuous improvement of your swing can be quite simple and enjoyable. The rest of this chapter is an invitation to explore Self 2's natural learning process—learning from experience—as it applies to your golf swing.

As with Inner putting and chipping, the golf swing can be best learned by developing feel and learning from your own swings. This is done by *paying attention* to certain critical swing variables without trying to make any changes. Change takes place as a spontaneous result of increased awareness—at whatever level of proficiency your swing may be. Technical knowledge can be used to identify which critical variables to observe and to give a hint about the direction of change that might occur.

This chapter looks at the golf swing in terms of several important learning outcomes: increased balance and stability; improved rhythm, tempo, and fluidity; increased power; and increased accuracy. Not all the variables for each of these outcomes will be discussed, but each will be discussed enough to allow the golfer to begin to make desired swing improvements. The principal aim is to apply a *method of learning* that uses focused awareness and trust as the primary tools. Once you feel comfortable with this method, you may use any source of sound technical knowledge, whether it is from your professional, a golf instruction book, magazine, or video to help you improve any aspect of your golf swing now and in the future.

Increasing the Feel of Your Swing

The first step to making any improvement in your swing lies in *increasing* the feel in your swing *as it is*. This is not a complicated process. Anyone can do it. Some people say, "I can't feel what I'm doing wrong," or "I can't get back the feel I used to have." Some even say, "I can't feel anything." Let's start with the last statement. If you think you can't feel your swing at all, shut your eyes and take a swing. Did you take the swing? How do you know? You didn't see it, smell it, or taste it, and probably you didn't hear much of it. So if you know you took a swing, you must have felt something. That's where you start. You feel whatever you feel. Maybe you feel something tight or loose, a little jerky or quite fluid; you may feel balanced or off balance, awkward or coordinated, fast or slow. The important thing is to feel without judgment of right or wrong. Why? Very simply because if you start judging what you feel as wrong, you are apt not to want to feel it. There's an old saying, "If you can't feel it, you can't heal it." It's a corollary to the law of awareness: Awareness itself is curative.

You might say, "Well, I'm very aware of my slice, and it doesn't change." I suggest that you are aware that you slice because you observe the ball taking wild turns to the right. But that is far different from *feeling* your slice. Feeling your slice is different from analyzing the cause of the slice. Really feeling it during the swing would mean you could tell without looking whether one particular ball sliced more or less than the one before it. And it would mean you could tell another person how you knew that you sliced more or less. Feeling is knowing. Knowing adds real control. Analyzing is intellectual speculation. This approach aims to shine more light on your swing through developing your feel.

One more distinction: Feeling your swing does not mean trying to feel the way it felt on that round in which you shot ten strokes below your handicap. You can feel your current swing only the way it is—not the way it was or the way you think it should feel someday. It's a funny thing about *should* and *was*; you just can't *feel* them. Why? Because they don't exist.

Only the swing you swing right now exists—and it won't for long—so pay attention while it's happening.

First Step to Greater Feel: Shifting from Broad to Narrow Attention, Then Back to Broad

Where do you start in this process of learning to increase the feel of your swing? Just take a few swings. Allow your attention to focus on the general feel of your swing. Don't try to focus on anything in particular at first. Just sense your body during these initial swings. In reality, there are thousands of things happening in your swing whether you are a total beginner or a pro. But you won't be able to notice all of them at the same time. One or two particular things will stand out. Without your planning it, some part of Self 2 will select a few sensations to serve up to your conscious awareness. Start with the feeling that was the most obvious, and focus attention there. If it was a feeling of tightness, then on the next few swings you can focus attention on exactly where in your body that tightness occurs and when.

Once you locate them in time and space, you can notice any changes in the degree of tightness. Don't be surprised if, within a few shots, you can't find the tightness anymore. It probably diminished on its own as you paid attention to it. Why? Because it felt better when you didn't tighten. Relaxing is a natural response to feeling overtightness. That's how simple natural learning is.

Let's take another example. Maybe you felt your right elbow doing something at the top of your swing. Okay. So you pay attention to your right elbow. Now you have to be careful here. You may think you know what your right elbow should or shouldn't do at the top of your backswing, but you can't let that get in the way of your attending to what it *is* doing. If you try to make your elbow "do it right," it will be hard to ever really know what it is doing. When you can catch it in the act of doing whatever it is doing, only then does it have a chance to self-correct.

But you will have to discipline your attention to make as accurate an observation as possible, without any "good-bad" judgment. Observe and allow any change that's going to take place to do so. Maybe on one swing the elbow goes higher and on the next it stays lower. How it feels, how it affects each shot, and whatever understanding you may have of the golf swing will all come into play in the process of natural change. You don't have to force it. Soon the change will stop, your elbow will find the location that feels best and works best for you at this time in your swing development, and then you move on.

You can use this same method to go through every single part of your body from head to feet and every part of your swing from setup to finish. The process is effective as long as you stay interested. When you lose interest, forget about focusing on anything at all and just hit the ball without any particular focus. That's a good way to take a break. Then, when you feel like focusing again, do it. (For beginners, I don't recommend narrow focus right away. It's best to keep your attention on the overall feel of the club for a while. Only when broad focus gets boring and something in particular presents itself would I recommend shifting to narrow attention.)

As the next step in swing development, you may want to make an improvement in one of the basic elements of a sound swing. We start with balance and stability.

IMPROVING BALANCE AND STABILITY

Balance is a good place to learn about natural learning precisely because it is so natural. You can't learn to balance a bike by reading a book or being taught how to balance. You have to feel the difference between balance and imbalance. At first you can feel only the big differences— and by that time it is usually too late because you've already fallen. But with attentiveness, you learn to feel smaller or more subtle differences in balance and learn to make automatically subtle adjustments that enable you to ride without falling. In golf, learning to maintain balance is a prerequisite of obtaining consistent power and accuracy in your swing. And you learn this balance in the same way: by feeling it at ever-increasing degrees of refinement.

Finding Your Balance by Finding Your Imbalance

If you notice that you were off balance only at the end of your swing when your right leg has had to spin around to keep you from falling, then, as it is with riding a bike, it is too late. You have to find where the imbalance *begins* to occur in your swing. The process is simple. Look for any instance of being off balance in your setup and/or your swing. When you find one, don't do anything about it. Simply bring attention to the moment and place in your swing where the imbalance occurred. Chances are it will not repeat itself. If it does, keep your attention focused on the same place until Self 2 finds out how to self-correct.

Focusing on balance is not only a good place to begin to develop trust in natural learning, it is also an easy exercise to use with practice swings. Just take a few initial swings without any intention other than to notice balance and imbalance. Could you detect anything other than perfect balance in the swing? If so, where? Perhaps you noticed a slight sense of imbalance on your left foot at the follow-through, or maybe you noticed your arms pulling you slightly ahead of yourself on the downswing. What you are able to feel will depend on how experienced a golfer you are and just how aware you are of the swing. But the process itself is the same. Once you detect an imbalance, just focus attention on the exact time and place you noticed it and allow the self-correction to take place.

In the process of looking for moments of imbalance, you may fix more than your balance. You may notice, for example, that imbalance during your backswing has something to do with the speed with which you take the club back. Then you can shift your focus to the speed of your take-away. You may find that after a few swings both tempo and balance self-correct.

Learning Stability

Stability and balance are very closely related. Almost every golf teacher and playing professional will say that the importance of having a stable setup posture and a stable lower body during the swing cannot be overemphasized. The details of the setup posture are not within my area of expertise, but they are readily available in every golf instruction book or magazine. (You can find a few of them in the Inner Swinging Chart on pages 133–135.) But the fundamental importance of stability in the swing is the same as it is with putting and chipping. It is only by having a dynamic stability in the lower body that the shoulders, arms, and hands are allowed to generate club-head speed and direction.

You learn stability the same way you learn balance: by noticing instances of instability and placing attention there until changes occur that contribute to increased stability. There are many elements of your initial setup to which you should pay attention. Critical variables include the distance between your feet in relation to your shoulders, the degree of bend in your knees and hips, ball position, weight distribution, and relative position of shoulders, hips, knees, and feet. Technical instructions can give you a clue, but you must discover for yourself the feel of the posture that will result in balance and stability. If you are trying to remember what a book said when you stand before the golf ball, you may or may not be in the best physical posture, but you can be almost sure you will *not* be in the best mental posture. But if you take the attentiveness to feel your way into *your* best posture, what feels stable and natural for you, then it is more likely you will stay focused in the feeling mode and produce *your* best swing.

Stacking

One of the most important elements of swing stability is the relative position of shoulders, hips, knees, and feet. To describe the proper positions and then attempt to get your body to conform to them during the swing would be nearly impossible. But I can imagine my feet, knees, hips, and shoulders being stacked like a pile of dominoes or poker chips. Then as I swing, I can notice if the stack stays straight or if one part or another gets out of vertical alignment. Being a tennis player, I found I had a tendency to sway a bit from left to right during my swing, and my center of gravity would sometimes swing outside my feet. I was able to achieve greater stability by observing the moment and degree of weight shift to the right until it didn't happen anymore. Learning stability by means of simple awareness may have saved me a lot of pain and suffering.

Discovering Your Rhythm

Rhythm is easier to experience than to define. When your golf swing is rhythmic, you know it, and when it's not, you can tell immediately if you are at all aware. Because we can feel rhythm, we can increase control over it.

Do not start by trying to swing "rhymically." Just swing the way you swing and notice the rhythm. Getting caught up in mechanics or even focusing too narrowly can take the music out of any swing. Rhythm is one aspect of the swing that you definitely don't want to try to match to someone else's or try to mold to some concept of what is "correct." You already have a rhythm. You walk with a rhythm, breath with a rhythm, and dance with a rhythm. It is a matter of experimenting with different rhythms, and, when you find yours, it will feel comfortable and more confident. But one caution: Don't just choose a rhythm that happened to produce a good result on one or two golf shots. You are looking for something that beats in time with your own inner pulse, so look inside for what feels best to you.

Harriet, a young woman who came to me for an Inner Golf lesson, felt that although she tried hard to swing correctly, something was keeping her from getting good results. Watching her take a few swings, I found my attention drawn to the full stop she took at the back of her swing. Deliberately obeying all the "rules," she took the club back, stopped as if to shift gears, and then swung forcefully down toward the ball.

I asked Harriet if she liked to dance, and she nodded. "Then do a dance called the 'golf swing.' Forget about results for a while, and all the rights and wrongs; just create a movement that has a pleasing rhythm to you." This was easy for her; inside of five minutes, her swing was completely different. She lost none of her effective elements of technique but picked up so much rhythm and timing that her stroke really became a swing. Not only did her power and consistency increase, but her obvious enjoyment in the movement itself was striking. "For the first time swinging this club isn't a chore that I'm worried about doing right, but something I like doing," Harriet said. "But I'm surprised that the results are there, too. It's like hearing that you can do what you've always really wanted to and it will work out okay." This seemed to me an apt definition of how the golf swing can be.

The golf stroke, like the tennis stroke, is basically a two-beat rhythm: back and forth. These two beats are fundamental to most movement—the rhythm of breathing, for example. We don't have to force it; it is there. Two common errors in swinging—failure to complete the backswing and forcing or rushing the downswing—are fundamentally errors of interference with that natural rhythm. Either we want the swing to descend before the backswing has been completed or we doubt that the transition will happen without help and so we force it.

The club will come down and accelerate itself as the tension produced by the full backswing builds to its limit and begins to uncoil. The key is to let the swing's rhythm control itself.

Not only is paying attention to rhythm tension-reducing, it is also a good way of freeing the body from the awkwardness and stiffness that result when you try to perform according to do-instructions. Like balance, it can also distract Self 1, in playing conditions, from anxiety over results. Self 1 doesn't really have many ideas about how to achieve balance and rhythm, and consequently it offers less interference in the guise of advice.

An adaptation of the da-da-da-da exercise in Chapter 2 is useful for "hearing your rhythm." After a few swings, insert "da's" at the key places in your swing, such as the moment the club is all the way back, the moment of impact, and the moment of swing completion. You can add as many da's as you like, but remember to keep your awareness on the club head so that you can say each one at the exact place in your swing that it represents. By listening to the da's, you can sharpen your sense of rhythm. Do this exercise for about five minutes at a time as part of your range practice. Your own rhythm does not remain static from day to day, so it's not a bad idea to locate it again each time you play. Let the body find its own sense of rhythm for a particular day, or even for a particular shot. Your job is simply to let it happen and to stay attuned to it. If you do so, your swing will gradually find a basic rhythm that is suitable to your body size and type, temperament, and skill level.

HEARING YOUR RHYTHM

DISCOVERING YOUR TEMPO

Tempo means rate of motion. In the golf swing it is determined by the relative speed of the arms on the backswing and downswing. You can feel your tempo by sensing the rate of your backswing, downswing, and follow-through.

Little is needed to improve tempo other than to become more aware of it and to be alert to Self 1's slightest tendency to interfere. Self 1 can't really describe tempo; however, Self 1 can destroy it by trying to speed it up beyond the natural pace of your Self 2 swing or by slowing it down too much through overdeliberateness. But simply being aware of the tempo of your swing can keep Self 1 from interfering.

As I experimented with my own tempo, I found that if I took the club back too slowly, I increased my tendency to swing down harder with my right arm. Although in point of fact the speed of the backswing shouldn't affect the speed of the downswing, my Self 1 *thinks* it does, so it makes up for a slow backswing by giving it the gun on the way down. I noticed that as I let the tempo of my backswing increase just a little, a slight momentum would build at the top of the swing that would heighten my sense of coil and increase my confidence that the club would descend at a reasonable speed. When my club came to rest at the top, I felt more inclined to force the club down to the ball. Bringing the club down willfully is nowhere near as effective as letting it descend as a response to the coiling of the backswing.

When practicing on the range, it is useful to explore different tempos, but when actually playing I would not recommend experimenting; merely be aware of your tempo as a focus for your attention. Consciously trying to influence tempo is likely to throw off your timing or some other aspect of your swing. If you think you would like a faster or slower tempo on a particular swing, translate that desire into a muscle thought by moving your arms in the desired tempo before the swing and then trust Self 2 to do it.

Experimenting with different tempos on the practice range will give Self 2 a chance to explore the feel of various speeds and choose what is best for you.

Take a few swings with your attention on tempo but without trying to change anything. Using a scale of 1 (slow) to 10 (fast) as a measure, rate your present backswing and downswing. How can you best differentiate between variations in speed? For me the left arm gives the best information about tempo. Without a club in your hand, feel the rate of your arm moving back and then the rate coming down. Which is faster? By how much? Paying attention to the speed of the left arm gives a valuable clue, especially since—at least in my case—it is the overeager right arm that destroys the tempo.

After you have determined what your present swing's tempo is, experiment with several different ones (back 7, down 3; back 3, down 7; back 5, down 5; back 8, down 8; and so forth). By consciously swinging in these different ways, you are broadening the scope of your experience. Often this is a valuable method for going beyond our present limits, both physical and mental. Then let go of conscious control and let Self 2 swing, calling out the numbers corresponding to the speeds you feel. At first you will probably notice some variations. Self 2 will be experimenting for a while to discover what feels and works best. Gradually, it will stabilize at a consistent tempo as the learning process is completed. Then you should keep swinging for a while to groove your new tempo.

These three general aspects of the swing—balance, rhythm, and tempo—are similar in that they relate to the whole swing and are too complex for Self 1. To focus awareness on them, you don't have to break down the swing or analyze its parts. Therefore, they are excellent focal points for attention during play, when focus on a specific part of the body or aspect of the swing could throw your stroke off balance. Trying to conform to specific mechanical details during a swing under pressure is asking for trouble, yet too often this is what we try to do in moments of self-doubt.

It is also worth mentioning that experiencing balance, rhythm, and tempo provides much of the enjoyment of golf.

SETUP POSITION

Accuracy in golf begins with the way you set up to the ball. Your initial alignment of feet, knees, hips, and shoulders relative to the target line makes Self 2's most difficult job—controlling direction—much easier.

My main suggestion on this subject is that you allow yourself to experiment and don't become locked into an absolute doctrine. Use awareness exercises to experiment with alternatives in ball placement relative to your feet (both in and out and forward and back), with open, closed, or square stance; shoulder or hip alignment; head position; and amount of knee bend. The goal in each of these experiments is to find a position that (1) is comfortable for *your* body, (2) allows you to swing freely from a stable, centered platform, and (3) gives Self 2 a vivid sense of the target line.

When setting up while on the course, it is especially important to let your body sense its position in relation to the target. Before hitting each ball, your body needs to know where the target is not only visually but through feedback from the position of your feet, hips, and shoulders. Let it *feel* the target line, not just *see* it. One way to facilitate this is to move your feet in place several times before settling into your final position. This simple action, plus attending for a few seconds to the alignment of hips and shoulders, will tell your body where you want it to hit the ball and thus help Self 2 determine what kind of swing will accomplish the result.

When a beginner first hears all the so-called rules of a correct stance, he can grow so concerned that he's doing something wrong on the setup that he's tense before he even hits the ball. After some experimenting I found that even if I didn't obey those rules, my Self 2 could hit the ball straight. This was a great relief to me. I even played around with radically open and closed stances, with the ball much too far in front or back. In the most extreme positions, I couldn't hit the ball straight, but in all the moderate positions Self 2 seemed to be able to make the adjustments necessary to hit the ball toward the target. This built up my trust in Self 2 and made me feel a lot less intimidated by instructional dogmas. It also made it far easier to relax over the ball.

Still, there's no need to make it harder for Self 2 than necessary, especially if you are looking for consistency, so let him show you what's easiest for you. Use professional instruction if it helps, but make your Self 2 the final authority. After all, Self 2 is the one—not your teacher—who has to hit your shots.

INCREASING ACCURACY

Control over the direction of the ball is a major focus of golf instruction. But there are only two factors that influence direction: the angle of the club face at impact and the path of the club head. From an Inner Game perspective, it stands to reason that the key to increasing your control over direction lies in increasing your feedback from these two critical variables.

A golf ball can be hit out of bounds with a perfect grip, a perfect stance, a straight left arm, and a still head—in short, with everything right, except that the club face is too open or closed in relation to the target. Conversely, a ball can be hit accurately with an awkward grip, terrible stance, bent arm, and wobbling head—as long as the club face is square at impact. In fact, one of the few universally agreed-upon principles for accuracy in every golfing situation requires the club face to be square to the target at impact. For this reason, awareness of the angle of the club face is crucial in learning to increase accuracy. If the club face is either open or closed at impact, it will impart a sideways force to the ball, as well as sidespin, and produce either a slicing trajectory (open face) or a hooking trajectory (closed face).

Learning to sense the angle of your club face at impact on drives requires a greater degree of concentration than in putting because of the higher speed of the club face. Realizing that your club face was open after you see your ball slice into the woods won't help you change it. The art of control comes from being able to acquire information from your body early enough during the swing so that the body can correct any misalignment *before* impact. This correction cannot be made consciously, but Self 2 can perform subtle last-minute adjustments below the threshold of conscious awareness if he is trusted to do so.

The path of the club head in relation to the target—not the angle of the club face—should determine the ball's initial direction. But sensing that direction is one of the most difficult kinds of awareness to achieve in golf.

Hit a few balls and guess their direction without looking. Ask a friend to check your accuracy. If you can't feel where the ball is going, it's hard to control it.

It took me a long time to truly sense my club-head direction by feel alone; I always had to look at my divot mark. Obviously, it was too late when I did so, but at least it told me that I was off line and that I should pay more attention in practice to this aspect of the swing.

One of the best ways to focus on your club-head direction is to practice making vastly out-of-line swings—far "outside-in" or "inside-out." Only by feeling the enormous difference between these two extremes did it become easier for me to sense the smaller differences.

There is much speculation about the cause of outside-in swings. To me, one reason seems predominant: It's more natural. Since the body is standing inside the target line, it is natural to swing across your body or in the direction of the body. If you try hitting from an extreme inside position to the outside, your body is in the way. You can experience the same unnaturalness by trying to throw a ball outward to the right of your body (assuming you're a right-hander). It's much easier to throw a ball across your body, to the left.

An extreme outside-to-inside swing, which is therefore the more common error of the two, is destined to start the ball off the club head to the left. To compensate for this, the club face is usually open at contact, producing the beginner's banana ball, which goes left off the club face before curving widely to the right. In an attempt to correct for the slice, the golfer often opens his stance toward the left; then the swing becomes even more outside-to-inside and the slice correspondingly greater. Various compensations for this problem produce many of the swing patterns that test Self 2's ingenuity in hitting even a few decent shots.

Control of this flaw can best be gained by learning to sense the difference between outside-in and inside-out swings and by learning to sense the difference between an open and closed face, both at setup and during the stroke itself.

CLUB PATHWAY AWARENESS EXERCISE

Exercises to develop control of accuracy and speed require subtle degrees of concentration and should be used only on the practice range when learning is more important than performance.

Learning to discriminate the feel of the path of the club in relation to the target can be developed by aiming for different targets on the ball itself. Imagine the face of a clock on the top of the ball, with the point closest to the target representing the noon position. For an inside-to-outside, or draw, swing, aim at the 6:00 to 7:00 position on the ball and follow through in the 12:00 to 1:00 position. For an outside-to-inside, or fade, swing, aim at 5:00 to 6:00 and follow through at 11:00 to 12:00: It may help to imagine that you yourself are the ball. Which point of contact would give you the best trajectory to the target?

For true accuracy, awareness of the angle of the club face and of the path of the club head must be integrated. The effects of the spin imparted to the ball by an open or closed club face will cause it to veer to the right (open) or left (closed). Even with a square club face you will fade if the club comes through a little outside-in; if a little inside-out, you will draw. But these awarenesses have to be developed separately on the practice range. In play, it's best to surrender control and trust Self 2 to integrate what he has learned about both aspects.

INCREASING POWER

The first error most beginning golfers make is to try for power. By attempting to force power into the stroke, Self 1 tightens too many muscles and, in so doing, restricts other muscles necessary to swing the club head through its arc. Overtightening freezes portions of the swing, and, even if it doesn't lock the wrists completely, it definitely throws off timing and rhythm.

Compensation for this error causes the second major impediment to power and the one most common among more experienced players. After many painful lessons learned from trying to hit the ball too hard, and with the encouragement of one of the most popular golf tips, the player tries to "swing easy." Fear of relinquishing control causes him to swing with too slow a tempo or, worse, decelerate as he approaches the ball. Learning to swing the club at different tempos is invaluable to the serious golfer, but slowing down the swing because of overcaution robs it of both power and accuracy.

Releasing optimum power on the swing comes from learning how to express your potential for it on the one hand and discovering how not to interfere with it on the other. The actual bodily process of producing power is extremely complicated, as it involves the contracting and relaxing of pairs of opposing muscle groups with a rapidity and timing that stagger the imagination. Self 2 can regulate this process perfectly if not interfered with.

As a way to quiet Self 1, I find it useful to think of the generation of power as a flowing river. Strength lends additional power to the muscles if used properly, but it's more important to generate a river of energy that can flow through your body. Overtightening restricts this flow and decreases power. I find that reminding myself before I swing to use energy, not strength, often results in a more powerful drive.

Whereas strength is a function of the development and reflexive abilities of our muscles, power is generated by muscles contracting and releasing, and so it has more to do with coordination than with force. Therefore, though it is the speed of the club head that imparts power to the swing, this velocity is the result of a complex and well-timed sequence of muscle contractions that build up tempo from one muscle group to the next. It starts in the legs. The velocity of our leg movement is not great, but built on it is the forward momentum of the hips, which in turn pull down the arms. The arms are also pulled down by their own muscles, and their velocity is the sum of the momentum building throughout the body and their own power. Then the wrists pick up that force, adding to it the momentum of their own uncocking.

Obviously, the intricacies of momentum are far beyond the abilities of Self 1 to master, especially in the two seconds it takes to swing a golf club. The entire sequence has to be coordinated by unconscious parts of the nervous system. All that can be grasped consciously is that the power swing is really a series of momentums, each building on another. No single one of them is very fast in itself, but the total velocity imparted to the ball is enormous when the timing is right. Imagine a man standing on the flatbed of an open railway car moving at 60 mph who shoots a gun in the same direction at 800 mph. The speed of the bullet when it hits its target is 860 mph.

The timing of the muscle-releasing process is more important to power than the strength of any single muscle group. This is the reason why trying for power by flexing different muscles to the maximum can, in fact, impede the velocity of the club head.

EXERCISES FOR INCREASING POWER

To explore your own potential for power, swing your club with the intent of increasing the flow of energy through your body. Pay attention to anything that seems to be restricting this flow. Wherever you find the flow in your body restricted, pay attention to whatever is happening there. As you focus on it, it will free itself of its own accord. Don't tell yourself to relax, as this will probably produce more tension. Do this exercise until you experience your body as a channel through which energy is flowing unrestrictedly. It doesn't help to push the flow; the best you can do is let the water build up behind the dam and then let it release. For me the exhilaration I experience with this release is one of the greatest enjoyments in the game.

Increasing the stability of the swing will also enhance power. Beginners seem to believe that power comes mostly from the hands and arms. The experienced player knows, consciously or unconsciously, that the momentum that ends with the high speed at which the club head strikes the ball begins in the feet. Imagine what would happen to your power if you were suspended in a harness two inches above the ground. How much club-head speed could you generate? No matter how strong you are, the results would not be impressive.

To get a feel for the amount of stability you do have and how to increase it, here is an exercise you can do with the help of a friend. Take your normal setup position as if you were about to hit a drive off the tee. Ask your friend to test your stability by pushing you in the upper body, front, back, and sides to see how easy it is to topple you off balance. Teachers of the martial arts are famous for using this technique to demonstrate to their students the value of a stable center.

Now make a conscious effort to ground yourself. Settle into your center as you did in the balancing exercise and let your belly hang as if it's resting on the ground, but without changing your physical posture. Relax any tension in your upper body. Ask your friend to try again to topple you, using the same amount of force. Unless your posture is already very stable, within a few minutes you'll experience a measurable increase in your stability. The greater the stability of the setup position, the more power and accuracy are introduced into the swing.

In golf the drive is one of the few opportunities we have to release our total power in action, and to me it's worth even a lost ball now and then to experience that sensation fifteen or so times a round. Driving is my favorite part of the game for this reason—not because I let myself swing fully but because I allow myself to enjoy it fully. I've found that almost everything I let myself enjoy fully I soon am doing well because enjoyment and learning go hand in hand. When they don't, usually it's because not much learning is taking place, and performance inevitably suffers.

Inner Swinging Chart for Self-Discovering Technique

DESIRED OUTCOME	CRITICAL VARIABLE	LEARNING GOAL (TECHNICAL HINT)
Increased balance and stability	• Balance/imbalance	• Remain in balance with little or no movement of head
	• Degree of head movement	
	• Distance between feet	• Approximately as wide as shoulders
	• Weight distribution	• Even distribution on balls of each foot at setup
	• Firmness of legs	• Firm legs, knees in
	• Degree of knee bend	• Knees slightly bent at setup
	• Degree of bend of waist	• Slight bend at waist
	• Location of center of gravity	• Keep it low, at belt-buckle. Should never go outside the feet
	• Stacking (vertical alignment) of feet, knees, hips, and shoulders	• Turn upper body over stable lower body. Keep vertical alignment as if swinging in a barrel.
Increased fluidity of swing	• Tightness of grip	• As you might hold a bird or a tube of toothpaste
	• Smoothness/jerkiness, at takeaway	• Smooth, one-piece takeaway
	• Speed of transition between backswing and downswing	• Complete your backswing before starting your downswing
	• Degree of tightness of right biceps at transition	

DESIRED OUTCOME	CRITICAL VARIABLE	LEARNING GOAL (TECHNICAL HINT)
Better tempo and rhythm	• Speed of backswing	• Arms, shoulder, and hips complete the backswing at the same time
	• Aliveness of arms	• Arms swing through to opposite side of body
	• Cadence	• Slight bow out of elbows at address to relax arms
Distance: Increased power	• Speed of club head at impact	• Head slightly behind ball at impact
	• Weight transfer during swing	• Stance a little wider than shoulders
	• Plane of swing, vertical to horizontal	• Almost full weight on back leg at the top of the swing and almost full weight on front foot at finish
	• Radius of clubhead pathway	• As extended as possible
	• Extent of turn of shoulders and upper body	• Shoulders turn twice as hips; back faces target
Direction: Increased accuracy	• Alignment of feet, knees, hips, and shoulders to target line	• Parallel to target line at address
	• Club face relative to target line	• Bottom leading edge is perpendicular at set up and impact. Club face looks at target thru impact.
	• Direction of swing path relative to target line. Inside out, outside in.	• On or near target line

DESIRED OUTCOME	CRITICAL VARIABLE	LEARNING GOAL (TECHNICAL HINT)
Direction: Increased accuracy (cont'd)	• Angle of back of left wrist at impact	• Similar to position at address
	• Degree of bend in left elbow	• Little if any bend until just after impact
	• Direction of shoulders at impact	• Square to slightly open at impact

There are many focal points on which to concentrate the attention that will aid in the production of more power, and any of them are helpful during practice on the range. Stick with one area for at least five minutes, but let Self 2 help you to find the focal point that it wants to stress.

In *Golf My Way*, Jack Nicklaus writes of the importance he places on visualizing the target and the shot before hitting it:

> I never hit a shot, even in practice, without having a very sharp, in-focus picture of it in my head. It's like a color movie. First I "see" the ball where I want it to finish, nice and white and sitting up high on the bright green grass. Then the scene quckly changes and I "see" the ball going there: its path, trajectory, and shape, even its behavior on landing. Then there's a sort of fade-out, and the next scene shows me making the kind of swing that will run the previous images into reality. Only at the end of this short, private, Hollywood spectacular do I select a club and set up the ball.

Much has been written on the subject of visualization and mental rehearsal. These techniques can have a powerful effect on performance, but many people, including myself, don't "see" pictures distinctly when they visualize. The primary advantage to targeting in this way is that it can give Self 2 a clear goal in a language that it understands: imagery. Before putting, to tell yourself in words that you want the ball to go into the hole is much less effective than actually picturing the ball doing so. You will get the best results if you think of it as a way of communicating a request to Self 2. If you make it an order in the form of a picture from Self 1 to Self 2, you will induce doubt, and you will *try* to accomplish what you visualized; probably you won't get the results you visualized, and you will soon abandon the technique.

TARGETING

To me this is the most important issue in visualization: using it to make a demand on Self 2, or as a gimmick, undermines trust in Self 2 and your proper relationship to it. *Asking* Self 2 by offering an image of the results you want is very different from *demanding* them, and affects the success of the technique as well as your general state.

When visualizing the target, it is best to hold the image in your mind throughout the swing. If you were shooting an arrow, throwing a baseball, or bowling, your eye would constantly be focused on the target. Since this is impossible with the golf swing, the best one can do is to "remember" the target constantly. "Remembering" does not mean trying to steer the swing; it simply means holding the position of the target as vividly as possible in your mind so that Self 2 can direct the swing.

SELF 2 TARGETING

I have so much respect for Self 2 that sometimes I think that picturing where I want my drive to go is presumptuous of me. I figure he knows better than Self 1 where to hit the ball. When I feel this way, I stand behind the ball and look down the fairway, letting Self 2 do the looking. I also let him decide whether to hit a fade or a draw to the left or right side of the fairway. It's exciting and requires more trust than willpower. When I address the ball, I don't really have any idea where it's going, and I don't find out until it rolls to a stop. This is a good antidote to overcontrolling, especially to steering. How can I steer if I don't know where I'm going? Letting Self 2 pick the goal is quite different from simply stepping up to the ball and hitting it anywhere; you make a conscious choice to let Self 2 make the decision and then trust it to execute the shot. Self 2 understands whether or not I'm sincere in surrendering the target as well as the shot-making. When I have faith, he almost always surprises me pleasantly—often with a much better shot than I could imagine.

I remember one particular shot that seemed impossible to me on a day when I was playing Pebble Beach with Michael Murphy. I had admired Mike's book *Golf and the Kingdom* and had looked forward for a long time to playing with him. The fact that Pebble Beach put on its best weather for us was a much-appreciated bonus. I had been playing pretty well up to the twelfth hole, a tricky, well-trapped par three of 184 yards, where I hit a three iron that faded into a trap ten yards in front and to the right of the green. The ball came to rest directly under the trap's six-inch border. There was no way I could hit it toward the green without ricocheting off the border. "What on earth can I do in a situation like this?" I asked Mike, a much more experienced golfer. "Well, there's not much you can do but blast it out of the trap and hope you can chip it close enough on your next shot to sink the putt and settle for a four." This made perfect sense, but somehow I just couldn't do the reasonable thing.

Okay, I said to Self 2, I sure as hell don't know how to hit this shot. I don't even know where to aim. You hit it. When I addressed the ball, I found myself facing a good seventy degrees left of the pin. I swung down, without the slightest preconception, through a point about two inches behind the ball with three-quarters force. Almost immediately after contact with the sand my club banged into the trap border, but the ball itself bounced off the border in a direction thirty degrees to the *right* of the pin, and, by virtue of spin and the break of the green, started a long curving roll toward the hole. I stood in awe as I saw it finally stop two inches from the cup. "I guess you should have hit it just a tad harder!" quipped Mike.

I leave it to my readers to do their own experimenting with Self 2 targeting. The key to success is a relaxed mind, faith, and the effort to surrender to Self 2. Of course, not all your shots are going to turn out the way you would like, and when this happens, how you deal with the situation is important. If you blame your lack of coordination or intelligence, or berate yourself in any such way, you can expect repeat performances. If you don't sense the immediate cause of the error, don't dwell on it or try to analyze it; it is almost certainly due to some kind of self-interference. All you can do next time is trust Self 2 more and put more effort into relaxed concentration. When you do, the past error doesn't affect the next shot.

To take full advantage of the curative faculties of awareness, a good practice is to tune up your body about once a month with a body-awareness scan exercise.

Begin by focusing your attention on your feet. Does anything draw your attention? Now focus on your calves, knees, thighs, lower body, upper body, right arm, left arm, wrists, and head. This tuneup will give you information about which areas require specific attention and will keep you from neglecting problems that may be affecting your swing.

Ideally, every practice session will be an enjoyable learning experience. The guidelines below are not meant to be followed rigidly but rather will give you an idea of the different components of a productive practice session.

Five Minutes of Pure Play

This period is for the purpose of warming up and preparing the mind and body for learning. Play is a good first step in most learning situations. Don't set any performance goals or try to practice anything. Don't try to focus on anything in particular or try to hit "good" shots. Make no judgment on any of your results—you are not going for results. This is the

BODY-AWARENESS SCAN

GUIDELINES FOR AN INNER GAME PRACTICE SESSION

time to take all the pressure off yourself. I sometimes even like to hit half swings, one-handed swings, hooks, and slices. The idea is to loosen up both mentally and physically. And have fun!

Twenty Minutes of Focused Swinging

This is the time to practice focusing on critical variables. You might want to start with self-generated variables you begin to notice (see p. 179). Next, think about a desired outcome for the practice session and start to focus on a variable recommended by your pro or one of the variables mentioned in the Inner Swinging Chart. Don't worry about results at this time. Trust that Self 2 will learn equally well from the good and from the bad. Your challenge with *all* awareness exercises is twofold: nonjudgmental focus of attention and letting go of conscious control. Simultaneously.

Generally speaking, I don't like to spend more than about five to seven minutes on any one variable at a time. But the best rule of thumb is to stay with it as long as it seems interesting to you and learning is taking place. I like to use three or fewer variables in the twenty-minute learning session. With each exercise, attempt to increase the awareness of feel for whatever aspect of the swing you are focusing on. Give any changes a chance to take place. Next, let the learning "groove" itself for a few shots, and then move on to the next focus. It's also a good idea to alternate between broad and narrow focus. You don't have to make sure that any swing change that takes place happens every time. You are primarily training your nervous system by giving it a range of focused experience.

Five Minutes of Play

Break from your period of focusing with a return to play. But here the play might be a little more results-oriented. You might want to swing with unrestrained power or hit with the same club to different targets.

Remaining Time: Performance

Use whatever time you have left to simulate playing conditions and to emphasize performance. Imagine actual golf holes; visualize the shot and select a club for each situation. Allow a longer period of time between shots, aligning yourself toward a different target for each one. Introduce psychological pressure by imagining more pressure than you would normally feel on the course. (This technique has the advantage of making real pressure less hard to handle.) Or set a goal for yourself and determine not to end the session until you achieve it.

Vijay Amritraj, undoubtedly the greatest tennis player who ever played for India, introduced me to Gene Malin, a highly ranked seniors tennis player, on the first tee at Spanish Hills Golf Club in Camarillo. The fourth player was Vijay's accountant, George, who was the last to hit. Before he did, Vijay whispered in my ear, "Don't be fooled by his swing."

I didn't know whether to expect a great swing and a not-so-good result or the other way around. The swing was astonishing! George stood over the ball, bent at the waist at almost a ninety-degree angle, with brand-new titanium clubs, waited for what seemed ten seconds without making the slightest motion, then, in an instant, reared up to an erect position, pulled his club back at lightning speed to about a half-swing position, and, without the slightest pause at the top, slashed into the ball, literally jumping forward as he did so, at one point with both feet off the ground. To call this the most idiosyncratic swing I had ever seen would be a major euphemism. His first drive went sky-high and about 150 yards out. He reached down and picked up his tee as if he'd gotten the kind of results he usually expected. The relatively smooth drives of the three tennis players were in the fairway between 225 and 250 yards out.

Then George hit a three wood, with the same swing, about 200 yards and a wedge within ten feet of the pin. Standing over his ball, he bent down so far that he could grasp the club a foot from the blade with his right hand. He sunk his putt for a par as if he had conducted business as usual. The tennis players, who had far better swings, came in with bogeys and a supreme wonderment about how they had been beaten by George.

A teaching pro would not know where to start correcting George's swing, and, as you might expect, he had never gone to one. Yet hole after hole he hit the fairways, chipped and one-putted more often than not, and came in with the lowest score.

I don't think George knew how "bad" his swing was. I don't think he cared. He knew what he wanted, and he felt confident he would get it. When he didn't get the results he wanted, he vented his feelings, but he did little analysis of what was wrong. He knew his swing was an aberration that would be better next time. At most he would say, "I wanted to draw that one, but I faded it." After watching him swing many times, we three tennis players would laugh in amazement that such a swing could produce the results he got.

George was very clear about his priorities. How his swing looked was not high on his list. Scoring was. A reporter once asked Ben Hogan who

Do You Want a Perfect Swing or the Ability to Score Well?

had the best golf swing he had ever seen. Hogan supposedly scratched his head, searched his mind for a long time, and finally said, "Oh, some guy I never heard of at some driving range in North Miami Beach." In golf as well as in life, it's very easy to get so caught up in the subgoals that you forget the goal itself.

YOU CAN'T CORRECT A BAD SHOT, SO WHY TRY?

Last summer I spent a few days with the PGA pros playing on the European circuit. A teaching pro named Jos, whom I had introduced to Inner Game methods, had been with the Tour for nearly the entire season. He had worked individually with over thirty of the touring pros, after which many of them made dramatic improvement in their scores. One Scottish pro who had never placed in the top twenty came in second in the next tournament after working with the Inner Game methods for less than a week. The next day, a full-page article about the "magic" of the Inner Game of Golf appeared in one of the London newspapers.

Interestingly, Jos, who gained a reputation for working Inner Game magic, never corrected anyone's swing. In fact, he knew very little about the mechanics of the game. His initial promise to his clients was that he would not do anything to change their swings—only their scores!

One evening, mid-tournament, I was asked to make a brief presentation to the pros. They listened attentively, looking for answers to questions about staying focused and keeping the pressures of tournament play from having a negative influence on their game—yet in private conversations, most of the pros asked about what really seemed to be on their minds: "How do I make a correction in my swing?" Their questions were usually preceded by descriptions of "technical failures" that I couldn't have commented on if I wanted to. But behind the complex descriptions of what had gone wrong, all the questions were the same: "There I was on the xth hole; I was striking the ball pretty well, when all of a sudden I [totally nonunderstandable technical jargon describing the swing mistakes they had made. And, of course, the ensuing bad results] tried to correct it by [more incomprehensible descriptions of technical manipulations to correct their swing], but I could never get myself back to my normal swing. So how can I correct a mistake like that?"

Finally, the answer dawned on me. You can't. Why? Because the swing that you want to correct has already occurred. Nothing you can do will change it. Thinking that any particular fault in a given swing needs to be corrected seems very natural, but it's based in doubt. What is the doubt? That the incorrect swing will happen again unless I actively do something about it. But you don't know that to be true! Yet the expectation that it will happen, no matter what you may do to try to prevent it, becomes a self-fulfilling prophecy. And in the process of "correcting," you can easily overcompensate and bring on the opposite problem. Attempting to correct prematurely for a golfing error is one of the greatest mental errors both professionals and weekend players make. We not only try to correct bad swings, but we try to repeat good ones. Both attempts are doubt-based. Neither one allows for true learning. Playing golf this way is playing in a *reactive* mind-set. Instead of hitting each shot as a perfectly new shot, which it is, I am swinging in reaction to past shots—good and bad. I assume that my swing will go off again unless I intervene and I assume that I can analyze what is wrong and correct it.

The only time it might be advisable to try to correct your swing is after the competition is over, and then only if you or another person has noticed enough repetitions of the stroke error that correction is called for. There are two kinds of stroke error—those you are aware of when they happen and those you aren't aware of until you see the unwanted result. If you are even aware of the approximate location of the swing error, Self 2 can correct it, without any manipulation from Self 1. The correction takes place spontaneously and really isn't a correction. A new swing is made, and the felt "error" is dropped. Trust in Self 2 means that you expect it to swing correctly, even more so after a faulty swing. Why? Because it's the nature of Self 2 to learn from experience, and it will if you don't let doubt and Self 1 control get in its way.

When I was playing tournament tennis and made an unforced error, I understood that the actual cause of my error was a momentary lapse in focus. I let the error be a wake-up call to come back to the present moment. I would make a conscious effort to let go of the past shot and focus my attention in the present moment. At the same time, I would ignore Self 1's inevitable comments on what I did wrong and how to correct my stroke and simply determine to trust Self 2 more. I admit this was counterintuitive. Just when my swing seemed to let me down, I would trust more. Every time I did this, I felt a kind of inner exaltation, not just *when* I hit a good shot but in knowing that I was not allowing myself to get pulled into the endless Self 1 cycle of error and correction.

CREATING YOUR SWING

It is very tempting to think you will excel at golf by training yourself to swing the same way every time. By repeating the same swing every time, you think you'll get the same result. This widely held belief is based on the observation that consistency seems to result from a foundation of similar elements—a steady balance, a steady rhythm, a steady movement through the striking zone. Good shots from the same player tend to look very much alike, from drives to putts. But to think of them as merely repetitions is an error. This is not so easy to explain. There is a distinct difference between *creating* a shot and *trying to repeat* a shot. Creation is free. It is not bound by the past, although it learns from the past. Only machines repeat themselves. Repetition soon gets boring, and with the boredom comes lack of attentiveness.

Creating your swing takes your full commitment to each shot. Even though you may get the exact results you are looking for, there is an element of the unknown. You don't know exactly how you will do it because you have never taken that swing before. The moment is a new moment, and you, in that new moment, are a slightly different person, hoping you have learned from past moments and therefore looking through slightly different eyes. Making new swing after new swing is the way of the creative golfer. A creative swing is not necessarily different from the last swing; it is just not an exact repetition. In this mode you are more awake and more exhilarated by each swing. The swing evolves organically, probably without your even knowing it. This is the way of nature and the way of natural learning.

Pursuing a swing that is repeatable could be a self-defeating effort. When something is the same every time, we have a hard time attending to it. For example, a constant noise in the room soon becomes unnoticed. The same is true of a golf swing. Swings that are merely repetitions are harder to feel. And when you lose feel, you lose control. I believe this is why people so often putt better temporarily when they make a change in their putter. The difference of the feel increases awareness. Increased awareness gives increased feel. Increased feel gives increased control. I believe this is also why players who practice the same shot too long often lose feel and are discouraged by the fact that they hit the first fifty balls better than the last fifty balls.

I suppose it is possible to make yourself into a kind of machine that can simply stamp out the same kind of shot at will. I know tennis players like that, and some are quite successful. I don't know what kind of a temperament it takes, but whatever it is, it's not for me. To get out of the numbing routines of machine golf, I recommend hitting the ball in a number of different ways on the driving range. Without making any efforts to get good results, explore different ways of swinging the club. Don't even look for a better way to swing. In fact, it's fun to try swinging "wrong" by exaggerating whatever errors you have a tendency to make. This exercise accomplishes two things. First, it helps you be nonjudgmental. You find that when you swing at the ball in the most horrendous way, lightning does not strike you down, you do not die of a heart attack, and, in fact, nothing at all happens except that the ball goes wherever it goes. Sometimes it will surprise you and be a better shot than you make when you are trying to swing correctly. The second and equally valuable result of this exercise is that it increases swing awareness. After five or ten minutes of unorthodox swinging, when you return to trusting Self 2 to hit the ball, you will feel the swing much more vividly. And again, the increased feel will increase Self 2 control and ultimately improve results.

CHAPTER 9

OF SLUMPS, STREAKS, AND FALSE EXPECTATIONS: BREAKING 80

As I learned to become more and more aware of my golf swing, my shot-making ability clearly improved. On the range and course I was hitting with greater distance and consistency than ever before. After six months, my score was holding consistently between 86 and 90 on courses of average difficulty. More experienced golfers said that scoring in this range was quite remarkable given that I'd been playing seriously for less than six months and only once a week. I began to think I was ready for a more challenging course, as I had thought before playing St. Andrews.

I had admired Michael Murphy's book *Golf in the Kingdom* and had been a friend of his since the early seventies. I knew he was an accomplished golfer, so it was with mixed feelings of friendship, respect, and some trepidation that I called him to make good on his casual offer to play Pebble Beach with him someday.

As we confirmed a date to play, both Mike and I admitted to being a little nervous, knowing that it is always easier to share philosophy about Inner Golf than to succeed in demonstrating it on the golf course. The day before leaving Los Angeles for this course, I opened the paper to a cartoon that seemed expressly designed for the two of us. It pictured two yogis, scantily clad, sitting on their respective beds of nails. One is saying to the other with a contemplative expression on his face: "You know,

PLAYING PEBBLE BEACH WITH MICHAEL MURPHY

OF SLUMPS, STREAKS, AND
FALSE EXPECTATIONS:
BREAKING 80

147

there is only one true test of humility, and that is to play Pebble Beach from the back tees, with the wind blowing in your face . . ." When I showed it to Mike, we both laughed and felt more relaxed because we both knew that humility was the worst that could happen to us. Nonetheless, we decided not to play from the back tees!

Except for an occasional round, Mike hadn't played in several years, but I was amazed at the ease of his swing and at the degree of concentration he mustered when he was near the pin. He didn't hit so many greens in regulation, but he got a lot of pars and ended the round with a birdie on the treacherous par-three number seventeen and a par on the long par-five eighteenth, giving him a respectable 82.

As for myself, I had decided that I didn't want Pebble Beach to intimidate me, nor did I want to fall into the trap of trying to impress Mike Murphy. Both of these had the potential to get to me if I let them. We had invited my father, who lives in Carmel and loves the Pebble Beach course dearly, to play with us. Just as we reached the club, I said to him, "I'm going to go for the enjoyment of the play today, no matter what games Self 1 wants to play. Pebble Beach is too beautiful and the companionship of Mike too rare to ruin the day worrying about how I'm playing."

By and large my resolve carried the day. It was threatened only at the times I began scoring better than I'd expected and started thinking about the possibility of breaking 80 at Pebble Beach. The thought "Wow, this would be great in the book" almost did me in a couple of times.

I had some jitters to overcome on the first hole, where I hit a long drive that was treacherously close to the woods on the right of the fairway. My only possible shot to the green was to stroke a four iron low and to the left, hoping to fade it into the green, which was invisible from where I stood. The only problem was that I didn't know how to hit a four iron low and fade it on purpose. It was my first chance to take a risk, and I did: "Self 2, I hope you know how to make this shot because I don't, and I'm going for it." The shot ended up fourteen feet from the pin. Dad was on in three and sank a fifteen-foot putt for a par. Mike was on the fringe in two and two-putted. I was in the garden spot, with a chance for a birdie. Self 1 was a little intoxicated by my unlikely approach, and I failed to notice how fast the greens were, so I hit my first putt past the hole by six feet. Coming back, I was thinking about making a par to at least tie the others, which proved to be an unnecessary and damaging thought, and I had to settle for a bogey. This showed me how little detached I really was. I had a sinking feeling in my stomach as I missed that putt and let my disappointment show. Mike responded to this: "That's good, Tim; it shows you care. One thing about this game; no one has too difficult a time really caring."

Mike and I both parred the second hole, but I hit an eight-iron approach on number three over the green and across the road, a misjudgment that cost me two strokes. Self 1 said, "That's not fair. You hit a good shot. It never occurred to you it could go OB. That's going to ruin your chances." I thanked Self 1 for his comment and remembered my initial intention to enjoy the day and do my best. The two-stroke penalty might teach me not to assume that you are ever out of the reach of trouble on the course, especially on one like Pebble Beach.

Mike finished the first nine with a double bogey on the ninth hole, which made his score a four-over-par 40. I was three over par after the third hole, and finished the round with par, bogey, par, par, bogey, bogey, for a 42. I was pleased with my score but more pleased that I was truly enjoying myself quite independently of the number of strokes I'd taken.

On the second nine I started with three pars in a row, while Mike went three over par. On the twelfth hole, I made that impossible sand shot described in Chapter 8 that ricocheted off the lip of the trap to within two inches of the cup. When I hit my longest drive of the day on the 555-yard fourteenth hole, Self 1 whispered innocently, "You know, Tim, in spite of your forty-two on the first nine, if you keep going like this you could break eighty. You can get a par on this hole easily. Then you could afford a bogey on one of the next four holes and still come in with a forty-two–thirty-seven for a seventy-nine." I was attracted to this thought, and on my next shot I was overconfident. I hit a clean three wood 220 yards, but it faded and dropped three feet outside the OB markers, on the front lawn of one of those beautiful fairway homes. My next shot came close to repeating the error, but landed three feet inside. Self 1 had managed to sabotage his dreams with a single shot.

Dad could see the disappointment on my face and consoled me with a story about Arnold Palmer, whom he had seen hit three shots on the same hole into an overhanging limb, each going OB near where I had. "The next day of the tournament that limb was missing from the tree," he said, "and it didn't look as if it had been sawed off!" I three-putted the green and carded an 8, but Dad's story made me feel better.

I was able to forget quickly and reengage my interest in enjoying each swing. I shot pars on the next two holes and bogeys on the last two, giving me a 42–42, 84. Mike shot a 42 on the second nine, which gave him an 82 for the day.

Throughout the day, I noticed that Mike took a lot of care with each shot. Even on two-foot putts he would study the lie carefully and prepare himself mentally as fastidiously as on more difficult shots. I realized that, for him, caring was a discipline that made the game of golf what it was. After a shot had gone astray, he would usually say something like "I lost consciousness in midswing" or "There was a big gap in my awareness on that shot; I wasn't very present."

Still, it seemed to me that caring too much can be as much a problem as not caring enough. Sometimes I care so much that I overtighten and mis-hit; other times I care too little and lose concentration and accuracy. For centuries Zen masters have wrestled with the problem of balance between these two extremes, and they eventually generated the ideal of "effortless effort"—caring without caring. To the Western mind this paradox is enigmatic. It defies intellectual logic but appeals to an intuitive sense that it is the true synthesis between the two extremes of caring too much and caring too little.

The answer here also seems to lie in the *nature* of the care—that is, what is doing the caring, and what does it care about? If what I am caring about is what Mike thinks of me as an Inner golfer, or what my score will be, Self 1 is doing the caring and is more interested in my image than in my experience. But if my caring takes the form of a natural desire to do my best for the fulfillment inherent in the action, then Self 2 is caring about expressing himself to the fullest, which is appropriate to the situation at hand. Effortless effort: the absence of Self 1 trying and the natural expression of Self 2 effort. It's a state of mind that can be achieved only by constantly choosing Self 2 over Self 1 whenever the choice is clear. Golf is an arena in which both selves vie constantly, and, more than in almost any other game, the feel of the action and its results gives a strong indication of whether it was Self 1 or Self 2 who was in control.

After this important round at Pebble Beach, I began to see that there might be more to mastering golf than course management and shot-making ability. I continued to score in the high eighties for a long time but seldom dipped below 85. I was about halfway through my experiment when I began wondering if breaking 80, the goal I'd promised my editor, was realistic. I asked myself a difficult question: Why wasn't my score improving in proportion to the obvious improvements in my shot-making ability? I was ready to explore an important area for anyone who wants to learn the most important lessons that the game of golf has to teach. It was time to delve into the underlying motivations and mind-sets that golfers bring to the game. Some of these are unconscious and not easy to uncover.

Shortly after I began this inquiry, a friend of mine named Al asked me a simple question that began to focus my thinking. We had been walking together while watching an LPGA tournament at Rancho Park Golf Course in Los Angeles. Pointing out one of the pros who had been playing well early in the Tour and then had seemed to fall apart, he asked, "How do we get out of slumps?"

My first response was more immediate and intuitive than analytical. "By not getting into them," I answered. Al paused. I knew what his next question would be, and I didn't know how to answer it.

"But what if you're already in one?" he asked on cue.

I'd thought a lot about the causes and cures of slumps but had no pat answer.

"Slumps don't exist," I found myself saying. "We create them in our minds. Some people say they're in a slump after two poor shots in a row; others don't feel they're in a slump until they've played poorly for two months. Therefore you're in a slump when you think you are. The deeper you think it is—the more deeply you believe in it—the harder it will be to get out of it. A slump is a belief that poor past performance is going to continue, and the best thing to do is not to believe it. Stay in the present, and let each shot, good or bad, stay in the past. The past doesn't have power over the present unless you surrender that power to it. If you find that you *have* been believing that you're in a slump, stop believing this the instant you recognize it. You created the belief, and you can un-create it."

I was a little surprised at the length of my answer, but it rang true. Al looked satisfied. "Just forget the bad shots and make each shot a new one," he concluded. "Yes, all the past is good for is that maybe it taught you something."

We each went our separate ways to watch the women professionals. But three hours later at the sixteenth hole, Al approached me again. "Tim, I have one other problem I'd like to ask you about. I'm a twelve-handicap; I play about twice a week. The other day I was playing in my usual foursome here, and I started off the day with par, birdie, par, par, birdie, par. By the time I reached the seventh hole, all I was thinking was, When is this going to end; it can't keep up much longer—and of course it ended on that hole. My question is, When you've got a streak going, how do you keep yourself from thinking it's going to end?"

I was struck by the parallel between Al's two questions, though he didn't seem to make any connection between them, and realized something I'd never seen so clearly before.

"That damned Self 1 gets us going both ways!" I exclaimed. "When you're playing badly, it tells you you're in a slump and will never get out, but when you're playing better than usual, it tells you that you're in a

How Do You Get Out of a Slump?

streak that can't last. It isn't even logical. On the one hand, it tries to get you to believe that negative experiences in the immediate past are bound to continue, but when the immediate past is positive, it tells you that your performance is bound to change for the worse!"

How do you get out of a slump, and how do you continue a streak? These two questions put side by side reveal something I find curious. The clear assumption behind the first is that once I'm "in a slump," unless I do something about it, I'm likely to stay in it. Therefore I ask, What should I do to get out of it? The second question assumes that if I am in a hot streak I need to do something to stay in it. Very interesting. When I'm playing below my expectations, I assume that the poor performance of the immediate past will continue unless I (Self 1) intervene. But when I am playing well, I do not assume that the good performance will continue unless I intervene. Self 1 is telling me that I have to do something to make the streak continue.

Even though each question seems logical on the surface, they all arise from opposite assumptions about how the past affects the future. It is as if Self 1 uses a faulty logic to convince us to expect the worst from ourselves in either situation! At the same time, I could see that Self 1 was establishing the importance of its own intervention. How many times have I seen players look for remedies to get out of slumps, and those remedies just dig the hole deeper? It's the spinning-your-wheel syndrome—the more you accelerate to get your car out of a rut, the deeper you dig the rut.

The key to understanding streaks and slumps seems to lie in the phenomenon of expectations. If I hit two bad shots in a row, what do I expect will happen on the next if I don't do anything to correct consciously? Do I expect to hit another bad shot, or do I expect that I will be more likely to hit a better one? In short, do I expect to learn from the past mistakes or to repeat them? This seemed to be a question worthy of further exploration. The golfer's assumptions about how the past affects the present lead to a set of expectations that clearly has great impact on his ability to perform in the future.

One day I played in a foursome, one of whose members commented as we walked down the first fairway, "Last week I ruined my stroke, and now my swing is totally out of sync. I'm really going to have to work it out during this round." How did he know this?

Similarly, if I start out with three poor shots, a voice inside may tell me, "You're way off your game today. Your swing is all screwed up." If I believe this, I do have a bad day all day—or at least a struggling one. All that really happened was that I hit three poor shots, and this doesn't say anything about my swing or about the future. But unconsciously I have set up negative expectations for myself, and, as often as not, I strengthen them by telling my partner, "I haven't played in two weeks, and last time I couldn't hit my hat, so don't expect much from me today."

What is particularly interesting about expectations is that they are a belief about the past that can affect the future. Expecting the best from yourself or another often contributes to that desired outcome. Expecting the worst can be equally self-fulfilling. The effects of "negative expectations" have been well documented, and an entire school of "positive thinking" has found broad appeal to those interested in succeeding at any enterprise.

THE EXPECTATIONS GAME

A step toward understanding the impact of expectations on performance emerged from a conversation with my father about his enjoyment of golf. When I asked him when he enjoyed the game, his answer was straightforward: "I enjoy golf when I play equal to or better than my expectations." I realized that for him this was very true, so true that my mother could come very close to "reading" his golf score by observing the expression on his face when he came home. She didn't have to ask how he had done and would sometimes tell me accurately, within a stroke or so, what he had scored that day. But, of course, she asked anyway.

I also noticed that Dad would often score very well on the first nine only to "even things out" by scoring poorly on the second nine. Surprisingly, this happened just as frequently the other way around. A terrible start would very often be balanced by a better-than-usual ending. Expectations alone seemed able to cause a swing of four or five strokes one way or the other. Interesting. I began to wonder if my expectations were keeping my score in the mid-eighties. I began to think more about the dynamics of expectations and their impact on my own performance.

I reflected on a somewhat painful round of golf I had recently played. Determined to break 80 and meet or exceed the expectations of my editor, as well as my own personal goal, I decided to play nine holes, and, if I broke 40, I would finish the round. I started well: par, par, par, birdie, par, bogey, par. I was even par going into the eighth hole. If I shot par in the next two holes, I would card my first 36 for nine holes. My tee shot on the five-par eighth hole was long, but it rolled into a fairway sand trap. Having a good lie, and with high expectations, I took out my four wood, hoping to reach the green. I then proceeded to hit three consecutive shots out of bounds and ended the nine holes with my accustomed six over par!

This got me thinking. If I am involved in a game that aims to meet or exceed my expectations, how can I "win" this game? At one level, the answer was obvious—I shouldn't set my expectations too high! If I feel confident I can shoot in the nineties, and that is all I expect, then most of the time I can meet my expectations and win the game. But if I shoot par on the first nine? Now my expectations are apt to shift. I might start thinking I can shoot in the high seventies or low eighties for the round. But what if I let myself succeed in shooting in the low forties on the second nine? What is going to happen? I'm going to feel great because I really busted my expectations! I'm going to celebrate my success, and probably I'm going to brag a little to my friends. And then—when I play next weekend—my expectations have changed. They have become higher! Now I must shoot in the low eighties to equal or exceed my expectations and those my friends have for me. That's going to be hard, and the probabilities of disappointment are greater. So what does Self 1 do? While telling me all along that I might break 80 if I try hard, it makes sure I shoot high enough on the second nine to bring my score back toward my handicap!

So what underlying purpose is served by projecting expectations? The only one I can think of is to preserve some sense of certainty about the future. Golf is clearly a game filled with uncertainties. And if I care about my results, I want to have some range of certainty about them. The part of Self 1 that feels uncomfortable with uncertainty and likes to project doubt creates an expectation. But because its purpose is to create certainty, it wants to be right. To be right, it does what it can to make its prediction come true. Expectations can create an identity, and remaining true to that identity can be a very strong motivating force. The reason you form an identity is to gain a sense of continuity or certainty. Surpassing the expectations of a formed identity can therefore feel threatening to one's stability. And sometimes this sense of stability is more important to a person than performance. There's a definite conflict of interest here that can have a significant impact on Self 2's performance.

Just as I was pondering the role of expectations in my own game, a poignant example of their impact on golf learning and performance came to my attention from a golfer named Harry Graham.

THE MAN WHO DIDN'T KNOW WHAT "PAR" MEANT

Harry Graham approached me after an Inner Game learning demonstration, during which a forty-year-old man who had never held a tennis racket before learned to serve and keep the ball in play, using proper footwork and changing grips, in about twenty minutes.

"Seeing how easily you helped him learn tennis," Harry said eagerly, "I was thinking that you might be able to help me with my golf."

"What seems to be the problem?"

He proceeded to tell a story that I might not have believed if I hadn't been convinced of his sincerity.

"About five years ago," Harry said, "I took up golf for fun and relaxation. I used to get off work at three and be able to play a round before dark. I worked on the weekends when my friends played, so I always played alone. About a year went by before I had the chance to play with some other people. I was surprised that they all shot in the high eighties or low nineties, and they were astounded that I'd shot seventy-four. 'How do you do that, after playing for only a year?' they asked in astonishment. 'If you're that good already, you could probably easily learn to break par and earn your living on the Tour. You should start taking lessons and go for it.'

"I didn't know how I'd done it; I didn't think it was any big deal to shoot par. I'd done it lots of times. In fact, that's what I thought 'par' meant—the score you were expected to make."

I looked at Harry incredulously.

"I thought par meant a kind of average score and felt quite happy about being average after only one year. Of course, I was playing every day, mainly because I thought the game was so much fun and it really was a nice break from work."

"Well," I said, "that sounds wonderful. What's the problem?"

"Well, I got to thinking about what my friends had said and decided maybe they were right. It *would* be a nice way to make a living, doing what I enjoyed the most, so I began taking lessons and working on the mechanics of my swing. To make a long story short, my problem over the last four years is that I haven't broken eighty-five once and don't enjoy the game anymore. I've tried everything, and nothing has worked. I'm very frustrated."

"Well, I can't make you forget what par means," I replied. "Once you know, you know. But you can make a choice to return to your original attitude toward the game, when you were playing for your own reasons and weren't trying to measure yourself against the expectations of others."

Harry and I talked for some time about natural learning and after a while he felt he could enjoy the game again. After I left him, I realized his story was a rare testimony both to the inherent power of Self 2 learning and to the power of expectations to impede it.

"THE THREE-BALL PLAYER"

While teaching tennis I ran into the same kind of identification with a certain level of performance, the same phenomenon, though perhaps not quite so rigid as it is in golf. When giving a demonstration of Inner Game methods, I would often ask for a volunteer from the audience who was a "three-ball player." When someone asked what that meant, I explained that a three-ball player was someone who, after he has hit the ball over the net three consecutive times, says, "Wow, that was a long rally!" People laughed, recognizing similar thoughts in their own experience. "What happens then?" I asked. "You miss!" was the unanimous reply. In fact, you don't always miss, but you do tend to get nervous. And if you hit another ball or two over the net, you're apt to get really nervous and say, "This isn't like me . . . it's got to end soon." What's interesting about this internal conversation is that the limit does not lie in the ability to hit more balls over the net; it lies in the phrase "This is not like me."

In the tennis demonstration, I found that changing the "expectations game" and replacing it with another game could dramatically alter the probabilities of going beyond one's expected limits. I would rally for a few minutes, with the volunteer who generally lived up to his or her expectation of hitting only three or four balls over the net before missing. Then we would have a short "coaching conversation" that went something like this: "How many balls would you like to be able to hit consecutively over the net?" Answer: "Ten would be great." "How about a thousand or, even better, never missing?" I would ask. "But that's an impossible goal." "We're not setting a goal but a direction," I would reply. "Wouldn't you like to move toward the direction of never missing?" "Okay. Sure. Sounds good to me." Then I would tell the volunteer to forget all about goals and instead concentrate on doing a simple exercise to increase her focus of attention, a skill she could use either on or off the court. At that point I would introduce the "bounce-hit" exercise. While focusing on saying "bounce" each time the ball hit the court and "hit" each time it hit either racquet, the three-ball player would start hitting ten or more balls without missing and without showing any signs of anxiety at passing a limit. Each time an error would occur, I would return the focus to the ball, not the miss, by asking whether she had said "bounce" or "hit" on time. After doing this exercise for a short time, the player could often return fifty or more shots before finally missing out of sheer exhaustion.

Focusing techniques such as bounce-hit also work in golf, as described in earlier chapters, though usually not so dramatically. This is partially due to the fact that in golf there is more time to think about your expectations and to lose your focus. It is also harder because of the handicap system, which creates such a strong tendency to form limiting self-identifications with specific levels of performance.

Golf can be a setup for creating limiting expectations. More than almost any other sport, it lends itself to precise measurement. It's one of the few sports where every shot is scored. This is not true in tennis, in which only winning or losing shots are counted, and these are erased by the game, and the game is erased by the set. The match is won by the person who won the most sets, which is not necessarily the person who won the most points or even the most games. In medal play, not only does every golf shot contribute to your score but the common practice of keeping a handicap means that every shot you take contributes to your handicap, a calculation based on all your past scores for a certain period of time.

When I play to a handicap, I have "evidence" upon which to base my expectations. Not only do I have evidence to form my own expectations about my performance, but those expectations are also held by the golfing community, which uses them to equalize my chances in handicap tournaments. When both you and "the world" believe in what can be expected of you, that can be quite a difficult barrier to break. For some reason, however, it seems to be more difficult to break this barrier on the side of lower scores than higher.

We tend to identify ourselves with our handicaps, thus making expectations about our performance even stronger. This fact comes home to me every time I play with strangers. After we exchange names and the social amenities are over, the first question asked is "What's your handicap?" This is a thinly veiled way of asking "How good are you?" Most people's response to this question will be "I'm a fourteen handicap," "I'm a four handicap," and so on. This is just like saying "My name is Bob, and you can expect me to shoot an 86 on this round . . . I'm an 86 kind of person!"

During the time that I had a twelve handicap, I played a round that brought this home to me sharply. The stranger with whom I was playing asked what my handicap was, and we made a small bet. I was playing exceptionally well that day for a twelve handicapper, a fact that did not escape the attention of my companion. He made several sarcastic comments during our round, and I myself felt self-conscious about the discrepancy between my handicap and my performance.

At the end of the day the man owed me a dollar. When I thanked him, he asked caustically, "What're you thanking me for?" I told him I'd enjoyed the opportunity to play.

"Well," he replied in a disgusted tone, "I didn't. I never enjoy playing with sandbaggers." With that observation, he walked away.

Driving home after the game, I felt angry at the man's insinuation that I had lied about my handicap. Having told him truthfully that my hand-

DON'T LET YOUR HANDICAP BE YOUR HANDICAP

icap was twelve, should I have played only as well as a twelve handicapper and fulfilled both our expectations?

Self 1's interest is in creating a self-image, and he loves to define himself. But his definitions are only limited imitations of your true Self 2 potential.

ARE EXPECTATIONS NECESSARY IN GOLF?

If playing the expectations game can limit my performance and enjoyment of the game, the question then arises: "Do I have to play the expectations game?" When I asked myself this question, I remembered a saying that had been passed along to me by a much-respected friend. "Blessed are they who have no expectations, for they shall not be disappointed." I wondered if it were possible to have neither low nor high expectations, nor anything in the middle, but to have *no* expectations. "Why do I need to have expectations in the first place?" I asked, realizing that the question itself was pushing my expected boundaries of thought. Maybe having expectations wasn't as much a necessity as I had thought but could be more of a choice.

I decided to look up the dictionary definition of "expectations." Its primary definition in my *Webster's Unabridged Dictionary* is "a looking forward to an event as about to happen." It is different from "hope" in two ways. "Hope" originates in desire and requires no reason to believe that what is hoped for will actually occur, while "expectation" is founded on some reasons that are thought to make the event probable. Also, as the dictionary points out, "Hope looks forward to some good; expectation looks forward to good or evil."

Now, in some situations in life, I actually need a bit of certainty in order to take intelligent action toward my goals. But this is not so much the case in golf. I don't really need to know that I am going to have a good day or a bad day. And do I really need to predict whether my next shot is going to be one of my best or my worst? Not really. If I want to know, all I have to do is wait a few moments. But if I want to know, I am apt to predict the worst, or at least not the best, and then my negative prophecy is apt to come about. What I have done, perhaps without knowing it, is to place my intolerance for uncertainty ahead of my desire to perform. To the extent that I don't need to be certain, I can be free of the limiting impact of expectations.

In short, the expectations game puts you in a double bind. To win it, you have to be "right" about your predictions about the future. And it's easier to be "right" and to "win" the expectations game if you keep your expectations low. But in order to keep your expectations low, you have to keep your scores high, so you thus have a game that is structured in such a way that it tends to keep players within a certain band of mediocrity. It is by its very design a limiting factor in the quest of excellence. One might then ask, "If negative expectations have a negative impact on performance, then how do you free yourself from them?" This can be a tricky matter. There is a common tendency for people to think they should simply replace negative expectations with positive ones. But it may not be as easy as that. If a person expects to slice by simply programming himself into saying to himself, "I expect to hit this straight . . . I expect to hit this straight," and so on, it probably won't work. Why? Because it is a positive thought that is meant to counter a negative one. Obviously, you believe the negative one to be true or you would not be trying to manipulate it away. So, in fact, you are reinforcing your negative belief in the very act of trying to counter it. There must be a better way.

While teaching tennis, I learned that it was difficult to combat negative programming head-on. If a person was convinced that he was a defensive volleyer, for example, it was hard to get him to attack the ball at the net just by telling him to do so. Even attempts at reprogramming were difficult if the negative self-concept was a long-standing one. Although *I* might have the faith that the student's Self 2 was capable of hitting aggressive volleys, his mind would prevent its expression.

One day I found a way to circumvent this, and the student's potential immediately began to develop. Since the same technique has proven effective in golf, I will explain it by means of an Inner Game lesson I gave to a golfer who told me that he'd always had a jerky and unrhythmic swing.

Since many people exaggerate when they tell a teacher what's wrong, I expected that when I saw Jeff's swing it wouldn't be as unathletic as he had described. I was wrong. Although he had played for over ten years and had an eighteen handicap, it seemed miraculous that he could break 100. "I have to agree with you, Jeff; those swings are not the epitome of smooth, coordinated movement. You weren't exaggerating." He looked a bit relieved that at least I could appreciate his concern. "But, of course, what I don't yet know is how you'd like to be able to hit the ball."

"Well, I'd like to be able to hit more smoothly and rhythmically—the way the pros do."

"Different pros swing in different ways. How would *you* like to be able to swing?"

"I'd like to be more—"

"No, don't *tell* me, *show* me. How would you swing?"

WHAT IF . . .

Jeff started hitting shots. Immediately, there was a marked increase in fluidity and rhythm, a different swing altogether. I gave no sign of surprise but, in a deadpan tone, remarked now and then, "Uh-huh, you'd like to swing a little more like that. . . . Yeah, I see, more like that . . ."

By the time Jeff had hit fifteen balls, his swing had transformed itself from that of a hacker to that of a swinger. I couldn't restrain my enthusiasm any longer. "Well, too bad you can't swing like that, Jeff. Maybe someday!" Jeff looked shocked as he realized what had happened. In his mind he hadn't been hitting smoothly; he was simply showing me how he would like to *if he could*.

Jeff's next swing was a disaster, a replay of his earlier tight and awkward swing. "Right, that's how you do swing," I said. "Now show me again how you'd like to be able to."

Again the smooth swing appeared. Jeff looked confused. The swings were completely different, yet he hadn't been taught anything new. "Which one is the real me?" he asked.

"It's your choice," I replied. "Both swings are there. The tight one is the one you thought was yours for over ten years, but the other one's been there all the time waiting to be let out."

That's how powerful negative programming can be. Self 1 is quite literal in his instructions. He will tell you a thousand times that you can't putt, and it will seem that you can't. Since everything you do to improve is based on the premise that you can't putt, nothing works for long; the identification with bad putting is too strong. Yet years of "I can't putt" can be circumvented by a single "But *if* I could . . ."

Likewise, a skier who hesitates going down a slope well within his capacity can be asked, "How would you ski if you weren't afraid of falling?" His style changes dramatically. A businessman who has been struggling with a decision to the point of desperation is asked, "If you knew the right decision, what would it be?" In both cases the "what if" often releases the potential that was being blocked by negative thinking.

Obviously, this trick can't be used to develop something that is not already within you. All it does is avoid the expectation that something is not there which in fact *is*. It works only when there is some trust between instructor and student, for it is embarrassing for the student to see that what he had been striving for was available all the time.

There are a couple of ways to use this trick on the practice range. One is to hit the way you'd really like to, regardless of the outcome, as suggested in the putting chapter. A good way to make this exercise more enjoyable and more acceptable to Self 1 is to practice what I call the "movie-star drill." Pretend that you are starring in a movie about a golfer whose form you admire. You don't have to get the same results as that golfer; you merely have to pretend that your swing resembles his and the director will splice in the shot later. Don't try to analyze how Jack Nicklaus swings and copy it; Self 1 will say, "I can't." Simply act the part of Jack Nicklaus.

We all tend to set expectations for ourselves that are commensurate with our past performance, even if they are optimistic ones. But when you play "what if" as Jack Nicklaus or Nancy Lopez, you'd be surprised what can sometimes be released when you really get into the role. You may not duplicate their swings, but parts of you that couldn't project beyond the self-image barrier of being only a weekend or average player emerge as soon as the barrier is circumvented in this way. Hidden parts of yourself are encouraged to simulate the attitudes and mannerisms of the pro.

Self 1 tends to notice a quality that seems to be missing from our golf swings or our characters and tries to replace it with some concept of the way we *should be*. All my life I've battled with my image of my own carelessness, and particularly in golf I've often wished I were more precise. Naturally, I've tried to improve in this regard, but until recently nothing seemed to work to make me more precise.

While working on this chapter it occurred to me that attempting to be precise puts me in the trying mode. Thereafter I stopped trying to put precision into my putting and chipping, which suffered most from this failing, and focused my attention on whatever precision was already there. My goal was to allow any precision I did possess its full expression. Through simple awareness my putting and chipping improved radically because I was giving all my attention to it.

On a piece of paper, list five or more qualities that describe your golf swing—not its results, but the swing itself. Here are a few sample self-portraits: Tony—tight, overcontrolled, correct, careful, muscled; Margo—powerless, cautious, unsure, precise, smooth; Jim—loose, off balance, wild, floppy, flowing.

Next, list some attributes you would like to see in your swing but which you feel it lacks. They don't have to be the opposites of your existing qualities, merely different. Tony's list might include "fluid, uninhibited, graceful, effortless, and unthinking." Write down each of these desired qualities four times, encouraging Self 2 to express their essence as you write. The experience of expressing the word as you write it is much richer than simply writing the word. Like golf, writing is a physical action and can therefore serve as a channel for the expression of Self 2 potential.

EXPRESSING QUALITIES

Another game that can be played with pencil and paper is one I call "paper golf." On a blank sheet of paper, mark points on the left-hand side to represent tees and draw circles on the right side to represent holes. Placing the pencil on the tee, close your eyes and draw a line to the center of the circle. After you've done this a few times, pick one desired quality from your list and draw the line from "tee" to "hole" expressing that quality. Do this a few times for each attribute you feel you lack. How do these lines compare with the first set of lines? How do they compare with each other? Take a look at the shape of the lines, as well as their accuracy. Which qualities were the most fun to express? Next time you're on the driving range, take your list with you. Consider each quality separately and reflect on it. Search your memory for an image that expresses it. (For example, Tony might picture a river as he thinks of fluidity or of a sapling bending in the wind as he thinks of gracefulness.) Then hold the image rather than the word in your mind as you swing. Don't *try* to express that quality; simply allow for the possibility that it already exists within you and let out whatever wants to express itself. Even if you think that little of the desired quality is coming through, notice whatever is there. Realize that you didn't force it to be there; it was already inside you. Continue with one quality until you have realized it to your satisfaction, then go on to another.

You will find that some of these desired qualities may improve your performance significantly, while others may make it worse. That's fine. You're not after performance right now; you're attempting to release certain generally desirable qualities. Then, when you are actually playing, the qualities you may need in a particular situation can emerge without conscious summoning.

Examples of qualities that you might want to consider include daring, trust, precision, finesse, mastery, gracefulness, coordination, rhythm, balance, power, straightness, and cleanness. The beauty of this exercise is that you discover parts of yourself that you had assumed didn't exist. This widens the scope of your possibilities; you don't have to develop a set style but can adapt it to fit the circumstances.

One day, after working at expressing various qualities that I hadn't associated with myself, I conceived the idea of expressing "Tim Gallwey." It was quite a different experience; instead of *being* Tim Gallwey, I tried to express my picture of "him" as detachedly as I had the other qualities I'd chosen. This experiment may sound odd, but it gave me a feeling of freedom, a sense that I wasn't limited by any qualities or even by the self-image conglomeration that is known as "Tim Gallwey." What I am is something more than my self-image and the qualities I can discern about myself. I can choose to present and express any of them.

One day I went out to play Perfect Liberty, a new golf course that had, so far, only nine completed holes. I didn't really have time to play eighteen holes, but I promised myself that if I broke 40 the first time through, I'd play them a second time. I was becoming increasingly aware that my last chance to break 80 before submitting the manuscript to my publishers was approaching. I had maybe another four weeks, and knowing this didn't exactly reduce the pressure.

I was playing with Tom Nordland and two other golfers, all of whom were going to complete the round. To walk away after nine holes would be embarrassing, but before we started I told them the conditions I'd imposed on my game.

I started with a bogey on the difficult uphill first hole, hitting a four iron to the fringe of the green but failing to get down in two. Still, I felt relaxed going to the second hole and absorbed in the awareness technique I had chosen.

I parred the next five holes and could feel the tension mounting as I approached the eighth tee. I was aware of the score and that breaking 40 was within reach, although the last two holes at this course had often been my downfall. A three wood well hit on the dogleg eighth hole would put the ball into a dry water hazard in the middle of the fairway. Although I'm not particularly fond of my two iron, Self 2 selected it as the best club for the situation. "The ball is already there, ten yards short of the water hazard . . . I can see it there. . . . Now, how would you like to swing this two iron?" I asked myself.

I heard the answer in my own head: "As if I knew how." And that's exactly how I swung. I hit it as if it were my favorite club. I felt wonderful as I swung; the swing was effortless, the crack off the club was clear, and I felt almost no vibration from the impact in my hands. The shot was clean, and the ball landed uncannily near the exact spot of grass where I had pictured it. I could do nothing but marvel at seeing what Self 2 can do without interference from Self 1. That shot gave me added confidence in the technique, and I parred the hole after missing a twenty-foot putt by half an inch.

To say I was truly confident on the ninth tee would not be accurate. The thought did pass through my mind: Wow, you could hit the drive OB and *still* break 40.

"That's right," I answered, overlooking the fact that this thought could have come only from Self 1. "I've got it made." Of course, my drive faded just enough to hit on the top of the hill a few feet on the wrong side of the OB marker. I waited to see if by luck it would roll down, but it stayed put, as if defying me.

Two shots later I was on the fringe of the green, needing to chip close

39–39 AT PERFECT LIBERTY

enough to one-putt to break 40. I remembered how only a few months earlier this situation would have scared me to death; at the very least I would have been thinking of some technique to keep me from yipping. But I hit the shot without a thought. Confidence in myself and in this latest technique was growing, and I felt very little pressure. The chip almost went in; I had only a two-inch tap for my 39 and a chance to play another nine, and a hope to break 80.

From time to time during the second nine I thought, I should be feeling more pressure than I am . . . I wonder when it's going to hit. But it never did. I didn't play spectacularly, but I made only a few mistakes. I missed a few birdie putts, failed to get out of a sand trap once, and hit another drive OB, putting me three over par, with a 78 for the round.

However, my enthusiasm for breaking the "80 barrier" was dampened by the fact that I did so playing the same nine holes twice. The second nine would not be completed until October, and for this reason I didn't feel I'd legitimately broken 80. But it felt good just the same.

THE CHOICE TO ACCEPT THE UNCERTAINTIES OF GOLF

Expectations can be a setup for disappointment. They can make it harder for me to break through to new levels of performance. And what do they provide in return? The promise of a temporary and, quite often, illusory sense of certainty.

It's true that sometimes I need to be somewhat certain about some things. If I deposit $1,000 in the bank, I expect that I can withdraw it on demand. If I stop at a red light, I expect that it will soon turn green. In these two cases my expectations about the future are firmly grounded in experience and reason. But when I'm standing on the first tee and I haven't hit a golf ball in a week, how grounded can any expectation be? Can I say to myself that if I just think, Swing easy and smooth, I can expect to hit it long and down the middle of the fairway? Or if I remember, Take a full turn until your left shoulder is just past the ball, is that a solid basis to expect a good first drive? Or even, "I will faithfully focus on da-da-da-da, to the exclusion of all other thoughts." Will that produce a result to meet my best expectation? Maybe if I envision the result and the perfect swing and then just let it happen? No! None of the above. Why not admit it? Nothing will bring true certainty into that shot. So why can't we give up on certainty? Self 1 is the kind of guy who doesn't like surprises. Then don't take him to the golf course!

Here is the alternative: Accept the uncertainty. Learn to tolerate it. Things change. Shit happens. Beauty happens. What's wrong with a little uncertainty? Doesn't it go with the territory of life? Doesn't it definitely go with the territory called golf? Besides, what's wrong with a few surprises? I've learned to like surprises. I'm surprised when that first drive goes down the middle, and I'm surprised when it doesn't. Actually, I can be relatively certain that in golf exactly what I expect will *not* happen. If I want to break through to a new level of understanding or a new level of performance, then I throw out the expectations game as a useless and limiting mind-set. This is easier said than done, but very much worth the effort.

Once I learn that I can be free from my own expectations, I can begin letting go of my unneeded expectations of others. Just as I want myself to be predictable, I want others to be predictable, too. When they are not, then I become disappointed, even upset. But why should I need them to be the way I expect? Sometimes I need them to keep their promises—that's a different matter. But they don't have to be the way I think they are going to be just so my little view of the world can have more stability in it. I'm coming to terms with the fact that there is very little in life that is stable, so I'm going to enjoy the part that is and let the rest be as unstable as it wants. This way I can see the possibility of freedom from the expectations game on or off the course.

My friend Tom Nordland was an excellent golfer who wanted to learn how to become an Inner Game instructor. We played many times during the period that my editor gave me to break 80. When I finally did, Tom asked if he could write an account of his observations of the evolution of my own golf game. I offer his narrative below.

TIM BREAKS 80!

It has been two years since Tim and I first played golf together. When I moved to Los Angeles from Minnesota, I thought I had done so in order to become involved with Inner Tennis, so it was a pleasant surprise when I learned that Tim was going to write a golf book.

When we started playing together, Tim had a long way to go. His swing was upright and uptight, and he had a unique way of lifting his arm and cocking his wrists as he swung the club. Although his typical shot was a slice, sometimes he would overpower the ball with his stronger right arm and pull the ball far to the left. He could hit the ball a long way when he connected just right, but his swing allowed for little consistency. His short game was equally erratic and showed that he hadn't played much. He would take mulligans and "gimmes" and fix his lie if it wasn't to his liking. I gradually let him know that serious golfers don't touch the ball between tee and green and that they count every stroke.

At the start, Tim's scores were consistently in the mid- to high nineties. Gradually, as he played more and practiced Inner Game exercises, his scores started dropping, breaking 90 and then moving toward 85. His improvement came from the fact that though he was playing only once a week, he was able to use concentration techniques he had transferred from tennis to golf effectively. But I had wondered if he would lower his score much more unless he played more and took some lessons. Although he had originally planned to take a lesson once a month, his first experiences with professional instruction weren't satisfactory. "My head gets clogged up with instructions, and I just don't have the time to devote to taking my swing apart and putting it back together," he said. So much for lessons.

Then Tim's business commitments began interfering with the regularity of his golf. When I reminded him of the need to play the game frequently if he hoped to improve, he replied, "There are a lot of golfers who can't play regularly. I'd rather prove that the average golfer can continue to improve with Inner Game techniques as well as the guy who can play all the time. Anyone knows that with enough practice he can improve. Besides, I can practice concentration anytime I remember to."

Tim started playing less and scoring better. I think it was after he came back from playing St. Andrews that I first noticed a change in his swing. Suddenly, he *looked* like a golfer rather than like a tennis player trying to play golf. He was hitting the ball straighter and more solidly than he ever had, and with less effort. He had developed some consistency. I don't know how it happened; there was simply a breakthrough. Tim said that he'd known it had to happen.

For a few months, Tim was playing in the low eighties consistently, and I thought that it wouldn't be long before he broke 80, having played a scant forty rounds from the time he was shooting in the high nineties. Then he was laid up with an illness that drained his energy and kept him off the course for three months. When he resumed, his scores shot up to the high eighties and he had to regain the consistency he'd attained earlier gradually. He took the setback as an Inner Game challenge and seemed more interested than discouraged. By the following summer he was again shooting fairly consistently in the low eighties.

We played Camarillo Springs Golf Course, northwest of Los Angeles, with Jon Wright and Al Forbes. The course is a relatively short par-71 but fairly challenging, especially with the strong wind that was blowing that day. We all knew that this was a "must" situation for Tim; time had run out on his book deadline. It was a real pressure situation, but Tim looked calm and composed as we teed off.

On the first hole, number ten, Tim reached the green nicely with a drive and a midiron and two-putted easily. He had hit both shots with authority, and I sensed he was up for the challenge. On the next hole, number eleven, he was explaining his "doctrine of the easy" drill to Jon, tried to cut across a dogleg, and hit his drive out of bounds by a few feet. He reached the par-four hole in two with his second ball, but three-putted for a triple bogey! I hoped he wouldn't be too discouraged, and his five-iron tee shot on the next hole, a par-three, showed that he wasn't. He hit it about eight to nine feet away and sank it for a beautiful birdie. He also birdied the next hole and almost birdied the fourteenth, leaving him one over par after five holes. He was playing beautifully.

After hitting the next three holes in regulation and getting easy pars, he came, still one over, to the par-three eighteenth, which was about 180 yards into a strong and sometimes gusting wind. Tim hit a three wood and skied it about halfway, his first really bad shot of the day. His fifty-yard pitch shot was held up by the wind and landed short in a trap; he blasted out fourteen feet from the pin and missed the putt for a double bogey and a 38, three over par.

On the first six holes of the front side Tim made only one bogey, the rest being pars. Some of them were tough because of the strong wind, but Tim was playing without error. His concentration was relaxed and steady. If he didn't reach a green in regulation, he was usually close enough to chip and putt for par. I was amazed by his accurate chipping all day long. During this interlude I wanted to ask him how he was feeling, but I didn't want to increase the pressure on him. Usually in such situations we made it a point to tease each other, but today was different. I sensed that Jon and Al felt the same way. We talked about Inner Game drills and concentration and avoided talk of his score.

The third-to-last hole was the crucial one. It was a medium-long par-three (155 yards), but again the wind made it difficult. Tim hit a six iron, didn't catch it fully, and landed in a water hazard. After taking a drop on the line of flight into the hazard, he was still forty to fifty yards from the green and lying two! I had been in similar situations before and knew that if he got nervous here and missed his recovery shot, he could easily get a double or triple bogey and blow the round. I watched with interest.

Tim didn't take much time and hit a beautiful, fluid approach shot, pin-high about six to seven feet from the hole, as nice an approach shot as I've seen under those circumstances. At that moment I knew that he was going to break 80. Though the putt lipped and he got a double bogey, it didn't matter; he had proved he could handle the pressure. He was now only six over with two holes to play. Neither tensing nor playing safe, he made pars on the last two holes, hitting the greens in regulation and two-putting. After he hit his second shot 150 yards to the green on the last hole and thus assured himself of his goal, we watched in amusement as he spent several minutes quacking at a flock of ducks in an adjacent pond. I wished I'd had a camera. The picture of the serene golf course at dusk, the lovely pond with its mallards, the mountains in the background, and the happy golfer with his bag on his shoulder seemed to symbolize something about the game, the recreation it offers and the reasons we play it.

"UTMOST SINCERITY"

When I began experimenting with expressing qualities, I naturally asked myself what was the most important quality to enhance golf. Many people would say self-confidence, and until recently I would have agreed if self-confidence is defined as reliance on Self 2. But there is an even more necessary quality on which the other attributes are based.

On the afternoon that I spoiled my chances for my best nine holes with four out-of-bounds on the eighth hole at Perfect Liberty Country Club in the Malibu Hills, one of the Japanese priests who tend the grounds approached me and asked how my book was going. "You believe in using your brain more than your arm?" he asked.

"I believe in both arm and brain," I said, "but I want to play with less ego interference."

"That's the most important thing," he said diffidently. "We like to say, 'Always use *utmost sincerity*.' If I could do everything with utmost sincerity, it would be very beautiful."

The phrase struck a deep chord in me. Utmost sincerity is what's left when you stop trying to *be* anything, when there are no more expectations or pictures to live up to. For me it sums up something I've valued highly ever since I began my excursion into the Inner Game. For the first thirty years of my life I dedicated myself to making something of myself— to being something more than my current self-image. The day I really became a player of the Inner Game I turned 180 degrees from this pursuit to that of discovering more and more of what I already am. By and large this has been a process of "un-becoming" my images of myself. It's like peeling off layers to get closer and closer to a simple core.

And what's at that core? Sincerity—something I can't describe. No matter what pictures I paint of this core, they are inaccurate. It can't really be pictured because it's so profoundly basic, but the closer I get to it, the more I can sense that it is natural, strong, and universal.

When that sincerity is the part of me that's predominant, I don't need to know if I'm going to play good or bad golf. I don't have to limit myself with expectations. I don't require any special results. Paradoxically, at times when I don't feel I need good results, I can't seem to avoid them. The minute I grow greedy for them and try to hold on to them or make them happen, I tighten a little, try to force them, and find that they tend to slip away. But the more I experience utmost sincerity, the more I realize that it is this quality—not the results—that feels good, and when I am in that mode I'm content to be what I am and to enjoy it as it leads me beyond my Self 1 limitations.

CHAPTER 10

RELAXED CONCENTRATION: THE MASTER SKILL

Over the years I have been asked to coach individuals and teams in a wide range of activities about which I had relatively little knowledge. Once when coaching the British Davis Cup tennis team, the Olympic pentathlon coach asked me to help train his team in riding, swimming, running, shooting, and especially fencing, none of which I had ever done competitively. After working with PGA golf professionals in Texas, I was asked by the Houston Philharmonic to give a coaching demonstration, and knowing full well that I never played any orchestral instrument, they picked their tuba player for me to work with. I accepted these invitations and many others, sometimes wondering what gave me or my clients confidence that I could help. Gradually, I realized that there was a common denominator in the achievement of excellence in all things. There is one *master skill* underlying the myriad of specialized skills required to excel at anything. I call it "relaxed concentration," and I call it the master skill because with it one can learn to improve any skill, and without it, it is difficult to learn anything. It is not easily defined or taught, but it can be learned and even successfully coached.

Everyone has experienced the state of relaxed concentration at one time or another during moments of peak performance or experience. In those spontaneous but all too elusive moments of heightened alertness and perception, actions seem artlessly excellent and life seems simple and whole. Even in complicated, demanding situations, the effort needed is clear and actions flow out of us that are uncannily appropriate. Golf shots are made as if they were the easiest ones imaginable, and we wonder what we ever thought was difficult about the game.

What is going on in your mind during your best performance, during a peak learning experience, or during a moment of total enjoyment? How does this state compare with your normal frame of mind during average or less-than-average performances? I made my initial observations about this on the tennis court and found that when playing badly my students' minds were filled with (1) a lot of self-instruction, (2) self-judgment, (3) various thoughts and feelings stemming from doubt and fear of failure. Yet when they were playing at their best, they reported that their minds were relaxed, absorbed, and quiet, free of these tensions. Often they would say that they weren't thinking at all and that their bodies seemed to know without conscious thought how to hit the ball.

WHAT IS RELAXED CONCENTRATION?

It is simply the capacity to focus totally. It occurs when commitment, abilities, and attention can be channeled in a single direction. It is being truly conscious and free of fear, doubt, and confusion. It is what enabled Ted Williams to say that sometimes he could see the baseball so well "that it almost stands still for me." Martial artists from East and West have long known that when totally focused, the mind is not interrupted by what we call "conscious thinking," and it is then that the most precise action occurs. Or as the master in Eugen Herrigel's *Zen and the Art of Archery* says, "A single conscious thought through the mind diverts the arrow from its course toward the target."

A more academic but insightful description of this state in both play and work has been written about extensively by Professor Mihaly Csikszentmihalyi of the University of Chicago. Calling it the "flow state," he writes,

> In the flow state, action follows upon action according to an internal logic that seems to need no conscious intervention by the actor. He experiences it as a unified flowing from one moment to the next, in which he is in control of his actions, and in which there is little distinction between self and environment, between stimulus and response, or between past, present, and future.

He goes on to say that the experience of this flow state is so *inherently* enjoyable that it is often sought for itself rather than for any extrinsic rewards that may result from it. He points out that this state has been experienced on the battlefield and in concentration camps, proving that it is attainable even during almost unendurable activities. Presumably, then, it might also be possible on the golf course!

And, of course, there are many descriptions from artists and athletes of all kinds, including golfers, who refer to playing "in the zone." Chess players, mountain climbers, race-car drivers, creative problem solvers, dancers, public speakers, even people in love have given similar descriptions of this elusive state. They praise it; they recommend it; they proclaim both its intrinsic value and the amazing results it often produces. Yet my experience of such people is that they are often surprised and humbled by the achievements they attain in this state, giving less credit to themselves than to something that is at least a step beyond their control. They usually shy away from trying to teach the attainment of this state, knowing intuitively that no words or formulas can promise to take student or teacher through the door to this valued experience.

Just as the state of relaxed concentration is often credited for contributing to one's best performances, the lack of it is frequently blamed for one's poorest performances. This holds true from the highest levels of athletic competence to the lowest. Likewise, when relaxed concentration is in the workplace, both individuals and teams work smoothly and effectively. But in its absence there is fragmentation of thought and action, leading to miscommunication and the inevitability of breakdowns in teamwork and performance. In both the individual and the team, divergence and conflict arise that prevent coherent, coordinated action.

There is no magic formula or method that automatically puts a person into the optimal state of mind. It may be that the state we look for is already there but that by mentally trying to figure out how not to think, we are, of course, thinking and thus endlessly chasing our tail. It's interesting that Self 1 will even propose ways to get rid of Self 1. It is even more interesting that we would believe it might succeed.

For a long time I was curious about descriptions of the state of relaxed concentration, like "I was totally lost in the action," "It just seemed to all come together at the right time," "I seemed to disappear and something else took over," or "I was playing out of my mind." These descriptions sound as if a person is being taken over by some alien force. But as I started to experience relaxed concentration a little more, I began to reach the conclusion that this "something else" that was taking over was not alien at all but was *me*. If anything was alien, it was the sensation that Self 1 was temporarily lost during total concentration. It sounded strange to hear myself say things like "I wasn't there and I never felt more at home."

So who is "lost" when we "lose ourselves in action" and who is found? For those who have followed the notion of Self 1 and Self 2 throughout

THE PARADOX OF "LOSING ONESELF IN ACTION"

RELAXED CONCENTRATION:
THE MASTER SKILL

173

this book, there is an easy explanation: Self 1 is lost—at least for a time—and Self 2 is found. Relaxed concentration is the natural state of mind of Self 2. Consequently, Self 2 is often more visible in the very young, who have not yet developed their Self 1 patterns of interference. For most adults, although it might seem easy when it is happening, a true state of relaxed concentration is usually not achieved without some degree of effort to focus attention and to prevent oneself from being swept away by Self 1 habits.

CONCENTRATION OF THOUGHT

Although conscious thought is often blamed for pulling us out of a state of relaxed concentration, one could reasonably ask, "Is there not such a thing as concentration of conscious thought?" Cannot thought itself be either focused or scattered, coherent and purposeful or disoriented and chaotic? How many times have you been in a conversation or at a meeting and suffered as the train of thought that starts out in one direction gets diverted into another direction, only to be switched to another, then another topic, seemingly without the choice or consent of those involved? Such fragmentation of thought is so commonplace that it often goes unnoticed. There's just that uncomfortable feeling at the end of the conversation that much was said but little accomplished. Of course, the same holds true *within* an individual. Concentration of thought cannot occur unless the thinker has learned to direct the flow of thought, slow it down, and, possibly, bring it to a stop. In this respect, thought is like the engine of a car; it needs brakes as well as an accelerator. And it helps if the driver has both hands on the steering wheel.

THE PRACTICE OF RELAXED CONCENTRATION

It is impossible to learn much about concentration without practicing it, and it is not until you start practicing it that you become aware of what it is, what its benefits are, and, perhaps, how unconcentrated you have been. Control over one's attention is a fundamental freedom. I was shocked at first to find how little control I consciously exercised.

When it comes to making the effort to practice, it is important to remember that the goal is *relaxed* concentration. Many people know that it is important to concentrate on what they are doing. Tennis players are repeatedly told to "watch the ball, watch the ball, watch the ball." We have all been told countless times to "pay attention to what we are doing" by parents, teachers, managers, and coaches. So we try to concentrate. But if we try too hard because we *doubt* that we will be able to achieve the desired concentration, then we will be subject to the law of doubt—when in doubt, tighten. The focus becomes forced and anything but relaxed. When you try too hard to concentrate, you will soon get tired because you are not actually receiving the benefits of the concentration. It's only a matter of time before distraction comes and you are happy to be distracted from your painful effort, and the time is usually pretty short. But relaxed concentration doesn't have to be forced. It is natural. It takes a *small but constant* effort to keep conscious and present enough to your immediate experience so that you don't get pulled away. It requires a nonjudgmental recognition when you do get distracted, followed by a gentle return to focus.

Can relaxed concentration be taught? I don't think so. Can it be learned through practice? Yes. In fact, I can think of no waking moment when a person cannot practice relaxed concentration—driving a car, standing in line, having a conversation with a friend, cooking dinner, solving a problem, hitting a ball, or walking the course between golf shots.

Human beings have the capacity to be conscious, but they can also lapse into unconsciousness. This choice is always present, and therefore so is the possibility of practicing staying conscious. The moments that we miss when unconscious do not come back so we can experience them again consciously. If we miss them, we miss them.

You can't make relaxed concentration happen any more than you can make sleep happen. It occurs when you allow—not force—yourself to become interested in each moment of your life. Undertaking to learn this master skill is a supreme challenge, but one with inestimable personal benefit.

Discipline

STEPS IN CONCENTRATION

The first step is to make a disciplined effort to focus your attention. Doing the simple back-hit-stop exercise requires such discipline. Your attention may want to fly away into thoughts about how to hit the ball or what will happen if you miss. One purpose of the exercise—indeed, of all the exercises in this book—is to provide a focus for your attention on something specific *here and now,* away from the interferences of past, future, should, shouldn't, and what might have been. Here and now the mind can begin to quiet itself, and the quieter it grows, the more feedback it gives Self 2 about what's happening.

Imagine that the mind is like a lake. When its surface is calm, reflections of trees, clouds, and birds can be seen clearly and in rich detail, as can whatever is in its depths. But when the surface is ruffled by the wind, it does not reflect clearly. Objects look darker, less distinct, even distorted. Likewise, the mind that is restless or agitated cannot make clear contact with reality, and then we have a difficult time dealing with our surroundings. Hence, quieting the mind is the first step in concentration.

Interest

Concentration reaches a deeper level when the mind becomes interested in its focus. It is difficult to keep your attention on something in which there is little interest. When there is discipline but no interest, it takes so much effort just to keep the mind still that concentration is generally superficial and of short duration.

Each individual needs to find his own focus of interest. Interest increases as you get into the subtleties; details are always more interesting than vague impressions. The path to this state of interest is to become ever more receptive to experience and to sustain your effort to make contact with what you are focusing on. If you try to force interest, it will evade you.

Absorption

A third level of concentration could be called absorption. It is a deepening of interest to the point where you begin to lose yourself in what you are attending to. A person becomes so absorbed that he is hard to distract. A golf professional absorbed in addressing an important shot won't hear people near him talking or be aware of cameras or his competitors because they are not relevant to his immediate task. This level of concentration is pleasurable as well as conducive to excellence, for you literally leave worries, doubts, and troubles behind. Most great athletic performances are accomplished in this state, where even the most strenuous action somehow seems effortless. There is no room for anxiety because your mind is so focused that you don't even hear doubt knocking at your door.

In an interview, Jane Blalock, an LPGA player, described the experience of absorption vividly: "It doesn't happen all the time, but when I'm playing well sometimes it's as if my eyes change. I can feel it. I just feel like Dr. Jekyll and Mr. Hyde—a transformation happens, I'm a totally different human being. I don't hear anybody, I don't see anybody, nothing bothers me, nothing is going to interfere with what I'm about to do."

In this state we experience an intensified contact with reality. Relevant details are seen more clearly: Golf balls and holes seem more distinct than usual, and actions flow with an uncommon ease even in the midst of extreme exertion. You just seem to know the best thing to do with each change in the situation.

Once absorbed in experience, one sometimes slips into a state that is difficult to describe because the "observer" who would describe it is no longer there. It's like falling asleep; you don't really know you did until you've awakened. But in this case it is falling awake, and you may not know it happened until you're looking back on it. As strange as it may sound, this state of absorption feels like the most natural thing when it happens. It is simple, effortless, and uncalculated.

From my own experience and the descriptions of others who have performed in an optimal state of mind, there seem to be three essential characteristics of relaxed concentration: (1) heightened awareness or perception, (2) strong and undivided desire or choice, and (3) heightened trust in potential and an absence of self-doubt. Awareness, choice, and trust are not merely ingredients but skills that can each be developed by practice. They become doors to relaxed concentration. As such, I see them as primary Inner Game skills that automatically increase performance, learning, and enjoyment in any activity.

Awareness skills increase our ability to focus our minds nonjudgmentally in the present moment, on details relevant to our purpose. *Choice skills* develop our ability to clarify goals, both short-term and long-range, and to find the energy and determination to overcome the inner and outer obstacles in order to achieve what we really want. They involve learning what your true goal is and making the effort to trust and be aware. *Trust skills* decrease doubt and give us confidence in our true potential. They involve learning to count on what is reliable for a particular end and to let go of dependence on what is not reliable. In Inner Game terminology, this means that the golfer learns to trust Self 2 to hit the ball rather than Self 1.

From this description it is easy to see that the three skills are interrelated. None can exist without the others, and a heightening of any one will automatically heighten the other two. However, the concentration produced by their combination is only as strong as the weakest link in the triad.

The essence of awareness skills is learning to see things as they are—that is, nonjudgmentally. When a golfer sees his swing in terms of "good" or "bad" he will not have a clear picture of it as it *is*. Awareness never judges; only Self 1 does. True awareness is like a flawless mirror; this principle is basic to Inner Game understanding. Awareness is curative only when there is no judgment, and when it is combined with purpose, effective action and learning can take place.

If the game of golf has to do with the controlling of a ball and a club with a body, and we understand that better control is accomplished by in-

THE ACT Δ

AWARENESS
SKILLS

creasing awareness, then the priorities for one's attention are narrowed to the ball, the club, the body, the course, and the target. Since the course, target, and ball (before contact) are immobile, they do not require the greatest concentration of the player's mind. Nevertheless, they should be observed, but not in a judgmental way. Your lie is not "bad," nor are the lake or the OB posts; nor are the trees you went into on your last round. Neither are they "good." They are best observed without attributing positive or negative values to them. Your lie is the way it is: in a divot, in the rough, buried in the sand, or sitting up smartly in the fairway. It's important to see the situation in clear detail. Negative judgments tend to obscure your vision of what you wish wasn't there and to cause doubt and tightening. Positive judgments tend to make you feel it's unnecessary to see details, and you become too casual.

Clearly, the most important focus for attention in golf is the body and the club. Golf is a game in which the sense of feeling is far more important than the sense of sight.

I can't resist telling a story about a blind golfer whose lifelong dream was to play a round with Arnold Palmer, his idol. Finally, after a tournament, he had the courage to introduce himself and ask Palmer. Understandably, Arnie was noncommittal. "Well, sure, sometime that would be fun," he answered, and then began talking to someone else. But the blind man would not be dissuaded so easily. Again he asked, and again he was put off politely. Finally, he made one more try, and, with a number of people standing around, he challenged Arnie: "Mr. Palmer, I know you're not the type to turn down a fair challenge. I have ten thousand dollars I'd like to wager on a single eighteen-hole medal-play match with you. Will you accept my challenge?"

"Sir, with all due respect," Palmer answered, "I don't want to take that money from you. Thanks anyway."

"Mr. Palmer, I'm not kidding. If you don't accept my wager, I'll feel justified in letting it be known that you weren't sure you could beat me."

Arnold Palmer has never been criticized for being uncompetitive. People were looking on and he was slightly annoyed by the persistence of the stranger, so finally he agreed: "Okay, if that's the way you want it, I'll play. Ten thousand dollars. You name the course and the time, and I'll be there."

"Very well," said the blind man. "I'll meet you on the first tee of Pebble Beach tomorrow at *midnight*."

According to the story, which may or may not be true, Arnie blushed, smiled, and capitulated. The blind man withdrew his wager, and they played a friendly daytime match.

Obviously, the blind man felt confident that he could play with feel alone. And, in fact, with just a little assistance, many blind people have learned to play excellent golf. This should tell us something about the relative importance of vision and feeling in golf. So where do you focus your attention? Not on thinking, not on seeing or even visualizing, but on feeling. It's okay to envision where you want the ball to go, but I question whether you want to en*vision* how to hit it. If anything, you may want to "en*feel*" how you are going to hit it. During the swing, it is feel, and not thought, that will control your movements.

How do you learn feel? By feeling whatever you can. In any activity you increase awareness by focusing attention on critical variables. A variable is anything that changes. A critical variable is a variable that is critically important to desired results. A few of these variables were itemized in Chapters 7 and 8. In golf, most of these variables must be attended to through the kinesthetic sense of feel or touch. People in our culture are more accustomed to being asked to look or to listen than to feel. When asked to feel something closely, whether it's an emotion or a physical sensation, they are often uncomfortable. The person being asked to feel the path of the club head may respond by asking, "What do you want me to do differently?" or "What do you want me to think about?" But there is a difference between doing, thinking, and feeling. This is a little cultural barrier that must be crossed to achieve relaxed concentration in golf. Though I was born and raised in California, I do not consider myself a stereotypical "touchy-feely" type. But I have to admit that golf is a game where you want to be very touchy-feely, not in relation to the people you play with but in relation to your own body and swing. To a great extent, excellence in golf is a function of how aware you are of the sensations of your body during the setup and swing. When you practice relaxed concentration in golf, give full and total attention to the feel of your swing during the few seconds of each and every shot. The much-discussed benefits of muscle memory are not derived so much from "good memories" as from vivid *feeling* experiences. In short, control in golf is inseparable from relaxed concentration on how the swing feels shot by shot, in practice, and on the course.

There are two ways to find a focus of attention on your swing. The first is to use a focus recommended by your teaching pro or perhaps one or more of the critical variables recommended in Chapter 8. The other, and by no means less valuable, way is to use a focus that is self-generated. You simply start attending to whatever catches your attention spontaneously. If you just pay general attention to how your swing feels on a given day, something in particular will stand out. Maybe you notice a jerkiness in

FOCUS ON CRITICAL VARIABLES

the rhythm or a good feeling of release of your wrists just before impact with the ball, an imbalance at the completion of swing, a feeling of awkwardness, and so on. Whatever stands out, pick that as your variable to attend to. Without judgment and without trying to make any kind of change, allow yourself to become more attentive to that particular variable. You can do this by feeling exactly *when* and *where* the variable occurs in the swing and then *to what degree*. If you can do this without any conscious control, the law of awareness dictates that beneficial change will result from your heightened awareness alone. When change has taken place, that particular variable will vary less and become less interesting. Something else in your swing will probably stand out. Attend to that. The focus can be as specific as the angle of the club head at impact or as broad as your rhythm throughout the swing. Generally speaking, I find a very narrow focus of attention more useful to practice on the range and practice green and a broader focus more conducive to play on the course. But I leave this to each player's experimentation.

CHOICE SKILLS

Choice is inseparable from concentration. You can't force concentration, and you can't be forced to concentrate. We attend only to what we have a desire to attend to. If our desires are scattered in several directions, our attention will be, too. Desire is like a force that has both strength and direction. About any particular desire a person can ask what its source is, where it is directed, and what its strength is. It is your desire to hit the golf ball that will direct your attention to the relevant components of the intended action—the ball, body, club, and target. The strength or singularity of your desire will contribute to the quality of concentration. If the desire is weak or confused, then focus will be more easily distracted; if it is strong and sincere, it will overcome both external and internal obstacles to reach its goal.

Without desire, there is no goal and no action. You can be very much aware of the ball sitting on the tee, but unless you have some urge to hit it, you won't. People generally have many different desires at the same time, somewhat like a boat that has many different forces acting on it. Maybe there is a twelve-mile-an-hour current from the west, a three-mile-an-hour tide from the southeast, and a twenty-mile-an-hour wind from the north. Perhaps the boat has a five-horsepower engine and the captain at the tiller is steering due west. The boat moves with a speed and direction that is the result of all these forces. Similarly, if a golfer has a small desire to shoot his best score ever, another to play it safe and not make a fool of himself, another to do only what he has to do to beat Joe, and a final desire not to break his normal expectations (see Chapter 9), the actual force and direction of desire brought to bear on a given shot will somehow be the result of these divergent desires. Confused desires diminish focus and are counterproductive.

Choice or commitment is like the engine in the boat. It allows some degree of maneuverability within a set of forces that it does not yet control. Here the analogy breaks down a bit because the winds, tide, and current represent unconscious desires that the captain of the boat has no control over. But human beings, by becoming aware of unconscious desires, can bring them under the control of conscious choice. Ultimately, when all the desires are moving in a similar or harmonious direction, full concentration can be achieved.

Choice, like awareness and trust, is a given. We can't *not* choose. We can pretend we don't, but to pretend you don't choose is a choice! Why would a person do that? In my experience, the answer is simple and somewhat embarrassing. I realize that choice has consequences. I don't like some of the consequences of my choices, so I choose to forget that I made the choice in the first place. Now I can pretend that the consequences are not my fault. I can even blame them on others, on destiny, or whatever else is convenient. Ouch. Painfully true. Of course there are consequences for not accepting the consequences of your choices. Your boat stops going in the direction you steer it and instead seems to be at the mercy of the winds and currents outside your control.

This point is illustrated by a conversation I had some time ago with a student who persisted in asking for advice on a certain matter. Guessing that he wanted to avoid responsibility for his own choice, I declined. When he continued to persist, I asked him, "If you were the only person in a car, would you rather be in the driver's seat with your hands on the wheel or in the backseat where you couldn't reach the wheel?" Without hesitating, he said, "Oh, I'd much rather be in the backseat." "Why?" I asked, incredulously. "Because one way or the other, I would probably get into an accident. But if I were in the front seat, with my hands on the wheel, then it would be my fault."

We come now to a very critical point in understanding the game of golf. What is the importance of results? In golf every single stroke you take is counted, tallied into your score for the round, and then averaged into your ongoing handicap. And the goal of each hole is precise: a little white ball going into a little dark hole. Very specific. Very measurable. By design, golf brings out our goal-orientedness. And the game is played mostly within cultures that themselves are very goal oriented, though most of our day-to-day goals cannot be measured with the precision of

OVERCONCERN ABOUT RESULTS

golf. If you look at most advertisements for golf equipment, training aids, or golf schools, most of them will entice you with the promise or suggestion of lower scores.

The question I would like to pose in the context of how to practice relaxed concentration is: Is it possible to be too goal oriented in golf? Does being goal-oriented produce the best scores? Do you think concentration comes easily to those who put everything into attaining good scores? Does it produce the deepest concentration? I don't think the answer to this question is easy, but for every serious golfer, it is worth asking.

THE PEL Δ

Granted, the rules of golf say that the goal of the game is to get around the course in as few strokes as possible. Performance is obviously important in all goal-oriented activity. But is it the only goal? It may be the only goal that is measured and scored. But is it the only result that counts? It is difficult for some golfers to see it any other way. But if you think about it, if all you really wanted was a low score, then the easiest courses would be the most popular. But it is usually the case that the most difficult courses are the most expensive and the most sought after. This is not consistent with a single-minded desire for low scores. "Well, challenging courses are more fun," the golfer replies. Yes, I agree, and often more beautiful. Does that mean there is another goal—fun or enjoyment perhaps? Is that a real result of golf? Or do you consider enjoyment just an incidental by-product of a good score? If you had to choose between having a low score and having a good time, which would you choose? Regardless of your answer, it is a fact that for the four to five hours you are playing eighteen holes of golf you are somewhere between misery and ecstacy. And human beings have a built-in preference toward the enjoyment side of the range of experience. So, almost by definition, enjoyment is a goal that comes with us while we're playing golf.

These questions are quite relevant to the subject of relaxed concentration. Generally speaking, those who value the inherent enjoyment in a given activity have an easier time finding a consistent focus.

Thus far, we have established at least two universal goals in golf: a performance goal (to score well) and an enjoyment goal (to have the best possible experience). Is there another? What about learning? Can you learn something valuable while playing a round of golf? Is what you can learn confined to golf, or can you learn things that will be useful outside of golf—like relaxed concentration, or confidence, or self-discipline, or honesty? And is it the person with the lowest score who necessarily learns the most? Obviously not. In any particular round of golf, learning and score are clearly distinct achievements.

So now we have three goals—performance, enjoyment, and learning—that are all present in golf. In fact, if you think about it, they are present in all activities in play or in work. Now comes an important question. Are these three goals related? Do they belong in a triangle indicating mutual interdependence? The obvious answer is yes. If a person is performing at a certain level but fails at learning and at enjoying the activity, what will soon happen to the performance level? Likewise, if a person does not enjoy the activity, it may be possible to keep up high levels of performance over the short haul but not the long one. On the other hand, if learning is happening, it is only a matter of time before it is bound to have impact on performance. Most great athletes and great performers in every field genuinely love what they do because of the experience that it brings them—not just because of the extrinsic results.

You can take performance, enjoyment, and learning as three mutually supporting aspects of sports or work, a relationship I will refer to as the PEL triangle. Many work teams who get caught up in the performance momentum alone don't get the necessary support from the other two sides of the triangle. This can have serious consequences if you are working in an environment of change. Learning is exactly that capability which enables us to adapt to change. It saves much more time than it takes. Thinking you don't have time to learn from mistakes is very time-consuming. Furthermore, learning from experience doesn't really take time because it happens while you are working. It's more a matter of attitude and personal and cultural priority, not time, that gets in the way. I have introduced the concept of balancing the PEL triangle in many work teams, and in almost every case a surprising improvement in *performance* has resulted along with the intrinsic benefits of increased learning and enjoyment at work.

The fact is that these three goals are the inherent goals of Self 2, so the simplest way to balance the triangle in any activity is simply to learn to *choose* Self 2. Given the chance and just a little encouragement, Self 2 always goes for enjoyment and learning. Its best performance is the natural result. This is inherent, but it is definitely a choice. Every such choice strengthens your connection with Self 2 and increases the probabilities of spending more time in a state of relaxed concentration.

Trust is the third component of relaxed concentration. Trust is the glue that holds awareness and choice together. It is the leap of faith that allows us to have greater and greater access to the potential that lies unactualized within us. Doubt is the great disrupter of that access. Self 1 is fundamentally a doubt-maker. When I listen to the conversation in my own head, I can reach no other conclusion than Self 1 simply does not like to trust Self 2. Obviously, this doubt undermines the flow of relaxed

TRUST SKILLS

concentration. "Can I really do this?" it asks, even midswing, midsentence, or midthought.

Do you ever wonder why Self 1 doubts you? Perhaps it is in doubting that Self 1 creates a role for itself. "You aren't really capable of living this life on your own, making your own choices correctly, and certainly not capable of hitting a golf ball correctly, so let me help you," it suggests. And how often do we doubt this doubt-maker? If someone else said the things about us that we say to ourselves in our own heads, would we tolerate it? Probably not. We would object or at least try to avoid that person. But when the little voice of self-doubt knocks at our door, we invite it in for tea and extended conversation. "You are probably going to miss this three-foot putt," it whispers. Your knees and wrists weaken. "Remember that last one you missed and how bad it felt?" "Yeah, I remember," we say. "What should I do to make sure it doesn't happen again?" "Well, whatever you do, don't leave it short again," self-doubt advises. You hit the ball four feet past the hole. "I told you that you'd miss," it says mockingly. "Next time concentrate more! And make sure you stay relaxed!" it might say. Is this a voice that is really out to help you? It's worth a thought. Do you really want to engage in conversations with it? Has it really ever helped you? Why not doubt the doubt-maker? Why not trust ourselves?

In his famous essay "On Self-Reliance," Ralph Waldo Emerson wrote, "Trust thyself, every heart vibrates to that iron string." I loved that quote from the first time I read it. But what does it mean to trust oneself? Not an easy question. Self-trust is such a basic act that it is sometimes easier to know it by its opposite. It is also easier to see in young children before it has been undermined. In a child, trust shows up as a simple and endearing quality. No one calls it egotistical or overconfident, as will happen all too soon. Trust is there when the child makes mistakes and when the child doesn't. Doubt does not seem to enter the picture at all, and, as a consequence, focus, learning, enjoyment, love, laughter, and all the human treasures are available to the child and are readily seen by others.

Trust is what enables us to relax enough to be ourselves. It is what makes it possible for you to go to sleep at night, or to laugh in the face of your worst nightmares, or to know that you are still all right even after three triple bogeys in a row. Trust does not make every shot we hit go long and true, but it allows us to think straight regardless of where the balls may go. In the face of the most challenging situations, trust allows us to pay attention to priorities and to access the capabilities we need. Trust is what allows us to learn and to acknowledge that we need to. Trust is the one and only channel we have to be who we really are, and, as such, it is the only true ticket to enduring enjoyment. For each individual, trust in oneself is an available choice at every moment. It is a choice because, after childhood, it doesn't just happen automatically.

Before going ahead, I must make it clear that I am not claiming that blind trust in itself is a virtue. The virtue is to learn to trust what is trustworthy. Obviously, it is not a virtue to trust a three-year-old to cross a street in traffic. And was it a virtue to trust the leader of your country if you lived in Germany in the thirties? Misplaced trust is the cause of much hurt, suffering, and loss of independence. But the greatest misplacement of trust of all occurs when we trust someone who tells us, directly or indirectly, that we are not worthy of our own trust. We can learn to trust others only to the extent that we can first trust ourselves. After all, if I can't trust myself, how can I choose who or what I *can* trust? I'll make a mistake, won't I? I'll pick the wrong book, the wrong leader, the wrong religion, the wrong things to believe. No. Life demands trust in life; existence demands that we trust our existence. It's the only way it works. And it does work.

I said in the foreword and in the first chapter that golf is a game about control. Trust takes place in the practice of letting go to Self 2 control. When I give total focus to the movement of my club head, to the feel of my swing, I have to trust that the ball will be hit, even though I can no longer hear the voice of Self 1 telling me how to do it. If I don't let go of the control of the swing, I can't really be fully aware of it. Why? Because I can't *feel* my swing at the same time I am *thinking* about how to swing. So trust and awareness go hand in hand. It is by letting go of Self 1 control that I gain control of my swing. Sometimes it is easier to trust when I am not aware. When I am unconscious, it's easier to swing freely, even wildly, without inhibition. But I cannot learn to swing well without bringing awareness into my swing. So I have to learn to be aware and let go at the same time. This is the heart of the Inner Game experiment and practice. Such is the practice of self-trust in golf. It does not guarantee that every ball will go long and true. Nothing will. But it does guarantee that you will not be at war with yourself and that you will learn to sustain greater and greater levels of relaxed concentration. This is the challenge of the Inner Game of Golf.

TRUST AND CONTROL

CHAPTER 11

PLAYING YOUR
OWN GAME

If you ask most golfers if golf is a pressure-filled game, most will agree that it is. But have we given much thought to where the pressure actually comes from? I contend that in golf itself there is *no* pressure. If we want to discover where the pressure comes from, we have to look somewhere else than the game of golf itself. Allow me to present my case.

Imagine, if you will, that a Martian has just landed his spacecraft somewhere near the eighteenth green at Pebble Beach during a Pro-Celebrity golf tournament. The president of the United States is standing over a five-foot, downhill, breaking putt. That he is feeling pressure is quite obvious from the fact that his hands, wrists, and knees are trembling noticeably. Perspiration is on his forehead as he tries to summon his concentration for what he hopes will be his last stroke of the tournament. The Martian is watching with great interest as the crowd stands in hushed silence. Unable to contain his curiosity, he turns to you and asks, "Tell me, sir, why is it that the leader of this, the most powerful country in the world, seems to be overcome by fear?"

Without hesitation, you give the obvious answer: "Well, sir, that's a downhill, breaking putt! It's not as easy as it looks."

The Martian acknowledges the point respectfully. "Yes, I can appreciate the difficulty of the task," he replies. "I'm quite sure I would not be

You Couldn't Explain the Pressures of Golf to a Martian

able to succeed myself. But if I may ask, what dreadful thing must happen if he is to miss? It must be quite frightening. Perhaps this is a kind of symbolic war and your country's enemy becomes the victor if he fails in this task? Or maybe his youngest daughter must be sacrificed to the gods if this shot is missed. . . . There must be something causing such dread in such a great and fearless leader."

"Well, you see, there is a lot of pressure on this last putt. If he misses, he will have to add another stroke to his score. It might affect his standing in the tournament, and it might even raise his handicap," you explain. "Yes," replies the Martian. "I am familiar with all the rules of golf and understand scores, handicaps, rankings, and the like. But nowhere have I read about the consequences of a high score or a high handicap. If there is no money involved in this match, what is actually at stake? What is won or lost?"

Now, answering the Martian becomes a little more difficult. You could try telling him that if the president misses the shot, people might consider him a "choker." Or you could say that it would be a blow to his self-confidence or self-esteem. You can imagine the Martian's response: "I didn't see anything about losing self-esteem—whatever that is—in the rules of golf." And he would be perfectly right. You can't really explain the pressures we feel playing golf because they have nothing to do with the game. The rules of golf just say you hit a ball with a stick, follow the rules, and count the number of strokes it takes you to go around eighteen holes. So where's the pressure?

As hard as it might be to explain to the Martian, the fact remains that plenty of pressure is felt on the golf course, and not just by professionals whose careers are on the line. Whatever is at stake, it is not a part of the game of golf but of the meaning that the players bring to the game. Put another way, the pressure is to be found in the games we play while we are playing golf, games made up in the culture and passed along quite efficiently from generation to generation. The reason the Martian can't understand is that he is not a part of the culture.

The importance of this distinction between the game of golf and the games we play while playing it is that while we cannot easily alter golf's rules, we are free to change the rules of our Inner Games. They are all individual or cultural inventions, and we can uninvent them or make up totally new games. If we don't like feeling the pressures that some of these games bring with them, and if we don't like the way they can limit our performance, this just might be worth a try.

After a lecture on the Inner Game of Golf as part of a UCLA Extension Continuing Education program, a middle-aged businessman approached me and asked urgently, "Can you give me a particularly strong concentration exercise that can keep me from becoming nervous on the last two holes?"

"Are you sure it's a concentration focus that you need?" I asked, guessing that he might be looking more for a gimmick than for a real solution to his problem.

"Yes," he said. "There's really nothing wrong with my game until I get to the end of the round. I've been playing all my life, and I love the game. I have a four handicap, and I believe in everything you say about the Inner Game, but I never par the seventeenth or eighteenth holes. Sometimes I'll even double- or triple-bogey them."

Over a cup of coffee, Joe began to speak about his game in general. "You know," he said, "I don't really have problems dealing with pressures in my business or home life; I seem to be able to handle anything that comes my way pretty easily. In a funny way, golf is the only part of my life that *really* matters to me. Every time I play, it's like a microcosm of my life. When I tee off on the first hole, I'm born. On the first few holes I'm growing up; on the middle holes I'm in my prime. And then . . ."

"Then at the last holes you approach death. No wonder you have trouble concentrating!"

Joe laughed. "I suppose you're right," he said. "Seriously, though, can you give me something to help maintain an old man's concentration through the eighteenth hole?"

"Well," I ventured, "don't you think that maybe if you reconsidered the meaning you attribute to the game—"

"No!" Joe cut me off abruptly. "Don't take away my game! That's what gives meaning to golf for me. Even if letting go of it were the only way I could score better, I wouldn't do it. I want to win the game *I'm* playing," he said with intensity.

Several years ago, I received a call from a highly ranked player on the LPGA Tour. She had been the winner of many major tournaments in her career and told me she needed only a few more victories to be included in the Hall of Fame. She asked if I would have time to help her with the mental aspects of putting. I agreed to meet her on the putting green at the Riviera Golf Club in Brentwood, California. After we introduced ourselves and chatted informally, she explained that the only time she had difficulty with putting was on the final holes of major championships

"GOLF IS A MICROCOSM OF LIFE"

"GOLF HAS MADE ME SOMEONE"

in which she was in contention: "Then, sometimes my hands tremble a little and I lose the feel of my stroke."

Not seeing how I was going to reproduce these circumstances so we could work on the problem as it occurred, I began asking her a few questions. "What is the goal of golf?" I asked. "To get around in as few strokes as possible," she replied succinctly.

"And why do you play?" I asked.

"That's a good question," she said, and then proceeded to give one of the most elegant answers I had ever heard. "First, I love the environment that the game is played in. Second, I love expressing a God-given talent. And third, I love competition." Her answer was so straightforward and so sincerely uttered that I have never forgotten it. I also didn't see that these motivations were potential sources of pressure.

"So far your hands aren't shaking," I said. "You will probably always be able to enjoy being on a golf course, expressing your talent and enjoying competition. These are not things you are apt to lose. Tell me, are there any other reasons you play?"

She thought for quite a while this time. "Well, yes," she said. "I owe something to golf. Golf has made me who I am today. Somebody. And I have many fans, and they count on me to do well. I don't want to let them down."

"Now how are your putting hands?" I asked.

"Trembling a bit," she admitted. "There is a lot at stake here. And getting into the Hall of Fame means a lot to me."

I was particularly interested in the sentence "Golf has made me who I am today." "If it is golf that made you someone, then golf can make you no one again," I remarked, pointing out the obvious. "Now I can understand why your hands might be shaking when you are in contention for a title. Someday your ability to compete will wane, and then what happens to who you are?"

The most poignant part of the conversation for her was not just how much meaning she had attributed to the Hall of Fame but how much she felt she owed to her fans, who somehow would also lose something if she didn't win. What became clear was that golf was one thing and "what's at stake" was something else. And this something else was not real but made up. When I hear TV golf announcers commenting that "the leader is six under par walking down the sixteenth fairway, and the pressure is really mounting," or something to that effect, I wonder how they know this. They say it as if it were as factual as a statement about the weather. But it's not. It's a matter of belief—a belief that is widely reinforced by everyone who believes in it—but, still, only a belief.

In fact, if you placed an elderly lady who had never played golf on the eighteenth green at Pebble Beach, gave her a putter, and asked her to try to putt the ball into the hole, she would probably experience no jitters at all. She might make the putt or miss the ball entirely. She would not "know" what was at stake. No, the pressure is not in golf. It is in the beliefs and meaning we bring to the game.

KATHY INVENTS HER OWN GAME

When I first met him, Joe worked as a human resources manager for the Coca-Cola Company. He had asked me to design a seminar on coaching skills for the managers in his division. The seminar I designed included a demonstration of the Inner Game as it applied to tennis, and Joe, upon seeing the results, wanted to know if they applied to golf as well. Joe, who was a low-handicap golfer, was also a Ph.D. in psychology and very interested in the learning process and what interferes with it. My work with Coke lasted for a period of six years, and Joe and I became close friends as well as collaborators on the Inner Game as it is applied to corporate management. During this time Leslye, my partner and adviser, also developed a close relationship with Joe, his wife, Kathy, and their two children. It was therefore particularly disturbing when we heard that Kathy had been diagnosed with a cancer that she had a low probability of surviving. There was little Leslye or I could do to bring comfort to this situation. Mostly we watched with the greatest respect and admiration as both of them lived with this fact. Neither giving up hope nor denying the seriousness of the disease, Joe and Kathy lived more fully, with greater intimacy and joy, than ever before. Their attitudes were the same—whatever happens, let's make the most out of our time together.

One of the things Kathy chose to do with her time was play an occasional round of golf with Joe, who was a near scratch golfer. One memorable afternoon Joe asked Leslye and me to join them for a round in Atlanta. Kathy was an advanced beginner, and, weakened and sobered by her condition, she didn't feel obliged to obey all the rules. She played for the pleasure of being in nature, for the camaraderie with her husband, for health and exercise, and for the joy she could find in the game. She swung at the ball with the abandon of a free spirit. If she hit a great shot, it brought a smile to her face. If she hit a terrible shot, it brought a smile to her face. If she got a little tired, she would just pick up her ball and carry it until she felt like hitting again. If she felt like hitting a couple of balls from the same place, then that's what she would do. She certainly was not worried about her score, her handicap, or impressing the people she played with. She seemed to take as much delight in the fortunes and misfortunes of the others in her foursome as she did in her own game.

What struck me is how independent her enjoyment was from her performance. And how easy it was for her to break all the rules of the game, written and unwritten. It was no big deal. She had given herself permission to follow her heart, to do it her way. Deep down we all knew that we were capable of doing the same thing. We could give ourselves the same permission to enjoy the game. It was a privilege to play with her and an inspiration to all who witnessed her.

ALMOST PERFECT LIBERTY

One of the most exhilarating moments in all my golfing experiences occurred one evening on the ninth tee at Perfect Liberty Golf Course. Starting at 4 P.M. after a day of writing, I had been unusually concentrated in my practice of "da-da-da-da" and wasn't aware of my score at all. As I approached the ninth tee, I checked my card and found that I had taken only thirty-two strokes—even par. I had a good chance to score my best nine holes ever. Of course I started thinking how good such a success story would look in the book. Looking down the narrow fairway, a longish downhill hole with OB on either side, I remembered that I had ruined many a good score on this hole before.

Then something clicked inside me; I realized it *really* didn't matter one iota whether I hit the ball OB or not. This may not sound like an event of epic importance, but it was to me. For a moment my heart knew what I grasped so well intellectually: The results in golf were not real. There was something else that was much more real, and how I scored on the course wasn't it. I can't say what made this perception so clear, but I remember an incredible sense of freedom as I stepped up to the ball and, concentrated but without concern, took a full swing. The ball left the club with a crack that seemed louder than any I'd heard before and soared off to the right, heading right toward the OB markers on the side of the hill. I remember thinking that it looked as if it would go OB and at the same time knowing more certainly than my eyes could see that it wouldn't. Part of this was knowing that it really didn't matter if the ball *did* go OB, and part of it was the feel when I'd hit it. But before the ball even began to draw, hit the side of the hill, and roll down onto the fairway, I let out a loud whoop. I felt a sense of victory that didn't come only from seeing a shot land well. Externally, I've hit better shots; internally, it was my best ever. In that moment there was a triumph that went far beyond managing to swing a stick correctly to make a ball go where I wanted it to. I had broken through an illusion. I felt as if I'd been freed from a tyrant. I could see that I had been trying to please the tyrant demanding external results because he rewarded me with praise and pride when I did what he wanted and punished me with feelings of self-contempt and helplessness when I didn't. But with that drive I had told him I didn't want to play his game anymore. He had taken the fun out of games and the art out of work, and he was an obstacle to getting the very results he demanded. His rewards weren't real and offered nothing but the illusion of happiness. I saw all this clearly as I walked to my ball. I felt no stronger, not even more confident, merely a lot less vulnerable.

The sun was setting behind the hills as I sank a four-foot putt for a par. I had scored my first par-36 for nine holes, and I felt no excitement. Yet I felt wonderful. I'm not ashamed to say that my eyes teared in gratitude.

For me, and obviously for many others, the illusion of the game had become so powerful that it had seemed real. Many people don't even like to speak of golf as a game. "You're going to have a hard time convincing the average golfer that his score isn't the most important thing," cautioned my father. "It's the score that makes them feel good." But it's believing that the results are so important that also creates most of the misery I see on the golf course. There *is* more to golf than the score. I've felt it, and I know there must be others who recognize that games are far more than results.

BREAKING THE GOLF ILLUSION

The illusion that the score is the most important thing about playing golf is so strongly engrained in most of our minds that it would be fatuous to think that it might be dispelled simply by some words written in a book. Intellectual assent to this proposition would not be hard to come by, but the real challenge is to break the hold that the score has on us at the visceral level—in our gut. Before we start down this path, let me say that I am not one of those people who thinks you should play golf without keeping score or that children should not be given grades in school. I have no quarrel with the rules of golf, just with the absurd meanings we have attributed to some of them.

First, forgive me for saying the obvious, but *golf is a game*. We all know this to be true when we are in our right senses. But sometimes we seem to forget the meaning of "game." "Game" means a "pretend" reality. "Game" means that we are going to make believe that it is important to hit a little white ball into a little black hole. I suppose if we really did believe it was important to have black holes filled with white balls for some reason, we wouldn't take them out once we had accomplished the task.

Monopoly is also a game. And if I land on Boardwalk with a hotel on it and have to pay $2,000 in Monopoly money, I may express exasperation, complain that I am going bankrupt, and make all kinds of gestures to represent my feelings about my misfortune. But I never for a moment think that my "real-life" bank account has been diminished. I never really think that anything meaningful has been lost when I lose the game. And I can't imagine losing sleep over the fact that my technique in the game needed work. But golf is a different story. We're not playing with Monopoly money anymore. We let our score and our performance be the measure of our self-esteem. We put our self-respect up for grabs—and something in golf is always ready to do the grabbing.

For those of you who know that golf is a game but still find yourselves pushed around by its pressures, as if the game were playing you, I have a strong remedy for you to try. I first concocted this remedy for Tom, a friend of mine who played to a four handicap and called me one day for "an Inner Game tip" just before he was going to play an "important match" with three of his friendly competitors. He should have known better than to ask me for a tip, and he didn't. But I could hear an intensity in his voice that gave away his intent to get a low score and impress his friends. So I advised him to forget about the competition for one round and "hit each ball for maximum enjoyment." He listened. A long pause followed as he thought about my proposition. Then he answered with undiminished intensity, "Okay. I'll try." His voice gave his thoughts away. What he was really saying was "Wow, maybe that will work." And "work," of course, meant "score better."

That brought out the devil in me. I adjusted my prescription slightly. "Yes, hit every ball for maximum enjoyment. But there are two more instructions you must follow. The first is that you may not under any circumstances score less than 86!" This time there was a short silence while he made sure he had heard me correctly, then an audible gulp on the other end of the line as the implications that he would have to shoot ten strokes higher than normal sunk in. "What's the third instruction?" he asked hesitantly. "The third instruction," I answered without the slightest expression of sympathy, "is that you may not tell anyone you are playing with about these instructions."

It was only because Tom was a good friend and a sincere student of the game in all its dimensions that he graciously accepted the challenge. "Okay. I'll do it," he said in a voice that was noticeably more sober.

That evening he called and I was eager to hear his report. "So did you follow the instructions?" I asked, not knowing what to expect. "Yes, I did," he replied succinctly. "And it wasn't exactly easy. Do you want to hear what happened?"

"I'm all ears."

Tom told his story with a mixture of pain and triumph. It was quite a story. The gist of it was that he started off the first nine feeling very relaxed with nothing to lose. By the time he got to the eighth hole, he was one under par and three strokes ahead of his nearest competitor. He then began thinking about his promise to come in with an 86. "I started looking for opportunities," he said. "Like when I was on the green, forty-five feet away from the pin, I said to myself, 'Now here's a good chance to three-putt without anyone expecting anything.' Then I would get up to the ball, barely taking aim, and nail it right into the hole. This must have happened three or four times," he said almost apologetically, "and when I arrived at the sixteenth tee, I was four under par. I couldn't miss a shot even when I tried."

"What did you do?" I asked, almost hoping that he had decided to forget the exercise and finish with his best score in a long time.

"I did what you said," he replied without emotion. "I teed the ball up on number sixteen and decided to see how far out of bounds I could hit it without it being obvious to the others what I was doing. In the last three holes, I was able to drop six shots per hole to par."

"Wow" was all I could manage to say.

"I tell you what," said Tom. "I wouldn't trade the experience for any score I could have made." I wondered what he could possibly mean. "Just to watch the reactions on the part of my friends! It was amazing." He went on to explain that when the second ball went out of bounds, they were joking with him and took some delight in the return of his mortality. Then, after a few more wasted strokes, there began to be some concern expressed. Finally, there was utter dismay. "They were truly suffering. I kept up the act and looked appropriately distraught, but they, they were besides themselves. They stopped kidding me and offered help; then they were simply silent. They ended up totally depressed. And all the while I was just watching how seriously everyone was taking it.

I didn't let on until we were sitting over beers in the clubhouse. I don't know how long it will last, but I don't think any of us will take the game so seriously again for a long time. I don't know what we learned, but I don't think we'll ever get quite so caught up in the delusion of golf again."

RE-CREATING THE GOLF ILLUSION

Games are simulations of reality devised by man to create a "safe" environment in which to hone skills and develop the qualities useful in real life. Because the consequences of a game are not real, it is safer to experiment and take risks that, if taken in the "real world," might be too costly.

So on the one hand it is too bad when we take a game and make it more real than life. On the other hand, it is equally in violation of the spirit of any good game not to play it *as if* the consequences were real. What does this mean? It means that to get the most out of the learning experience and enjoyment that games and sports have to offer, you have to pretend the consequences are real. If you don't, there is no reason to exert yourself, to dig deep for an effort of utmost sincerity. There is no reason to go beyond yourself. And that is the point of the game, to provide an environment in which you can safely go beyond previous boundaries. That's what makes it a learning experience. It's also what makes it fun. So the key is to pretend that the game is real while knowing that it is not. You re-create the illusion, but you don't get caught up in it. We knew how to do this as children playing cops and robbers and hide and seek. We had the right idea. Play it as if your life depended on it; then, in an instant, be able to leave it and laugh, no matter the outcome. Could it not be the same with golf? I wondered. Play *as if* each shot of the round were of the greatest consequence, and walk off the course, treating the best or the worst of scores with knowing disregard.

BALANCING THE PEL Δ

In the last chapter, I stated that to attain a true state of relaxed concentration there must be a balance between the three aspects of any human endeavor: performance, experience, and learning. When Self 2 emerges over the ego-centered interferences of Self 1, three things always occur: The person performs at or near his or her best, a natural enjoyment arises from whatever he or she is doing, and the person learns.

Golf is just one of the activities in which we have gotten so caught up in the importance of results that we sacrifice the enjoyment and learning legs of the PEL triangle. Instead of a mutually supporting balance, our triangles are lopsided, with one really long leg in the direction of performance and two stunted ones representing our commitments to the quality of our experience and of our learning. The irony is that in the process of sacrificing all for the sake of performance, we sacrifice performance as well. Why? Because, over the long run, high-level performance requires continuous learning and is sustained by enjoyment. It's nearly impossible to perform consistently if you're on a roller coaster between elation and deflation.

So if you want to escape the "golf illusion," I recommend that you balance your PEL triangle. This means that you can play more than the "performance game" while playing golf. You can play the "learning game" and the "enjoyment game" as well. After all, it takes four to five hours to play a round of golf. Why not go for maximum enjoyment and maximum learning as well? Yes, I know that no one keeps score in these games. But they count nonetheless. You take something home with you when you win these games—something perhaps more valuable than a score. If you are able to set and achieve learning and enjoyment goals in golf, it is very possible that you will find it easier to bring the same balance into your work life and other activities. This is natural—the way it was meant to be. And it works. I truly believe that if we aren't enjoying and aren't learning, something is wrong and we should step back, whether we are on the golf course or in the workplace, and ask ourselves, "What is really important to me?" During twenty years as a business consultant, I have introduced this concept of balance to work teams at many different levels in a number of different kinds of organizations. Never once have I found a team whose members did not think they were overbalanced in their emphasis on performance results compared to learning and enjoyment. Time and again, efforts to rebalance the triangle have resulted spontaneously in improved performance.

Recently, I played with a former golf pro who had virtually given up the game since he had failed to qualify for the pro tour the year before.

Barry was raised on golfing technicalities and knows a hundred dos and don'ts for every swing in every possible situation. Predictably, his swing was mechanical, tight, and now, returning to the game, anything but consistent. He just couldn't seem to keep from hitting thin. He was obviously uptight and becoming more tense as the day wore on and his former game refused to return. He was using the back-hit-stop exercise but admitted, "I really have no idea where the club is at the back of my swing. Nothing works for me, anyway."

"Then when do you say 'back'?" I asked.

"I say it when I think the club should be there, but I don't feel it."

I asked if he wanted to try another exercise.

"I'd try anything at this point," he said.

"All right, why don't you try hitting the next drive as if it really doesn't matter at all, how well you hit it or where it goes. Just hit it any way you want to."

Barry proceeded to drive fifty yards farther than anything he'd hit all day, but he didn't look self-satisfied as he watched the shot—only surprised.

"What are you going to do next time?" I asked.

"I'm going to try to do the same thing again and hope for the same results."

"Maybe you'll get them, but the odds are you won't. You weren't going for results when you hit that shot, and if you start thinking to yourself, Hey, this method really works!, it probably won't. You can't use 'not caring about results' to get specific results, can you?"

Barry looked puzzled. "Then what do you suggest?"

"Well, you could change games for a while. Up till now you've been playing the achievement game—hitting the ball 'right' to get the best results."

"Until recently that's the only game I'd ever played—especially on the golf course."

"There is another game, and it's not the only one to play, but it's a good one to try when you're frustrated. It's called 'fun-o,' and there are only two rules. One is that you hit each shot in whatever way is the most fun for you in that particular situation. The second rule is that you relinquish entirely any concern for results. You still play golf—that is, you go for the hole with the least number of swings—but your goal is the enjoyment you get out of each stroke, regardless of the outcome."

We all played "fun-o" for the rest of the round, and soon Barry was acting like a kid out of school. When I asked him what he was doing differently, he said, "I'm just doing the opposite of everything I've been told throughout my golfing career. It feels terrific. I'm using my right hand instead of my left and slapping at the ball as if it were a hockey puck."

Barry enjoyed his rebellion for a couple of holes, whacking wildly at the ball. Then he grew tired of this and started hitting it the way he'd always wanted to. By the end of the round he was a different person.

After the game Barry told me, "I really dreaded playing again; I was sure it would take me a long time to reach my former standard. Frankly, even as a kid I got into this game as a way to achieve success. I was always afraid of failure, so I practiced all the current techniques for hours every day. In twenty years of golf, I don't think I ever really played for fun before."

PLAYING YOUR OWN GAME

In the final analysis of the game of golf, we can be sure of only a few things: the hitting of a ball with a club over a course and into the hole. The goal of the game is crystal-clear: Get the ball in the hole. Looking at the simplicity of the physical game of golf, I realize I succeed only eighteen times a round. In that I am equal to everyone who plays the full course. We vary only in how many times we *fail* to get the ball in the hole.

The second thing we can be sure of is that the meaning golfers attribute to this physical game is a matter of the golfer's choice. There is no inherent meaning in the game. The rules of the game give it no meaning. People give it meaning. When each of us first learned the game, we could not help but pick up on the meaning attributed to it by the person who taught us. And where did that person find meaning? You can choose to ignore the question of meaning, but it won't go away, and it will affect every shot you take and most of what you think and feel while playing the game. This is where the mental side of golf exists—in the agreed-upon meaning of the game.

But did you ever consciously agree with anyone? Did you ever say to yourself, "Yes, golf is a game where I have to prove something about myself . . . to my dad, my mom, my friends, or myself," or "Now I'm going to spend four hours to see if I can live up to my own expectations of myself," or "Golf is my chance to show that I am better than someone else"? Did you say, "If I can't learn to break eighty before I die, then my life is not worth living"? And did you ever wonder why you care so much about whether you're hitting the ball right, according to the current definition of "right"? Fragments of most of these games are in all of us, and they continue in varying degrees whether we like it or not. I'm not saying that these additional meanings are good or bad. But have you ever actually made a conscious choice about the meanings you are accepting?

There can be great benefit in making the choice consciously. There is something to be gained in stepping back each time you play and asking yourself, "Why am I playing?" There is an old saying, "If you don't stand for something, you will fall for anything." In the culture of golf, there are many things to "fall for." Many of them have the capability to drive people crazy or, if not crazy, at least closer to misery than enjoyment.

The foundation of mastering the mental side of golf is to take a stand on why you are playing. Once you decide that you are going to play for the fun of it, or for the friendship, or whatever, the other Inner games will come knocking at your door, the games you and the rest of us have been playing unconsciously. You will at least have a choice. In the choice to play your own game while playing golf you accomplish something more important than score. You accomplish a measure of human dignity. If you feel pressure, you know that it is the pressure you created. If you feel joy, you know why. And if you can play your own game on the golf course, and allow others to play theirs, then it becomes more possible to do the same in the rest of your life.

THE FUNDAMENTAL OF GOLF: WHY DO YOU PLAY?

CHAPTER 12

BEYOND FORMULA TO FEELING

Recently, the publisher of the 1946 golf classic *Live Hands* by E. M. Prain asked me to write the foreword for the book's republication. Noting that the original foreword was written by Bernard Darwin, a renowned golf writer and former captain of the Royal and Ancient Golf Club of St. Andrews, I wondered, "Why me?" and barely took the invitation seriously. It was only because of Leslye's advice that I even opened Prain's book to read a few pages. There were five short chapters. The first one, entitled "Searching for Formula," showed me that the golfer's compulsion to look for a simple "secret" of the game was not a new one at all and that I was not the first writer to express the irony of being caught up in the complexity of mechanics while looking for the single cure-all technique.

In his elegant English style, Prain describes the endless search for a formula that will unlock our dreams of being the golfer we think we could be:

> The trouble with the rest of us (all but the best players) is that we are always groping. We cannot grow as we should like because we have not roots. We are the earth's most changeable disciples, ever ready to try some new tag in the hope it will prove our salvation, equally ready to desert it for another if it does not give us what we want.

A scratch golfer himself, Prain describes the futility of his own search: "I do not know how many times I felt I had found Excalibur. One day my salvation lay in the movement of my hip, the next in the way my shoulder turned, and again I felt I had found it when I opened my somewhat closed stance."

Prain's search for formula takes on religious overtones: "I know the hopeless feeling which assails the changeable disciple. How fleeting are the moments of success and how often the new half-built castle tumbles about him in ruins." Many of Prain's golfing friends, caught up in the search for formula, would set out to enjoy the game, but soon after they teed off found themselves playing "as if under a cloud." As he explains, "In the course of one swing they were trying to do six or seven different things. But all that they achieved was an exaggeration of certain actions of that swing which deprived the whole of rhythm."

Had I not known when these words were published, I'd have thought they were written by someone who had read *The Inner Game of Golf*. It seems as if our appetite for formulas in golf and in life is as unending as the cycle of hope and disappointment that these illusory mental constructs engender. We want encapsulated wisdom. We want to read the formula in a book and apply it to our lives. We don't particularly want to think about the formula; it's enough to know that someone who calls himself an expert has thought about it. Our job is simply to follow it. A formula is a mental construct that tells you what to do in a given situation. In the face of uncertainty, the formula gives direction and certainty. If golf really worked that way, we would all be scratch golfers by now. And if life worked that way, we would all have happy lives.

My passion to transcend formulas does not come from a life free of them. Precisely the opposite—I was brought up with formulas for everything. Being Irish, I also had a bit of the rebel in me, so I turned against traditional formulas only to come up with untraditional (but equally problematic) formulas. Finally, I've arrived at the point where I'm ready to give up on formulas once and for all, except as they apply to routine matters like filing a tax return or installing a piece of software. As noted in Chapter 6, "Discovering Technique," I still believe that it is important to understand the technology of anything that you want to do excellently. But understanding and following formulas are two different things. I don't hit the ball with my understanding. My understanding contributes, in the background, to my execution. But in the execution itself, I am either following formula or following feeling. I am either coming from the mind or from the gut.

I have chosen feeling over formula. I want to play from feeling, write from feeling, live from feeling. Why? Because it feels *good*, and it works.

At least that's my experience. By feelings I obviously do not mean the fears and doubts that Self 1 generates. These are what create the uncertainty that has me looking for formulas in the first place. So I am not talking about Self 1 emotions, positive or negative, as the source of play. Rather, I am talking about the feelings generated naturally by Self 2. You can see them in young children all the time—not learned feelings but self-generated impulses, desires, instincts, and responses that are the most human part of human beings. For me, the whole point of quieting Self 1 thinking is not to hit the golf ball better but to access more easily the natural feelings of Self 2. All of us have these feelings, and all of us enjoy them. But most of us have been conditioned out of our belief in their value and, especially, in their practicality.

I want to enjoy and follow the feelings that come from the natural wellspring of my life. When it comes to golfing, this means my priority is to find the feeling and swing from it. As I stand before the ball, I am not thinking about how I should swing, nor am I trying to remember how the swing should feel. No. The first and most important thing I have to do is reach for the urge to hit the ball. This may sound strange. "I know I want to hit the ball, and I know where I want to hit the ball, and sometimes I even know how I want to hit the ball," I can imagine the reader saying. Yes, so do I. But I don't always *feel* it. There's a big difference between having an idea about where or how to hit the ball and responding naturally to the desire to do it.

It's like the difference between thinking that it's time for dinner and feeling hungry. Either will get you to the dinner table and through the act of eating a meal. But is there not a significant distinction between the meal eaten in conscious response to hunger, the water drunk in conscious response to thirst, and following the formula "It's time to eat and time to drink"? For some it doesn't matter. For much of my life, it didn't matter to me. With the attitude that I wanted to accomplish everything quickly, I often tried to read a newspaper, watch TV, and get something else done all at the same time. It was even okay to eat in the car while driving to an appointment. But when I eat from the feeling of hunger, the meal itself becomes important because there is a unique enjoyment in feeling and fulfilling the hunger.

In the same way, there is a unique enjoyment in hitting the ball exactly the way you want to. Not the way you think you want to but the way you feel you want to in the very moment you're hitting the ball. I don't have to name this feeling—in fact, it's better if I don't. Naming the feeling might turn it into a formula. I just have to go with the feeling, whatever it's called, and let it express itself in my shot. With each shot I execute this way, I become more myself. I become more human. There is a sweet satisfaction to each shot, from drive to hole. Only when I am willing to take this seeming risk of putting feeling first do I know that I am playing golf and not being played by golf. I become more important than the game. And that is the way it should be. I do not want to be a pawn in my own game. I want to be the player. When finding the feeling and expressing it take priority over everything else, the results are usually a happy surprise. On those occasions when the ball goes off course, I usually realize in a flash that I was also off course. I left the purity of the feeling and added in a little strength that wasn't felt, a little formulation to compensate for some doubt or fear generated by Self 1. Good. I thank the shot for showing me, for holding up the mirror. And I draw from the shot renewed motivation to reach for the purest urge the next time I swing.

Does Self 1 go away? No. Though it may offer less in the way of mechanical formulas, Self 1's next ploy is something like "Now, that was the right feeling on the last shot. You should try to feel that way the next time, too." Of course, I fall for that a few times because the Self 2 shot did feel great, so it's easy to believe that I should feel like that all the time. But my "feeling part" doesn't work that way, does it? If I like a certain feeling, Self 1 wants to reduce it to a formula—a repeatable sameness. I liked it, so I want to capture it, make it be there on demand. Press the button and say, "Now feel just like you did when . . ." In doing this, I am actually leaving the domain of feeling and reentering the domain of thought, the part that tries to reproduce mentally what it has experienced nonmentally.

The moment I try to reproduce a feeling, I take a step away from where natural feelings originate. I need to learn a little old-fashioned humility. I need to be willing to feel whatever is there at the moment, not just what I expected to find. The feeling I experience on the first tee may be quite different from the one I feel on the eighteenth, so why try to hit the eighteenth-tee shot with the first-tee feeling? Standing over the putt on the thirteenth green, I might not be able to retrieve the same sensation that sank the forty-foot putt on the twelfth green. I can't really control the spontaneous nor should I want to. But I can learn to reach for that place where the spontaneous occurs. I can sit at its door and listen to the music that plays there, to the drum that beats, and I can acknowledge the originality and sweetness of the song. And I can express that song in my swing as well as in my walk from one shot to the next.

This for me becomes true play. This is the way I can enjoy golf. And this is the only thing I have found to be more compelling than formulas. Thoughts about the golf swing still enter my mind, and that's okay. They have something to teach me, but nothing important. The minute I begin to think they have something important to tell me, the minute the result of the shot becomes more important than my connection with what I have called my Self 2, I have set myself up to be trapped once again, to be played by the game instead of being the player of the game. Initially, I was surprised to discover that even though I was putting feeling first, I still wanted to compete. I like competition and the challenge it provides. Competition serves a valid purpose and heightens my enjoyment. But there's true competition and false competition. False competition is the striving of Self 1 based on the (supposed) need to prove something to someone. As false competition pressures fall away, I find within myself the true competition—the striving for excellence. I was interested recently to learn that the word "competition" is from the Greek word meaning "to seek together." Two opponents seek excellence together while competing.

Maybe some readers would like me to name more specifically the feelings I am referring to. I leave them unnamed so that Self 1 can't so easily judge or manipulate them. I seek to protect their integrity by keeping them out of the domain of language. Then I am freer to hit each ball with the genuine enthusiasm of the moment and not from a particular feeling Self 1 tells me I *should* have. I call the feeling I hit the ball from "felt desire."

It is satisfying in itself when that urge is expressed accurately, and the satisfaction is independent of where the ball goes. It is this enthusiasm itself that I value the most. It is of life, and it is living. Here words begin to fail. My choice to play this way is part of my choice to live my life with utmost sincerity and with the enthusiasm that I recognize was a natural part of my early life—and the life of every child. While pitching and chipping one day, I was thinking about Prain's title, *Live Hands*. My hands did feel more alive, and I was much more aware of their subtle and very complex movements. But I had no desire to interfere or manipulate. The more connected I am with this living feeling, the more alive I feel— my hands, my legs, and every other part of my body. I noticed my body learning technique without needing to analyze what it was learning. Things work that way only when feeling is given top priority.

I feel an enthusiasm in writing about this, but not that of a salesperson or an evangelist. It is something I have to offer, something that I have discovered that seems of utmost importance to me. It is not important to me that it be important to you, but I wouldn't want to keep it a secret either. Take from it what you will. If what I am saying is valid for any reader, it is because the reader already knew it to be true before reading these words and the words are just a reminder. That is what they are to me. I need this reminder because so much of what I run into every day is the result of formulaic thinking and behavior. We are trained to believe that formulas will take us where we want to go, in golf, in work, in relationships, in life. So attached do we become to our particular formulas that we will fight bloody, cruel fights to defend them and to promote their global acceptance.

A Different Kind of Enjoyment

I spent many long hours rewriting Chapter 9, trying to bring together my understanding about the impact of expectations on the golfer and his golf—not an easy subject, as you might have gathered. By five in the afternoon my brain was tired and my body restless for movement. Too much writing, not enough doing, I said to myself. Off to the nearest golf course I went in the hope of getting in at least nine holes before dark.

I had just been given a set of irons by the Southern Cal representative of Spalding, and I was eager to try them out. The Westlake golf course was a relatively short but challenging 18-hole course with only two par-five holes. Par was 67. I decided to play with only a five iron, a seven, a pitching wedge, and a putter. This would give me a good chance to try my new irons and allow me to move quickly. It would also ease any indecision about club selection! I started on the tenth hole and hit two five irons to the green and left my twenty-foot putt an inch short. The next hole was 420 yards, and two five irons left me ninety yards short of the green. But my first shot with my new pitching wedge landed a foot from the pin for an easy tap-in for par. "My clubs haven't learned how to miss yet," I said to myself. By the time I met up with other players on the fifteenth hole, I had barely missed three birdie putts and was even par. The two foursomes in front of me looked slow, and I didn't feel like waiting. So I doubled back and played holes twelve, thirteen, and fourteen again. Three more pars. By now I could hear Self 1's voice quite distinctly calculating having my best round and trying to remember what I had just written about how to keep a streak going. I could also hear it rehearsing how it would brag to certain people about my "accomplishment." But there was also another voice present: "What do you really want to accomplish?" it asked. Fifteen was a 520-yard par five, and I hit my first off-line five iron of the day. It wasn't really bad, but it came to rest in the root system of a tree on the left edge of the fairway. I hit another ball, this time as well as any I'd hit all day. I played both balls in. I had to take a stroke penalty for an unplayable lie on my first. I ended up with a bogey on my first and a par on my second. One over. "What do I want to accomplish?" I asked again. My answer surprised me. "Really nothing at all. I just want to enjoy the experience."

What was the experience? I want to tell you about it because it taught me something important. The experience I was having while playing this round was not exalted. I was not on a high. I might even have said I wasn't experiencing much at all. I would just stand up to the ball and hit it. I didn't think about it or spend time lining up my shots or envisioning where I wanted the ball to go. I wasn't doing any Outer Game technique or any Inner Game technique either. I was just hitting the ball and watching it fly straight. There was not even the hint of wanting to say "YES" with the affirmative gesture of having conquered something. The whole thing was no big deal at all. The closest word to describe the feeling was "contentment."

I remembered having a similar feeling years ago when I was playing in the zone in tennis. But at that time in my life I remember feeling something was missing. I was missing the feeling of "I did it." I missed the feeling of accomplishment that comes from trying something and having it work. But on the course at Westlake, I didn't miss the feeling of conquering, the feeling of triumph. I liked the simpler, less dramatic feeling that was almost unnoticeable but nonetheless there. It felt constant and true, not something that would crumble easily. So my only choice was just to keep on appreciating that simple state as long as it lasted—not because it was producing par golf but because it felt comfortable. Self 1 made its effort, and I made my effort. I ended with pars on the last two holes, and the simple feeling just continued.

After another day of hard work at the computer, the urge to play overtook me again around 5:30. It had rained most of the day, so the Westlake course was almost empty. This time I wanted to try out my three iron. So I took it, my seven, my wedge, and putter, and, playing quickly, I was able to complete a full eighteen holes. I played the last two in the dark, chipping in on the eighteenth for a birdie. My game was not quite as consistent as the day before. I bogeyed seven of the eighteen holes but birdied three, giving me a 71 for the first time ever. What was nice was that there were only momentary interruptions of the simplicity, each one reminding me that I had to keep alert to Self 1's effort to enter and make things more complicated. At the end of the day, I felt I had learned how to play golf. Definitely not the final word on how to swing the club or on shot-making, but a very satisfying reason to play the game for the rest of my life.

THE FUTURE OF THE GAME

Though the rules of golf are relatively static, the use and meaning of the game vary with each individual and are affected by changes in the culture. I believe that in the next few years there will continue to be significant changes in the way golf is taught and played.

Already golf instructors I have spoken with admit that there is relatively little more to be learned about the mechanics of the golf swing; what teaching professionals need most is to learn how to help their stu-

BEYOND FORMULA
TO FEELING

211

dents put into practice what is already understood about the swing. The focus is shifting slowly to the art of learning as opposed to debating the content of what should be taught. There is a growing admission on the part of even the master technicians of golf that breaking down the elements of the golf swing and putting them back together again is a difficult and generally ineffectual way to master the game. There is also a growing recognition of the role of tension and other mental obstacles in golf. In short, we are seeing a shift of attention from the physics of the game to its psychology.

This shift from the outer to the inner in golf reflects a general rebalancing occurring in the culture at large. There is a growing realization that physical control over our external environment is limited. Without an ability to solve problems on the mental level, technology cannot get to the root of the causes of war, crime, famine, or our general dissatisfactions. It seems clear that the breakthroughs of the next age must come in the form of advances in our individual and collective abilities to tap existing human capabilities and to overcome the negative internal forces that interfere with their expression.

As our culture undergoes a necessary rebalancing of its outer and inner games, sports in general can find a new raison d'être. Potentially, sports have a greater value to a culture than as a mere outlet for releasing tensions or providing heroes. They can become the laboratory in which research and experimentation about human motivation, performance, and self-interference take place. Ancient cultures used sports to benefit and strengthen themselves. The Inner Game is hardly a new one, but we are pretty rusty at playing it. Sports can be a safe arena in which we relearn its importance and increase our skill at it. Sports can be both the showcase and the laboratory in which the culture can learn increasing self-control.

Golf has a particular role to play in this scenario. Admittedly, its players are not known for their openness to change; indeed, it is said that it is a conservative game played by conservatives. But it is, in fact, a game popular with a broad cross section of the population and one that demands self-control. A businessman who learns how to cope with stress on the golf course can save his management a lot of suffering and his business a lot of money. Likewise, a student can grasp the elements of learning and self-confidence on the golf course in such a way that it has a permanent effect on his life. Everyone should learn to respect that thin line existing between what is real and what is a game. As a culture, we would then come to understand the true value of competition. In short, the Inner Game aspects of the game of golf described in this book are exactly those issues that the culture at large needs to grapple with. If golf allows itself to become a medium for such experimentation, it would more than justify its existence.

This shift of attention will have a great significance for golf instructors. It will no longer be sufficient for a teacher of the game to be a good player and to know the mechanics of the swing. Forward-looking teachers will attempt to develop an understanding of the learning process. If they do, they will be more valued than in their old roles as swing mechanics, for they will be teaching such valuable inner skills as concentration, self-trust, will, and awareness. Such teachers will be recognized as making valuable contributions to the quality of a student's entire life.

But how many better ways are there to engage in the universal and ageless contest against oneself? If the game is played as Bobby Jones claimed to play it—as a conquest of oneself—it becomes truly recreational. It is a break from the routine and patterns of daily life that can truly enrich our existence. What players learn about themselves on the course can be transferred to every aspect of their lives and thus benefit the culture of which golf is only a small part.

Such a perspective would give the game a significance that would make it worth all the time and effort we enjoy putting into it. Although I don't expect a new way of looking at the game to take place overnight, it could happen quickly in this current era. But whether it comes gradually or as a revolution, it *will* take place, and golf will become more fun, more natural, and more in tune with the way games are meant to be played—in dynamic balance between the inner and the outer.

ABOUT THE AUTHOR

W. TIMOTHY GALLWEY is the author of the bestselling Inner Game series of books and founder of The Inner Game Corporation, which applies Inner Game principles and methods to the development of excellence in individuals and teams. He lectures worldwide, conducts team trainings, and coaches workshops. He can be reached at The Inner Game Corporation, P.O. Box 875, Agoura Hills, CA 91376 or on the Internet at www.theinnergame.com.

ABOUT THE TYPE

This book was set in Goudy, a typeface designed by Frederic William Goudy (1865–1947). Goudy began his career as a bookkeeper, but devoted the rest of his life to the pursuit of "recognized quality" in a printing type.

Goudy was produced in 1914 and was an instant bestseller for the foundry. It has generous curves and smooth, even color. It is regarded as one of Goudy's finest achievements.